First ACL Workshop on Ethics in Natural Language Processing

Held at the 15th Conference of the European Chapter of the Association for Computational Linguistics (EACL 2017)

Valencia, Spain
4 April 2017

ISBN: 978-1-5108-3864-2

First ACL Workshop on Ethics in Natural Language Processing

Held at the 15th Conference of the European Chapter of the Association for Computational Linguistics (EACL 2017)

Valencia, Spain
4 April 2017

EACL 2017

Ethics in Natural Language Processing

Proceedings of the First ACL Workshop

April 4th, 2017
Valencia, Spain

Introduction

Welcome to the first ACL Workshop on Ethics in Natural Language Processing! We are pleased to have participants from a variety of backgrounds and perspectives: social science, computational linguistics, and philosophy; academia, industry, and government.

The workshop consists of invited talks, contributed discussion papers, posters, demos, and a panel discussion. Invited speakers include **Graeme Hirst**, a Professor in NLP at the University of Toronto, who works on lexical semantics, pragmatics, and text classification, with applications to intelligent text understanding for disabled users; **Quirine Eijkman**, a Senior Researcher at Leiden University, who leads work on security governance, the sociology of law, and human right; **Jason Baldridge**, a co-founder and Chief Scientist of People Pattern, who specializes in computational models of discourse as well as the interaction between machine learning and human bias; and **Joanna Bryson**, a Reader in artificial intelligence and natural intelligence at the University of Bath, who works on action selection, systems AI, transparency of AI, political polarization, income inequality, and ethics in AI.

We received paper submissions that span a wide range of topics, addressing issues related to overgeneralization, dual use, privacy protection, bias in NLP models, underrepresentation, fairness, and more. Their authors share insights about the intersection of NLP and ethics in academic work, industrial work, and clinical work. Common themes include the role of tasks, datasets, annotations, training populations, and modelling. We selected 4 papers for oral presentation, 8 for poster presentation, and one for demo presentation, and have paired each oral presentation with a discussant outside of the authors' areas of expertise to help contextualize the work in a broader perspective. All papers additionally provide the basis for panel and participant discussion.

We hope this workshop will help to define and raise awareness of ethical considerations in NLP throughout the community, and will kickstart a recurring theme to consider in future NLP conferences. We would like to thank all authors, speakers, panelists, and discussants for their thoughtful contributions. We are also grateful for our sponsors (Bloomberg, Google, and HITS), who have helped making the workshop in this form possible.

The Organizers
Margaret, Dirk, Shannon, Emily, Hanna, Michael

Organizers:

Dirk Hovy, University of Copenhagen (Denmark)
Shannon Spruit, Delft University of Technology (Netherlands)
Margaret Mitchell, Google Research & Machine Intelligence (USA)
Emily M. Bender, University of Washington (USA)
Michael Strube, Heidelberg Institute for Theoretical Studies (Germany)
Hanna Wallach, Microsoft Research, UMass Amherst (USA)

Program Committee:

Gilles Adda	Fernando Diaz	Nikola Ljubesic	Molly Roberts
Nikolaos Aletras	Benjamin Van Durme	Adam Lopez	Tim Rocktäschel
Mark Alfano	Jacob Eisenstein	L. Alfonso Urena Lopez	Frank Rudzicz
Jacob Andreas	Jason Eisner	Teresa Lynn	Alexander M. Rush
Isabelle Augenstein	Desmond Elliott	Nitin Madnani	Derek Ruths
Tim Baldwin	Micha Elsner	Gideon Mann	Asad Sayeed
Miguel Ballesteros	Katrin Erk	Daniel Marcu	David Schlangen
David Bamman	Raquel Fernandez	Jonathan May	Natalie Schluter
Mohit Bansal	Laura Fichtner	Kathy McKeown	H. Andrew Schwartz
Solon Barocas	Karën Fort	Paola Merlo	Hinrich Schütze
Daniel Bauer	Victoria Fossum	David Mimno	Djamé Seddah
Eric Bell	Lily Frank	Shachar Mirkin	Dan Simonson
Steven Bethard	Sorelle Friedler	Alessandro Moschitti	Sameer Singh
Rahul Bhagat	Annemarie Friedrich	Jason Naradowsky	Vivek Srikumar
Chris Biemann	Juri Ganitkevich	Roberto Navigli	Sanja Stajner
Yonatan Bisk	Spandana Gella	Arvind Neelakantan	Pontus Stenetorp
Michael Bloodgood	Kevin Gimpel	Ani Nenkova	Brandon Stewart
Matko Bosnjak	Joao Graca	Dong Nguyen	Veselin Stoyanov
Chris Brockett	Yvette Graham	Brendan O'Connor	Anders Søgaard
Miles Brundage	Keith Hall	Diarmuid O'Seaghdha	Ivan Titov
Joana J. Bryson	Oul Han	Miles Osborne	Sara Tonelli
Ryan Calo	Graeme Hirst	Jahna Otterbacher	Oren Tsur
Marine Carpuat	Nathan Hodas	Sebastian Padó	Yulia Tsvetkov
Yejin Choi	Kristy Hollingshead	Alexis Palmer	Lyle Ungar
Munmun De Choudhury	Ed Hovy	Martha Palmer	Suresh Venkatasubramanian
Grzegorz Chrupala	Georgy Ishmaev	Michael Paul	Yannick Versley
Ann Clifton	Jing Jiang	Ellie Pavlick	Aline Villavicencio
Kevin B. Cohen	Anna Jobin	Emily Pitler	Andreas Vlachos
Shay B. Cohen	Anders Johannsen	Barbara Plank	Rob Voigt
Court Corley	David Jurgens	Thierry Poibeau	Svitlana Volkova
Ryan Cotterell	Brian Keegan	Chris Potts	Martijn Warnier
Aron Culotta	Roman Klinger	Vinod Prabhakaran	Zeerak Waseem
Walter Daelemans	Ekaterina Kochmar	Daniel Preotiuc	Bonnie Webber
Dipanjan Das	Philipp Koehn	Nikolaus Pöchhacker	Joern Wuebker
Hal Daumé III	Zornitsa Kozareva	Will Radford	François Yvon
Steve DeNeefe	Jayant Krishnamurthy	Siva Reddy	Luke Zettlemoyer
Francien Dechesne	Jonathan K. Kummerfeld	Luis Reyes-Galindo	Janneke van der Zwaan
Leon Derczynski	Vasileios Lampos	Sebastian Riedel	
Aliya Deri	Angeliki Lazaridou	Ellen Riloff	
Mona Diab	Alessandro Lenci	Brian Roark	

Invited Speakers:

Graeme Hirst, University of Toronto (Canada)
Quirine Eijkman, Leiden University (Netherlands)
Jason Baldridge, People Pattern (USA)
Joanna Bryson, University of Bath (UK)

Table of Contents

Workshop Program

Tuesday, 4 April, 2017

9:30–11:00   **Morning Session 1**

9:30–9:40   *Welcome, Overview*
Dirk, Margaret, Shannon, Michael

9:40–10:15   *Invited Talk*
Graeme Hirst

10:15–10:50   *Invited Talk*
Joanna Bryson

11:00–11:30   **Coffee Break**

11:30–13:00   **Morning Session 2 - Gender**

11:30–11:45   *Gender as a Variable in Natural-Language Processing: Ethical Considerations*
Brian Larson

11:45–12:00   *These are not the Stereotypes You are Looking For: Bias and Fairness in Authorial Gender Attribution*
Corina Koolen and Andreas van Cranenburgh

12:00–12:25   *Paper Discussion*
Authors and Discussant

12:25–13:00   *Invited Talk*
Quirine Eijkman

Tuesday, 4 April, 2017 (continued)

13:00–14:30   Lunch Break

14:30–16:00   Afternoon Session 1 - Data and Design

14:30–15:05   *Invited Talk*
Jason Baldridge

15:05–15:20   *A Quantitative Study of Data in the NLP community*
Margot Mieskes

15:20–15:35   *Ethical by Design: Ethics Best Practices for Natural Language Processing*
Jochen L. Leidner and Vassilis Plachouras

15:35–16:00   *Paper Discussion*
Authors and Discussant

16:00–17:00   Afternoon Session 2 - Coffee and Posters

16:00–17:00   *Building Better Open-Source Tools to Support Fairness in Automated Scoring*
Nitin Madnani, Anastassia Loukina, Alina von Davier, Jill Burstein and Aoife Cahill

16:00–17:00   *Gender and Dialect Bias in YouTube's Automatic Captions*
Rachael Tatman

16:00–17:00   *Integrating the Management of Personal Data Protection and Open Science with Research Ethics*
Dave Lewis, Joss Moorkens and Kaniz Fatema

16:00–17:00   *Ethical Considerations in NLP Shared Tasks*
Carla Parra Escartín, Wessel Reijers, Teresa Lynn, Joss Moorkens, Andy Way and Chao-Hong Liu

16:00–17:00   *Social Bias in Elicited Natural Language Inferences*
Rachel Rudinger, Chandler May and Benjamin Van Durme

16:00–17:00   *A Short Review of Ethical Challenges in Clinical Natural Language Processing*
Simon Suster, Stephan Tulkens and Walter Daelemans

16:00–17:00   *Goal-Oriented Design for Ethical Machine Learning and NLP*
Tyler Schnoebelen

16:00–17:00   *Ethical Research Protocols for Social Media Health Research*
Adrian Benton, Glen Coppersmith and Mark Dredze

16:00–17:00   *Say the Right Thing Right: Ethics Issues in Natural Language Generation Systems*
Charese Smiley, Frank Schilder, Vassilis Plachouras and Jochen L. Leidner

17:00–18:00   Evening Session

17:10–17:45   *Panel Discussion*
Panelists

17:45–18:00   *Concluding Remarks*
Dirk, Margaret, Shannon, Michael

Gender as a Variable in Natural-Language Processing: Ethical Considerations

Brian N. Larson

Georgia Institute of Technology
686 Cherry St. MC 0165
Atlanta, GA 30363 USA
`blarson@gatech.edu`

Abstract

Researchers and practitioners in natural-language processing (NLP) and related fields should attend to ethical principles in study design, ascription of categories/variables to study participants, and reporting of findings or results. This paper discusses theoretical and ethical frameworks for using *gender* as a variable in NLP studies and proposes four guidelines for researchers and practitioners. The principles outlined here should guide practitioners, researchers, and peer reviewers, and they may be applicable to other social categories, such as race, applied to human beings connected to NLP research.

1 Introduction

Bamman et al. (2014) challenged simplistic notions of a gender binary and the common quest in natural-language processing (NLP) studies merely to predict gender based on text, making the following observation:

> If we start with the assumption that 'female' and 'male' are the relevant categories, then our analyses are incapable of revealing violations of this assumption.... [W]hen we turn to a descriptive account of the interaction between language and gender, this analysis becomes a house of mirrors, which by design can only find evidence to support the underlying assumption of a binary gender opposition (p. 148).

Gender is a common variable in NLP studies. For example, a search of the ACL Anthology (`aclanthology.info`) for the keyword "gender" in the title field revealed seven papers in 2016

alone that made use of personal (as opposed to grammatical) gender as a central variable. Many others used gender as a variable without referring to gender in their titles. It is not uncommon, however, for studies regarding gender to be reported without any explanation of how gender labels were ascribed to authors or their texts.

This paper argues that using gender as a variable in NLP is an *ethical issue*. Researchers and practitioners in NLP who unreflectively apply gender category labels to texts and their authors may violate ethical principles that govern the use of human participants or "subjects" in research (Belmont Report, 1979; Common Rule, 2009). By failing to explain in study reports what theory of gender they are using and how they assigned gender categories, they may also run afoul of other ethical frameworks that demand transparency and accountability from researchers (Breuch et al., 2002; FAT-ML, nd; MacNealy, 1998).

This paper discusses theoretical and ethical frameworks for using *gender* as a variable in NLP studies. The principles outlined here should guide researchers and peer reviewers, and they may be applicable to other social categories, such as race, applied to human beings connected to NLP research. Note that this paper does not purport to select the best theory of gender or method of ascribing gender categories for NLP. Rather, it urges a continual process of thoughtfulness and debate regarding these issues, both within each study and among the authors and readers of study reports.

In summary, researchers and practitioners should (1) formulate research questions making explicit theories of what "gender" is; (2) avoid using gender as a variable unless it is necessary to answer research questions; (3) make explicit methods for assigning gender categories to participants and linguistic artifacts; and (4) respect the difficulties of respondents when asking them

1

Proceedings of the First Workshop on Ethics in Natural Language Processing, pages 1–11,
Valencia, Spain, April 4th, 2017. © 2017 Association for Computational Linguistics

to self-identify for gender.

Section 2 considers theoretical foundations for *gender* as a research construct and rationales for studying it. Section 3 proposes ethical frameworks for academic researchers and for practitioners. Section 4 examines several studies in NLP that are representative of the range of studies using gender as a variable. Section 5 concludes with recommendations for best practices in designing, reporting, and peer-reviewing NLP studies using gender as a variable.

2 Gender and rationales for its study

2.1 Three views of gender

There are many views of how gender functions as a social construct. This section presents just three: the common or *folk* view of gender, a *performative* view of gender, and one social psychological view of gender. None of these views can be seen as correct for all contexts and applications. The view that is appropriate for a given project will depend on the research questions posed and the goals of the project.

A *folk* belief, as the term is used here, refers to the *doxa* or beliefs of the many that may or may not be supported by systematic inquiry—common beliefs distinguished from scientific knowledge or philosophical theories (Plato, 2005). In the folk conception, the "heteronormative gender binary" (Larson, 2016, p. 365) conflates sex, the chromosomal and biological characteristics of people, with gender, their outward appearances and behaviors. The salience of these categories and their binary nature are taken as obvious and natural. Consequently, the options available on a survey for the question "Gender?" are frequently "male" or "female" (sex categories) rather than "masculine" or "feminine" (gender categories). There is a growing understanding in contemporary western culture, however, that some individuals either do not fall easily into the binary or exhibit gender characteristics inconsistent with the biological sex ascribed to them at birth—these persons are sometimes referred to as being "transgender," while those whose sex and gender are congruent are "cisgender" (DeFrancisco et al., 2014). Various communities of persons who are not cisgender have other names they prefer to use for themselves, including "gender non-conforming," "non-binary," and "genderqueer" (GLAAD, nd b). According to one academic report, there are 1.4 million trans-

gender people in the United States alone, and for these persons, the language used to characterize them can function as respectful on the one hand or offensive and defamatory on the other (GLAAD, nd a). Note that the gender labels that transgender persons ascribe to themselves do not include "other." The folk view of gender might be an appropriate frame for the NLP researcher seeking to explore study participants' use of language in relation to their own conceptions of their genders.

Another view of gender sees it as *performative*. So, according to DeFrancisco et al. (2014, p. 3) gender consists in "the behaviors and appearances society dictates a body of a particular sex should perform," structuring "people's understanding of themselves and each other." According to Larson (2016), an actor's gender knowledge comprises components of the actor's cognitive environment—beliefs about behaviors the actor expects to have a particular effect or effects on another based on knowledge about a typified situation in the actor's cognitive environment. Among these behaviors is language. Butler (1993) characterized gender as a form of performativity arising in "an unexamined framework of normative heterosexuality" (p. 97). According to all these theories, gender performativity is not merely *performance*, but rather performances that respond to, or are constrained by, norms or conventions and simultaneously reinforce them. This approach to gender could be useful, for example, in a study exploring the ways that language might be used to resist folk views of gender, especially in a context like transgender communities, where resistance to gender *doxa* is essential to building identity. Similarly, it could be useful in studying cases where persons of one gender attempt to appropriate conventional communicative practices of another gender without adopting a transgender identity. Bamman et al. (2014) made specific reference to this family of theories in their study of Twitter users.

A third approach to thinking about gender is to assume a gender binary, identify characteristics that cluster around the modes of the binary, and assess the gender of study participants based on their closeness of fit to these modes. This is exactly the approach of the Bem Sex Roles Inventory (Bem, 1974) and other instruments developed by social psychologists to assess gender. This approach allows the researcher to break gender down into constituent features. So, for example, the BSRI associates self-reliance, independence, and athleticism with masculinity and loyalty, sympathy, and sensitivity with femininity (Blanchard-Fields et al., 1994). This approach might be useful, for example, for an NLP practitioner seeking to identify consumers exhibiting individual characteristics—like independence and athleticism—in order to market a particular product to those consumers without regard to their gender or sex. Such approaches may not be available to NLP researchers, though, as they require participants to fill out surveys.

These are only three of many possible approaches to gender, and as the examples suggest, they vary widely in the kinds of research questions they can help to answer.

2.2 Rationales for studying gender

Broadly speaking, NLP studies focused on gender stem from two sources: researchers and practitioners. Borrowing from concepts in the field of research with human participants, we can characterize *research* as "activity designed to test an hypothesis, permit conclusions to be drawn, and thereby to develop or contribute to generalizable knowledge" (Belmont Report, 1979). Practitioners, by contrast, are interested in providing solutions or "interventions that are designed solely to enhance the well-being of an individual. . . client"—in other words, the development of commercial applications. These two rationales can blend when academics disseminate research with the intention of attracting commercial interest and when practitioners disseminate study findings to the academic community with a goal, in part, of attracting attention to their commercial activities. Practitioners may also intend to develop applications that serve the needs of multiple clients, as when they seek to sell a technical solution to many players within an industry.

The practitioner may have more instrumental objectives, hoping, for example, for insights about consumer behavior applicable to an employer's or client's commercial goals. Practitioners engaged in such studies need not be concerned about the finer points of academic-researcher ethics. They should be conscious, however, of the social effects of their research when it is disseminated, covered in the news, etc. Even if their research is used only internally for their companies or clients, they may use variables in machine learning applications in

such a way as to cause "algorithmic discrimination," where "an individual or group receives unfair treatment as a result of algorithmic decision-making" (Goodman, 2016). The ethical frameworks discussed in the next section provide reasons to avoid such discrimination.

3 Ethical frameworks

Academic researchers and commercial practitioners may draw their ethical principles from different ethical frameworks, but they have similar ethical obligations for ascribing category labels to persons and for using and reporting the research resulting from them.

In the United States, academic researchers are generally guided by principles articulated in the Belmont Report (1979), which calls on researchers to observe three principles:

- *Respect for persons* represents the right of a human taking part or being observed in research (sometimes called a "subject" or "participant") to make an informed decision about whether to take part and for a researcher "to give weight to autonomous persons' considered opinions and choices."

- *Beneficence* requires that the research first do no harm to participants and second "maximize possible benefits and minimize possible harms."

- *Justice* demands that the costs and benefits of research be distributed fairly, so that one group does not endure the costs of research while another enjoys its benefits.

Under regulations of the U.S. Department of Health and Human Services known as the Common Rule, "all research involving human subjects conducted, supported or otherwise subject to regulation by any federal department or agency" must be subjected to review by an institutional review board or IRB (Common Rule, 2009). As a practical matter, most research universities in the United States require that all research involving human participants be subject to IRB review. The Common Rule embodies many of the principles of the Belmont Report and of the Declaration of Helsinki (World Medical Association, 1964).

Other authorities argue that academic researchers have ethical responsibilities regarding their research, even if it does not involve human participants. In that context, internal and external validity (or validity and reliability) of research findings are ethical concerns (Breuch et al., 2002; MacNealy, 1998). Not being explicit about what the researcher means by the research construct *gender* raises a problem for readers of research reports, as they cannot evaluate a researcher's claims without knowing in principle what the researcher means by her central terms. Not being explicit about the ascription of the category *gender* as a variable to participants or communication artifacts that they create brings into question internal and external validity of research findings, because it makes it difficult or impossible for other scholars to reproduce, test, or extend study findings. In short, doing good science is an ethical obligation of good scientists.

Practitioners are bound by ethical frameworks that are applicable to all persons generally. In the West, these may be drawn from normative frameworks that determine circumstances under which one can be called ethical: "virtue ethics"— having ethical thoughts and an ethical character (Hursthouse and Pettigrove, 2016); "deontological" ethics—conforming to rules, laws, and other statements of ethical duty (Alexander and Moore, 2016); and "consequentialism"—engaging in action that causes more good than harm (Sinnott-Armstrong, 2015). Other western and non-western ethical systems may prioritize other values (Hennig, 2010). Deontological ethics is drawn from sets of rules, such as religious texts, industry codes of ethics, and laws. Deontological theorists derive such rules from theoretical procedures, such as Kant's categorical imperative, where "all those possibly affected" can "will a just maxim as a general rule"; Rawl's "veil of ignorance," in which participants cannot know what role they will play in the society for which they posit rules; or Habermas's discourse ethics, rules resulting from a "noncoercive rational discourse among free and equal participants" (Habermas, 1995, p. 117). In a sense the Belmont Report provides a set of rules for deontological evaluation.

Consequentialist ethical systems like utilitarianism evaluate actions not by their means but their ends. They are thus consistent with the Belmont Report edict that research's benefits should outweigh its costs. But neither the Belmont Report nor other ethical systems typically permit actors to ignore the means they use to pursue their ends.

Some researchers/practitioners have argued for *fairness, accountability,* and *transparency* as ethical principles in applications of machine learning, a technology commonly used in NLP. Consider, for example, Hardt (2014) and Wallach (2014), and the group of researchers and practitioners behind FAT-ML (FAT-ML, nd). In this literature, it is not always clear what these three terms are meant to represent. So, for example, *fairness* appears to be a social metric similar to the Belmont Report's *beneficence* and *justice*. Wallach refers to it almost strictly in the phrase "bias, fairness, and inclusion." This seems concerned with fairness in the distributive sense of the Belmont Report's *justice* rather than the aggregate sense of consequentialist ethical systems. Wallach's uses of *transparency* and *accountability* echo the ethical principles for researchers suggested by Breuch et al. (2002) and MacNealy (1998). She appears to view them as principles to which researchers and practitioners should aspire.

FAT-ML could be operationalized as an ethical framework this way: NLP studies would expose their theoretical commitments, describe their research constructs (including *gender*), and explain their methods (including their ascription of gender categories). The resulting *transparency* permits *accountability* to peer reviewers and other researchers and practitioners, who may assess a given study against principles intended to result in valid and reliable scientific findings, principles designed to ensure respect for persons, justice, beneficence, and other evolving ethical principles under the rubric of *fairness*. Identification of the applicable rules awaits the rational non-coercive discourse of which the First Workshop on Ethics in NLP is an early and important example.

4 Applying frameworks to previous studies

This section considers how previously published and disseminated studies satisfy the ethical frameworks noted above and whether those frameworks may challenge the studies. Note that consideration of these particular studies is not meant to suggest that they are *ethically flawed*; they have been selected because they are recent studies or high-quality studies that have been widely cited. Generally, the studies discussed in this section included very careful descriptions of their methods of data collection and analysis. However, though each purported to tell us something about gender, hardly any defined what they meant by "gender" or "sex," many did not indicate how they ascribed the gender categories to their participants or artifacts, and some that did explain the ascription of gender categories left room for concerns.

A great many studies have explored gender differences in human communication. An early and widely cited study is Koppel et al. (2002), where the researchers used machine learning to predict the gender of authors of published texts in the British National Corpus (BNC). Koppel and colleagues noted that the works they selected from the BNC were labeled for author gender, but they did not indicate how that labeling was done.

Like Koppel et al., many study authors allow the ascription of the gender category to be the result of an opaque process—that is, they do not fully embrace the transparency and accountability principles identified above, making the validity of studies difficult to assess. For example, in a study of computer-mediated communication, Herring and Paolillo (2006) assigned gender to blog authors "by examining each blog qualitatively for indications of gender such as first names, nicknames, explicit gender statements... and gender-indexical language." The authors did not provide readers with examples of the process of assigning these labels—called "coding" here as it is frequently by qualitative researchers, and not to be confused with the computer programmer's notion of "coding" or writing code—a coding guide, which is the set of instructions that researchers use to assign category labels to persons or artifacts, or a statement about whether the researchers compared coding by two or more coders to assess inter-rater reliability (Potter and Levine-Donnerstein, 1999).

Rao et al. (2010) examined Twitter posts ("tweets") to predict the gender categories they had ascribed to the texts' authors. They identified 1,000 Twitter users and inferred their gender based upon a heuristic: "For gender, the seed set for the crawl came from initial sources including sororities, fraternities, and male and female hygiene products. This produced around 500 users in each class" (2010, p. 38). Of course, using linguistic performances (profiles and tweets) to assign gender to Twitter accounts and then using linguistic performances to predict the genders of those accounts is very like the "house of mirrors" that Bamman et al. (2014) warned of above.

The approach of Rao and colleagues and Herring and Paolillo also appears to put the researcher in the position of deciding what counts as male and female in the data. This raises questions of fairness with regard to participants who have been labeled according the researchers' expectations, or perhaps their biases, rather than autonomous decisions by the participants.

Other studies make their ascription of gender categories explicit but fail to cautiously approach such labels. For example, two early studies, Yan and Yan (2006) and Argamon et al. (2007), used machine learning to classify blogs by their authors' genders. They used blog profile account settings to ascribe gender categories. Burger et al. (2011) assigned gender to Twitter users by following links from Twitter accounts to users' blogs on blogging platforms that required users to indicate their genders. More recently, Rouhizadeh et al. (2016) studied Facebook users from the period 2009–2011 based on their self-identified genders (but these data were gathered before Facebook's current gender options, see below), and Wang et al. (2016) looked at Weibo users, collecting self-identified gender data from their profiles.

None of the studies in the previous paragraph described how frequently account holders indicated their own genders, what gender options were possible, or how researchers accounted for account holders posing with genders other than their own. The answers to such questions would make the studies more transparent, helping readers to assess the their validity and fairness. For example, if many users of a site refused to disclose their genders, it is possible that the decision not to disclose might correlate with other characteristics that would make gender distinctions in the data more or less pronounced. The Belmont Report's concern about autonomy would best be addressed by understanding the options given to participants to represent themselves as gendered persons on these blogging platforms. If there were only two gender options—probably "male" and "female"—we might well wonder whether transgender persons may have refused to answer the question, or if forced to answer, how they chose which gender.

One study deserves special mention: Bamman et al. (2014) compared user names on Twitter profiles to U.S. Census data which showed a gender distribution for the 9,000 most commonly appearing first names. Though some names were ambiguous—used for persons of different genders—in the census data, 95 percent of the users included in the study had a name that was "at least 85 percent associated with its majority gender" (p. 140). They then examined correlations between gender and language use. This approach might fall prey to criticisms regarding category ascription similar to those leveled at the studies above. Bamman et al., however, exhibited much more caution in the use of gender categories than any of the other studies cited here and engaged in cluster analyses that showed patterns of language use that crossed the gender-binary boundary. By describing the theory of gender they used and the method of ascribing the gender label, they made their study transparent and accountable. Whether it is fair is an assessment for their peers to make.

5 Guidelines for using gender as a variable

This section describes four guidelines for researchers and practitioners using gender as a variable in NLP studies that fall broadly under these admonitions: (1) formulate research questions making explicit theories of what "gender" is; (2) avoid using gender as a variable unless it is necessary to answer research questions; (3) make explicit methods for assigning gender categories to participants and linguistic artifacts; and (4) respect the difficulties of respondents when asking them to self-identify for gender. It also includes a recommendation for peer reviewers for conference-paper and research-article submissions. Note that this paper does not advocate for a particular theory of gender or method of ascribing gender categories to cover all NLP studies. Rather, it advocates for exposing decisions on these matters to aid in making studies more transparent, accountable, and fair. The decisions that practitioners and researchers make will be subject to debate among them, peer reviewers, and other practitioners and researchers.

5.1 Make theory of gender explicit

Researchers and practitioners should make explicit the theory of gender that undergirds their research questions. This step is essential to make studies accountable, transparent, and valid. For other researchers or practitioners to fully interpret a study and to interrogate, challenge, or reproduce it, they need to understand its theoretical grounds.

Ideally, a researcher would provide an extended discussion of the central variable in his or her study. For example, Larson (2016) offered a definition of "gender" used in the study along with a lengthy discussion of the concept. Both the discussion and analysis in Bamman et al. (2014) engaged with previous theoretical literature on gender and challenged the gender constructs used in previous NLP studies. But articles using gender as a variable need not go to this extent. The goal of making gender theory explicit can be achieved by quoting a definition of "gender" from earlier research and giving some evidence of actually having read some of the earlier research. In the alternative, the researcher may adopt a construct definition for gender; that is, the researcher may answer the question, "What does 'gender' measure?" Thus, researchers can either choose definitions of "gender" from existing theories or identify what they mean by "gender" by defining it themselves.

Practitioners may take a different view. Consider, for example, a practitioner working at a social media site that requires its users to self-identify in response to the question "gender." It is reasonable for this practitioner to use NLP tools to study the site's customers based on their responses to this question, seeking usage patterns, correlations, etc. But a challenge arises as social media platforms recognize nuances in gender identity. For example, in 2015 Facebook began allowing its users to indicate that their gender is "female," "male," or "custom," and the custom option is an open text box (Bell, 2015). A practitioner there using gender data will be compelled to use many labels or group them in a manner selected by the practitioner. Using all the labels presents difficulties for classifiers and for the practitioner attempting to explain results. Grouping labels requires the practitioner to *theorize* about how they should be grouped. This takes us back to the admonition that the researcher or practitioner should make explicit the theory of gender being used.

5.2 Avoid using gender unless necessary

This admonition is perhaps obvious: Given the efforts that this paper suggests should surround the selection, ascription, use, and reporting of gender categories in NLP studies, it would be foolish to use gender as a category unless it is necessary to achieve the researcher's objectives, because the effort is unlikely to be commensurate with the pay-off. It is likely, though, that the casual use of gender as a routine demographic question in studies where gender is not a central concern will remain commonplace. It seems an easy question to ask, and once the data are collected, it seems easy to perform a cross-tabulation of findings or results based on the response to this question.

The reasons for avoiding the use of gender as a variable unless necessary are grounded in all the ethical principles discussed above. A failure to give careful consideration to the questions presented in this paper creates a variety of risks. Thus, researchers should resist the temptation to ask: "I wonder if the women responded differently than the men." The best way to resist this temptation is to resist asking the gender question in the first place, unless it is important to presenting findings or results.

A reviewer of this paper noted that following this recommendation might inadvertently discourage researchers and practitioners from checking the algorithmic bias of their systems. Indeed, it is thoroughly consistent with values described here for researchers and practitioners to engage in such checking. In that case, gender is a necessary category, but where such work is anticipated, the other recommendations of this Section 5 should be carefully followed from the outset.

5.3 Make category assignment explicit

Researchers and practitioners should make explicit the method(s) they use to ascribe gender categories to study participants or communication artifacts. This step is essential to make the researcher's or practitioner's studies accountable, transparent, and valid. Just as the study's *theory* of gender is an essential basis for interpreting the findings—for interrogating, challenging, and reproducing them—so are the *methods* of ascribing the variable of study. This category provides the largest number of specific recommendations. (In this section, the term "researcher" refers both to researchers as discussed above and to practitioners who choose to disseminate their studies into the research community.)

Researchers have several choices here. Outside of NLP, they have very commonly ascribed gender to study participants based on the researchers' own best-guess assessments: The researcher interacts with a participant and concludes that she is female or he is male. For small-scale studies,

this approach will not likely go away; but the researcher should consider at the time of study design whether and how to do this. Researchers reporting findings should acknowledge if this is the approach they have taken.

A related approach makes sense where the researcher is studying how participants behave toward each other based on what they perceive others' genders to be. For example, if studying whether a teacher treats students differently based on student genders, the researcher may need to know what genders the *teacher* ascribes to students. The researcher should give thought to how to collect information about this category ascription from the teacher. The process could prove challenging if the researcher and teacher operate in an environment where students challenge traditional gender roles or where students outwardly identify as transgender.

But participant self-identification should be the gold standard for ascribing gender categories. Except in circumstances where one might not expect complete candor, one can count on participants to say what their own genders are. On the one hand, this approach to ascribing a gender label respects the autonomy of study participants, as it allows them to assert the gender with which they identify. On the other hand, it does not account for the fact that each study participant may have a different conception of gender, its meaning, its relation to sex, etc. For example, a 76-year-old woman who has lived in the United States her whole life may have a very different conception of what it means to be "female" or "feminine" than does a 20-year-old recent immigrant to Germany from Turkey. Despite this, each may be attempting to make sense of her identity as including a female or feminine gender.

In theory, the researcher could address the concerns regarding participant self-identification using a gender-role inventory. In fact, one study looking for gender differences in writing did exactly that, using the Bem Sex Role Inventory (BSRI) to assess author genders (Janssen and Murachver, 2004). The challenge with these approaches is that gender is a moving target. Sandra Bem introduced the BSRI in 1974 (Bem, 1974). It has since been criticized on a wide variety of grounds, but of importance here is the fact that it was based on gender role stereotypes from the time when it was created. Thus a meta-analysis by

Twenge (1997) of studies using the BSRI showed that the masculinity score of women taking the BSRI had increased steadily over 15 years, and men's masculinity scores showed a steady decrease in correlation over the same period. These developments make sense in the context of a gender roles inventory that is necessarily validated over a period of years after it is first developed, resulting in an outdated set of gender stereotypes being embodied in the test, stereotypes that are not confirmed later as gender roles change. This does not mean that these inventories have no value for some applications; rather, researchers using them should explain that they are using them, why they are using them, and what their limitations are.

Researchers should consider the following specific recommendations: First, if a study relies upon a gender-category ascription provided by someone else, as does Koppel et al. (2002), it should provide as much information as possible about how the category was ascribed and acknowledge the third-party category ascription as a limitation. This supports the goals of research validity, transparency, and accountability.

Second, if the researchers relied upon self-identified gender from a technology or social media platform, the study report should show that the researchers have reflected on the possibility that users of the platform have not identified their genders at all (where the platform does not require it), that users may intentionally misidentify their genders, that transgender users may be unable to identify themselves accurately (if the platform presents only a binary), or that they may have been insulted by the question (if the platform presents them with "male," "female," and *other*," for example). All these reflections address questions of validity, transparency, and accountability. The final two, however, also implicate the autonomy and respect for persons the Belmont Report calls for.

Third, if researchers use a heuristic or qualitative coding scheme to assess an author's gender, it is critically important that readers be presented with a full description of the process. This includes providing a copy of the coding guide (the set of instructions that researchers use to assign category labels to persons or artifacts) and describing the process by which researchers checked their code ascriptions, including a measure of inter-rater reliability. Studies that use automated means to ascribe category labels should include copies of computer code used to make the ascriptions. This supports the goals of accountability, transparency, and validity.

Fourth, researchers who group gender labels collected from participant self-identification or use a heuristic to assign gender categories to participants or artifacts should consider "denaturalizing" the resulting category labels. This challenge is only likely to increase as sites like social media platforms recognize nuances in gender identity, as this section previously noted with regard to Facebook. For example, Larson (2016) asked participants to identify their own genders, giving them an open text box in which to do it. (See also the detailed discussion of methods in Larson (2017).) This permitted participants in the study to identify with any gender they chose, and respondents responded with eight different gender labels. Larson explained his grouping of the responses and chose to denaturalize the gender categories by not using their common names. The article thus grouped "F," "Fem," "Female," and "female" together with the category label *Gender F* and "Cis Male," "M," "Male," and "Masculine" with the label *Gender M*. Such disclosure or transparency supports the goals accountability and fairness.

The steps described here would have strengthened already fine studies like those cited in the previous section. Of course, they would not insulate them from criticism. For example, Larson (2016) collected self-identified gender information and denaturalized the gender categories as explained above, but the result was nevertheless a gender binary consistent with that prevalent in the folk-theory of gender. The transparency of the study methods, however, provides a basis for critique; had it simply reported findings based on "male" and "female" participants, the reader would not even be able to identify this basis for critique.

5.4 Respect persons

One final recommendation is applicable to researchers and to practitioners who may have a role in deciding how to collect self-identified gender labels from participants. Here, the practitioner or researcher should take pains to recognize differences and difficulties that respondents may face in ascribing gender to themselves or to others. For example, assuming that one is collecting demographic information with an online survey, one might offer respondents two options for gender:

"male" and "female." In contemporary western culture, however, it is not unusual to have respondents who do not easily identify with one gender or another or who actively refuse to be classed in a particular gender. Others are confidently transgender or intersex. Thus, two options may not be enough. However, the addition of an "other" might seem degrading or insulting to those who do not consider themselves to be "male" or "female." Another option might be "none of the above," but this again seems to function as an othering selection. There are so many ways that persons might choose to describe their genders that listing them might also be impractical, especially as the list itself might have reactive effects by drawing special attention to the gender question. Such effects might arise if the comprehensive nature of the list tips research participants off that gender is an object of study in the research. But even the "free-form" space discussed above presents difficulties for practitioners and researchers.

Grappling with this challenge, and in the case of researchers and practitioners disseminating their research, documenting that grappling, is the best way to ensure ethical outcomes.

5.5 Reviewers: Expect ethical practices

The way to ensure that researchers (and practitioners who disseminate their studies as research) conform to ethical principles is to make them accountable at the time of peer review. A challenge for researchers and peer reviewers alike, however, is space. A long paper for EACL is eight pages at the time of initial submission. A researcher may not feel able to report fully on a study's background, data, methods, findings, and significance in that space and still have space to explain steps take to ensure the use of the *gender* variable is ethical. At least two possible solutions come to mind.

First, researchers may make efforts to weave evidence of ethical study design and implementation into study write-ups. It may be possible with the addition of a small number of sentences to satisfy a peer reviewer that a researcher has followed the guidelines in this paper.

Second, a researcher could write up a supplemental description of the study addressing particularly these issues. The researcher could signal the presence of the supplemental description by noting its existence in the first draft submitted for peer review. If the paper is accepted, the supplemental description could be added to the paper before publication of the proceedings without adding excessive length to the paper. In the alternative, the supplemental description could be made available via a link to a web resource apart from the paper itself. ACL has provided for the submission of "supplementary material" at least at some of its conferences "to report preprocessing decisions, model parameters, and other details necessary for the replication of the experiments reported" (Association for Computational Linguistics, 2016). Other NLP conferences and technical reports should follow this lead. In any case, it may be helpful if the peer-review mechanisms for journals and conferences include a means for the researcher to attach the supplemental description, as its quality may influence the votes of some reviewers regarding the quality of the paper.

6 Conclusion

This paper represents only a starting point for treating the research variable *gender* in an ethical fashion. The guidelines for researchers and practitioners here are intended to be straightforward and simple. However, to engage in research or practice that measures up to high ethical standards, we should see ethics not as a checklist at the beginning or end of a study's design and execution. Rather, we should view it as a process where we continually ask whether our actions respect human beings, deliver benefits and not harms, distribute potential benefits and harms fairly, and explain our research so that others may interrogate, test, and challenge its validity.

Other sets of social labels, such as race, ethnicity, and religion, raise similar ethical concerns, and researchers studying data including those categories should also consider the advice presented here.

Acknowledgments

Thanks to the anonymous reviewers for helpful guidance. This project received support from the University of Minnesota's Writing Studies Department James I. Brown fellowship fund and its College of Liberal Arts Graduate Research Partnership Program.

References

Larry Alexander and Michael Moore. 2016. Deontological ethics. In Edward N. Zalta, editor, *The Stanford Encyclopedia of Philosophy*. Metaphysics Research Lab, Stanford University, Winter 2016 edition.

Shlomo Argamon, Moshe Koppel, James W. Pennebaker, and Jonathan Schler. 2007. Mining the blogosphere: Age, gender and the varieties of self-expression. *First Monday*, 12(9).

Association for Computational Linguistics. 2016. Call for papers. the 55th Annual Meeting of the Association for Computational Linguistics | ACL Member Portal, November. Retrieved February 17, 2017 from https://www.aclweb.org/portal/content/55th-annual-meeting-association-computational-linguistics.

David Bamman, Jacob Eisenstein, and Tyler Schnoebelen. 2014. Gender identity and lexical variation in social media. *Journal of Sociolinguistics*, 18(2):135–160.

Karissa Bell. 2015. Facebook's new gender options let you choose anything you want. *Mashable*. Retrieved January 1, 2017, from http://mashable.com/2015/02/26/facebooks-new-custom-gender-options/.

Belmont Report. 1979. The Belmont Report: Ethical principles and guidelines for the protection of human subjects of research. Retrieved January 24, 2017, from https://www.hhs.gov/ohrp/regulations-and-policy/belmont-report/index.html.

Sandra L. Bem. 1974. The measurement of psychological androgyny. *Journal of Consulting and Clinical Psychology*, 42(2):155–162.

Fredda Blanchard-Fields, Lynda Suhrer-Roussel, and Christopher Hertzog. 1994. A confirmatory factor analysis of the Bem Sex Role Inventory: Old questions, new answers. *Sex Roles*, 30(5-6):423–457.

Lee-Ann Kastman Breuch, Andrea M. Olson, and Andrea Frantz. 2002. Considering ethical issues in technical communication research. In Laura J. Gurak and Mary M. Lay, editors, *Research in Technical Communication*, pages 1–22. Praeger Publishers, Westport, CT.

John Burger, John Henderson, George Kim, and Guido Zarrella. 2011. Discriminating gender on Twitter. Technical report, MITRE Corporation, Bedford, MA.

Judith Butler. 1993. *Bodies That Matter: On the Discursive Limits of "Sex"*. Routledge, New York.

Common Rule. 2009. Protection of Human Subjects. 45 Code of Federal Regulations Part 46. Retrieved February 13, 2017, from https://www.hhs.gov/ohrp/regulations-and-policy/regulations/45-cfr-46/.

Victoria Pruin DeFrancisco, Catherine Helen Palczewski, and Danielle Dick McGeough. 2014. *Gender in Communication: A Critical Introduction*. Sage Publications, Thousand Oaks, CA, 2nd edition.

FAT-ML. n.d. Fairness, accountability, and transparency in machine learning. Retrieved January 23, 2017, from http://www.fatml.org/.

GLAAD. n.d. a. Gay and Lesbian Alliance Against Defamation. GLAAD media reference guide. In focus: Covering the transgender community. Retrieved January 23, 2017, from http://www.glaad.org/reference/covering-trans-community.

GLAAD. n.d. b. Gay and Lesbian Alliance Against Defamation. Glossary of terms: Transgender. Retrieved January 23, 2017, from http://www.glaad.org/reference/transgender.

Bryce W. Goodman. 2016. A step towards accountable algorithms? algorithmic discrimination and the european union general data protection. In *29th Conference on Neural Information Processing Systems (NIPS 2016)*, Barcelona. NIPS Foundation.

Jurgen Habermas. 1995. Reconciliation Through the Public use of Reason: Remarks on John Rawls's Political Liberalism. *The Journal of Philosophy*, 92(3):109–131.

Moritz Hardt. 2014. How big data is unfair: Understanding sources of unfairness in data driven decision making, September. Retrieved January 23, 2017, from https://medium.com/@mrtz/how-big-data-is-unfair-9aa544d739de#.jr0yrklo0.

Alicia Hennig. 2010. Confucianism as corporate ethics strategy. *China Business and Research*, 2010(5):1–7.

Susan C. Herring and John C. Paolillo. 2006. Gender and genre variation in weblogs. *Journal of Sociolinguistics*, 10(4):439–459.

Rosalind Hursthouse and Glen Pettigrove. 2016. Virtue ethics. In Edward N. Zalta, editor, *The Stanford Encyclopedia of Philosophy*. Metaphysics Research Lab, Stanford University, Winter 2016 edition.

Anna Janssen and Tamar Murachver. 2004. The relationship between gender and topic in gender-preferential language use. *Written Communication*, 21(4):344 –367.

Moshe Koppel, Shlomo Argamon, and Anat Rachel Shimoni. 2002. Automatically categorizing written texts by author gender. *Literary and Linguistic Computing*, 17(4):401 –412.

Brian N. Larson. 2016. Gender/genre: The lack of gendered register in texts requiring genre knowledge. *Written Communication*, 33(4):360–384.

Brian N. Larson. 2017. First-year law students' court memoranda. Web download LDC2017T03, Linguistic Data Consortium, University of Pennsylvania, Philadelphia, February. http://catalog.ldc.upenn.edu/LDC2017T03.

Mary Sue MacNealy. 1998. *Strategies for Empirical Research in Writing*. Longman, Boston.

Plato. 2005. Meno. In *Plato: Meno and Other Dialogues*, pages 99–143. Oxford University Press, Oxford.

W. James Potter and Deborah Levine-Donnerstein. 1999. Rethinking validity and reliability in content analysis. *Journal of Applied Communication Research*, 27(3):258–284.

Delip Rao, David Yarowsky, Abhishek Shreevats, and Manaswi Gupta. 2010. Classifying latent user attributes in Twitter. In *Proceedings of the 2nd International Workshop on Search and Mining User-generated Contents*, pages 37–44, Toronto, ON, Canada, October. ACM.

Masoud Rouhizadeh, Lyle Ungar, Anneke Buffone, and Andrew H. Schwartz. 2016. Using syntactic and semantic context to explore psychodemographic differences in self-reference. In *Proceedings of the 2016 Conference on Empirical Methods in Natural Language Processing*, pages 2054–2059. Association for Computational Linguistics.

Walter Sinnott-Armstrong. 2015. Consequentialism. In Edward N. Zalta, editor, *The Stanford Encyclopedia of Philosophy*. Metaphysics Research Lab, Stanford University, Winter 2015 edition.

Jean M. Twenge. 1997. Changes in masculine and feminine traits over time: A meta-analysis. *Sex Roles*, 36(5-6):305–325.

Hanna Wallach. 2014. Big data, machine learning, and the social sciences: Fairness, accountability, and transparency. Retrieved January 23, 2017, from https://medium.com/@hannawallach/big-data-machine-learning-and-the-social-sciences-927a8e20460d#.czusepxiz.

Yuan Wang, Yang Xiao, Chao Ma, and Zhen Xiao. 2016. Improving users' demographic prediction via the videos they talk about. In *Proceedings of the 2016 Conference on Empirical Methods in Natural Language Processing*, pages 1359–1368. Association for Computational Linguistics.

World Medical Association. 1964. *Declaration of Helsinki: Ethical Principles for Medical Research Involving Human Subjects*. World Medical Association, Ferney-Voltaire, France, October 2013 edition.

Xiang Yan and Ling Yan. 2006. Gender classification of weblog authors. In *AAAI Spring Symposium: Computational Approaches to Analyzing Weblogs*, pages 228–230, Palo Alto, CA, March. Association for the Advancement of Artificial Intelligence.

These are not the Stereotypes You are Looking For:
Bias and Fairness in Authorial Gender Attribution

Corina Koolen
Institute for Logic, Language and
Computation, University of Amsterdam
`c.w.koolen@uva.nl`

Andreas van Cranenburgh
Institut für Sprache und Information
Heinrich Heine University Düsseldorf
`cranenburgh@phil.hhu.de`

Abstract

Stylometric and text categorization results show that author gender can be discerned in texts with relatively high accuracy. However, it is difficult to explain what gives rise to these results and there are many possible confounding factors, such as the domain, genre, and target audience of a text. More fundamentally, such classification efforts risk invoking stereotyping and essentialism. We explore this issue in two datasets of Dutch literary novels, using commonly used descriptive (LIWC, topic modeling) and predictive (machine learning) methods. Our results show the importance of controlling for variables in the corpus and we argue for taking care not to overgeneralize from the results.

1 Introduction

Women write more about emotions, men use more numbers (Newman et al., 2008). Conclusions such as these, based on Natural Language Processing (NLP) research into gender, are not just compelling to a general audience (Cameron, 1996), they are specific and seem objective, and hence are published regularly.

The ethical problem with this type of research however, is that stressing difference—where there is often considerable overlap—comes with the tendency of enlarging the perceived gap between female and male authors; especially when results are interpreted using gender stereotypes. Moreover, many researchers are not aware of possible confounding variables related to gender, resulting in well-intentioned but unsound research.

But, rather than suggesting not performing research into gender at all, we look into practical

solutions to conduct it more soundly.[1] The reason we do not propose to abandon gender analysis in NLP altogether is that female-male differences are quite striking when it comes to cultural production. We focus on literary fiction. Female authors still remain back-benched when it comes to gaining literary prestige: novels by females are still much less likely to be reviewed, or to win a literary award (Berkers et al., 2014; Verboord, 2012). Moreover, literary works by female authors are readily compared to popular bestselling genres typically written by and for women, referred to as 'women's novels,' whereas literary works by male authors are rarely gender-labeled or associated with popular genres (Groos, 2011). If we want to do research into the gender gap in cultural production, we need to investigate the role of author gender in texts without overgeneralizing to effects more properly explained by text-extrinsic perceptions of gender and literary quality.

In other words, NLP research can be very useful in revealing the mechanisms behind the differences, but in order for that to be possible, researchers need to be aware of the issues, and learn how to avoid essentialistic explanations. Thus, our question is: *how can we use NLP tools to research the relationship between gender and text meaningfully, yet without resorting to stereotyping or essentialism?*

Analysis of gender with NLP has roughly two methodological strands, the first *descriptive* and the second *predictive*. First, descriptive, is the technically least complex one. The researcher divides a set of texts into two parts, half written by female and half by male authors, processes these with the same computational tool(s), and tries to explain the

---

[1] We are not looking to challenge the use of gender as a binary construct in this paper, although this is a position that can be argued as well. Butler (2011) has shown how gender is not simply a biological given, nor a valid dichotomy. We recognize that computational methods may encourage this dichotomy further, but we shall focus on practical steps.

Proceedings of the First Workshop on Ethics in Natural Language Processing, pages 12–22,
Valencia, Spain, April 4th, 2017. © 2017 Association for Computational Linguistics

observed differences. Examples are Jockers (2013, pp. 118–153) and Hoover (2013). Olsen (2005) cleverly reinterprets Cixous' notion of *écriture féminine* to validate an examination of female authors separately from male authors (Cixous et al., 1976).

The second, at a first glance more neutral strand of automated gender division, is to use predictive methods such as text categorization: training a machine learning model to automatically recognize texts written by either women or men, and to measure the success of its predictions (e.g., Koppel et al., 2002; Argamon et al., 2009). Johannsen et al. (2015) combines descriptive and predictive approaches and mines a dataset for distinctive features with respect to gender. We will apply both descriptive and predictive methods as well.

The rest of this paper is structured as follows. Section 2 discusses two theoretical issues that should be considered before starting NLP research into gender: preemptive categorization, and the semblance of objectivity. These two theoretical issues are related to two potential practical pitfalls, the ones which we hope to remedy with these paper: dataset bias and interpretation bias (Section 3). In short, if researchers choose to do research into gender (a) they should be much more rigorous in selecting their dataset, i.e., confounding variables need to be given more attention when constructing a dataset; and (b) they need to avoid potential interpretative pitfalls: essentialism and stereotyping. Lastly, we provide computational evidence for our argument, and give handles on how to deal with the practical issues, based on a corpus of Dutch literary novels (Sections 4 through 6).

Note that none of the gender-related issues we argue are new, nor is the focus on computational analysis (see Baker, 2014). What is novel, however, is the practical application onto contemporary fiction. We want to show how fairly simple, commonly used computational tools can be applied in a way that avoids bias and promotes fairness—in this case with respect to gender, but note that the method is relevant to other categorizations as well.

2 Theoretical issues

Gender research in NLP gives rise to several ethical questions, as argued in for instance Bing and Bergvall (1996) and Nguyen et al. (2016). We discuss two theoretical issues here, which researchers need to consider carefully before performing NLP research into gender.

2.1 Preemptive categorization

Admittedly, categorization is hard to do without. We use it to make sense of the world around us. It is necessary to function properly, for instance to be able to distinguish a police officer from other persons. Gender is not an unproblematic category however, for a number of reasons.

First, feminists have argued that although many people fit into the categories female and male, there are more than two sexes (Bing and Bergvall, 1996, p. 2). Our having to decide how to categorize the novel by the transgender male in our corpus published before his transition is a case in point (we opted for male).

Second, it is problematic because gender is such a powerful categorization. Gender is the primary characteristic that people use for classification, over others like race, age and occupational role, regardless of *actual* importance (Rudman and Glick, 2012, p. 84). Baker (2014) analyzes research that finds gender differences in the spoken section of the British National Corpus (BNC), which indicates gender differences are quite prominent. However, the context also turned out to be different: women were more likely to have been recorded at home, men at work (p. 30). Only when one assumes that gender causes the contextual difference, can we attribute the differences to gender. There is no direct causation, however. Because of the saliency of the category of gender, this 'in-between step' of causation is not always noticed. Cameron (1996) altogether challenges the "notion of gender as a pre-existing demographic correlate which accounts for behavior, rather than as something that requires explanation in its own right" (p. 42).

This does not mean that gender differences do not exist or that we should not research them. But, as Bing and Bergvall (1996) point out: "The issue, of course, is not difference, but oversimplification and stereotyping" (p. 15). Stereotypes can only be built after categorization has taken place at all (Rudman and Glick, 2012). This means that the method of classification itself inherently comes with the potential pitfall of stereotyping.

Although the differences found in a divided corpus are not necessarily meaningful, nor always reproducible with other datasets, an 'intuitive' explanation is a trap easily fallen into: rather than being restricted to the particular dataset, results can be unjustly ascribed to supposedly innate qualities of all members of that gender, and extrapolated to all members of the gender in trying to motivate a result. This type of bias is called essentialism (Allport, 1979; Gelman, 2003).

Rudman and Glick (2012) argue that stereotypes (which are founded on essentialism) cause harm because they can be used to unfairly discriminate against individuals—even if they are accurate on average differences (p. 95).

On top of that, ideas on how members of each gender act do not remain descriptive, but become prescriptive. This means that based on certain differences, social norms form on how members of a certain gender *should* act, and these are then reinforced, with punishment for deviation. As Baker (2014) notes: "The gender differences paradigm creates expectations that people should speak at the linguistic extremes of their sex in order to be seen as normal and/or acceptable, and thus it problematizes people who do not conform, creating in- and out-groups." (p. 42)

Thus, although categorization in itself can appear unproblematic, actively choosing to apply it has the potential pitfall of reinforcing essentialistic ideas on gender and enlarging stereotypes. This is of course not unique to NLP, but the lure of making sweeping claims with big data, coupled with NLP's semblance of objectivity, makes it a particularly pressing topic for the discipline.

2.2 Semblance of objectivity

An issue which applies to NLP techniques in general, but particularly to machine learning, is the *semblance* of neutrality and objectivity (see Rieder and Röhle, 2012). Machine learning models can make predictions on unseen texts, and this shows that one can indeed automatically identify differences between male and female authors, which are relatively consistent over multiple text types and domains. Note first that the outcome of these machine learning classifiers are different from what many general readers expect: the nature of these differences is often stylistic, rather than content-related (e.g., Flekova et al. 2016; Janssen and Murachver 2005, pp. 211–212). For men they include a higher proportion of determiners, numerical quantifiers (Argamon et al., 2009; Johannsen et al., 2015), and overall verbosity (longer sentences and texts; Newman et al. 2008). For women a higher use of personal pronouns, negative polar-

ity items (Argamon et al., 2009), and verbs stands out (Johannsen et al., 2015; Newman et al., 2008). What these differences mean, or why they are important for literary analysis (other than a functional benefit), is not generally made sufficiently evident.

But while evaluations of out-of-sample predictions provide an objective measure of success, the technique is ultimately not any more neutral than the descriptive method, with its preemptive group selection. Even though the algorithm automatically finds gender differences, the fact remains that the researcher selects the gender as two groups to train for, and the predictive success says nothing about the merits (e.g., explanatory value) of this division. In other words, it starts with the same premise as the descriptive method, and thus needs to keep the same ethical issues in mind.

3 Practical concerns

Although the two theoretical issues are unavoidable, there are two practical issues inextricably linked to them, dataset and interpretation bias, which the researcher should strive to address.

3.1 Dataset bias

Strictly speaking, a corpus is supposed to represent a statistically representative sample, and the conclusions from experiments with corpora are only valid insofar as this assumption is met. In gender research, this assumptions is too often violated, as potential confounding factors are not accounted for, exacerbating the ethical issues discussed.

For example, Johannsen et al. (2015) work with a corpus of online reviews divided by gender and age. However, reflected in the dataset is the types of products that men and women tend to review (e.g., cars vs. makeup). They argue that their use of abstract syntactic features may overcome this domain bias, but this argument is not very convincing. For example, the use of measurement phrases as a distinctive feature for men can also be explained by its higher relevance in automotive products versus makeup, instead of as a gender marker.

Argamon et al. (2009) carefully select texts by men and women from the same domain, French literature, which overcomes this problem. However, since the corpus is largely based on nineteenth century texts, any conclusions are strongly influenced by literary and gender norms from this time period (which evidently differ from contemporary norms).

Koppel et al. (2002) compose a corpus from the

BNC, which has more recent texts from the 1970s, and includes genre classifications which together with gender are balanced in the resulting corpus. Lastly, Sarawgi et al. (2011) present a study that carefully and systematically controls for topic and genre bias. They show that in cross-domain tasks, the performance of gender attribution decreases, and investigate the different characteristics of lexical, syntactic, and character-based features; the latter prove to be most robust.

On the surface the latter two seem to be a reasonable approach of controlling variables where possible. One remaining issue is the potential for publication bias: if for whatever reason women are less likely to be published, it will be reflected in this corpus without being obvious (a hidden variable).

In sum, controlling for author characteristics should not be neglected. Moreover, it is often not clear from the datasets whether text variables are sufficiently controlled for either, such as period, text type, or genre. Freed (1996) has shown that researchers too easily attribute differences to gender, when in fact other intersecting variables are at play. We argue that there is still much to gain in the consideration of author and text type characteristics, but we focus on the latter here. Even within the text type of fictional novels, in a very restricted period of time, as we shall show, there is a variety of subgenres that each have their own characteristics, which might erroneously be attributed to gender.

3.2 Interpretation bias

The acceptance of gender as a cause of difference is not uncommon in computational research (cf. Section 1). Supporting research beyond the chosen dataset is not always sought, because the alignment of results with 'common knowledge' (which is generally based on stereotypes) is seen as sufficient, when in fact this is more aptly described as researcher's bias. Conversely, it is also problematic when counterintuitive results are labeled as deviant and inexplicable (e.g., in Hoover, 2013). This is a form of cherry picking. Another subtle example of this is the choice of visualization in Jockers and Mimno (2013) to illustrate a topic model. They choose to visualize only gender-stereotypical topics, even though they make up a small part of the results, as they do note carefully (Jockers and Mimno, 2013, p. 762). Still, this draws attention to the stereotype-confirming topics.

Regardless of the issue whether differences between men and women are innate and/or socially constructed, such interpretations are not only unsound, they promote the separation of female and male authors in literary judgments. But it can be done differently. A good example of research based on careful gender-related analysis is Muzny et al. (2016) who consider gender as performative language use in its dialogue and social context.

Dataset and interpretation bias are quite hard to avoid with this type of research, because of the theoretical issues discussed in Section 2. We now provide two experiments that show why it is so important to try to avoid these biases, and provide first steps as to how this can be done.

4 Data

To support our argument, we analyze two datasets. The first is the corpus of the Riddle of Literary Quality: 401 Dutch-language (original and translated) novels published between 2007–2012, that were bestsellers or most often lent from libraries in the period 2009–2012 (henceforth: Riddle corpus). It consists mostly of suspense novels (46.4 %) and general fiction (36.9 %), with smaller portions of romantic novels (10.2 %) and other genres (fantasy, horror, etc.; 6.5 %). It contains about the same amount of female authors (48.9 %) as male authors (47.6 %) and 3.5 % of unknown gender, or duo's of mixed gender. In the genre of general fiction however (where the literary works are situated), there are more originally Dutch works by male authors, and more translated work by female authors.

The second corpus (henceforth: Nominee corpus) was compiled because of this skewness; there are few Dutch female literary authors in the Riddle corpus. It is a set of 50 novels that were nominated for one of the two most well-known literary prizes in the Netherlands, the *AKO Literatuurprijs* (currently called ECI Literatuurprijs) and the *Libris Literatuur Prijs*, in the period 2007-2012, but which were not part of the Riddle corpus. Variables controlled for are gender (24 female, 25 male, 1 transgender male who was then still known as a female), country of origin (Belgium and the Netherlands), and whether the novel won a prize or not (2 within each gender group). The corpus is relatively small, because the percentage of female nominees was small (26.2 %).

5 Experiments with LIWC

Newman et al. (2008) relate a descriptive method

of extracting gender differences, using Linguistic Inquiry and Word Count (LIWC; Pennebaker et al., 2007). LIWC is a text analysis tool typically used for sentiment mining. It collects word frequencies based on word lists and calculates the relative frequency per word list in given texts. The word lists, or categories, are of different orders: psychological, linguistic, and personal concerns; see Table 1; LIWC and other word list based methods have been applied to research of fiction (e.g., Nichols et al., 2014; Mohammad, 2011). We use a validated Dutch translation of LIWC (Zijlstra et al., 2005).

5.1 Riddle corpus

We apply LIWC to the Riddle corpus, where we compare the corpus along author gender lines. We also zoom in on the two biggest genres in the corpus, general fiction and suspense. When we compare the results of novels by male authors versus those by female authors, we find that 48 of 66 LIWC categories differ significantly ($p < 0.01$), after a Benjamini-Hochberg False Discovery Rate correction. In addition to significance tests, we report Cohen's d effect size (Cohen, 1988). An effect size $|d| > 0.2$ can be considered non-negligible.

The results coincide with gender stereotypical notions. Gender stereotypes can relate to several attributes: physical characteristics, preferences and interest, social roles and occupations; but psychological research generally focuses on personality. Personality traits related to agency and power are often attributed to men, and nurturing and empathy to women (Rudman and Glick, 2012, pp. 85–86). The results in Table 1 were selected from the categories with the largest effect sizes. These stereotype-affirming effects remain when only a subset of the corpus with general fiction and suspense novels is considered.

In other words, quite some gender stereotype-confirming differences *appear* to be genre independent here, plus there are some characteristics that were also identified by the machine learning experiments mentioned in section 2.2. Novels by female authors for instance score significantly higher overall and within genre in Affect, Pronoun, Home, Body and Social; whereas novels by male authors score significantly higher on Articles, Prepositions, Numbers, and Occupation.

The only result here that counters stereotypes is the higher score for female authors on Cognitive

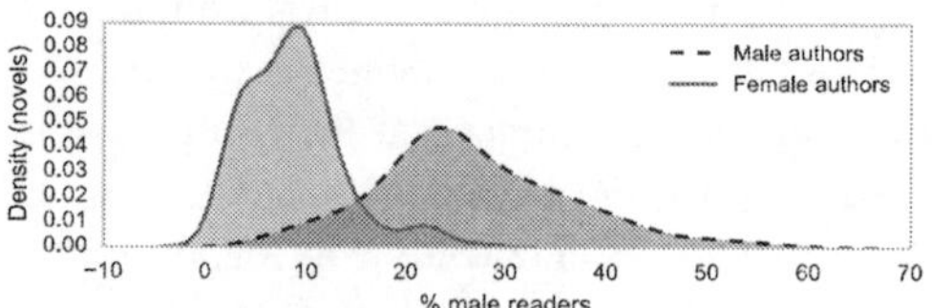

Figure 1: Kernel density estimation of the percentage of male readers with respect to author gender.

Processes, which describes thought processes and has been claimed to be a marker of science fiction—as opposed to fantasy and mystery—because "reasoned decision-making is constitutive of the resolution of typical forms of conflict in science fiction" (Nichols et al., 2014, p. 30). Arguably, reasoned decision-making is stereotypically associated with the male gender.

It is quite possible to leave the results at that, and attempt an explanation. The differences are not just found in the overall corpus, where a reasonable amount of romantic novels (approximately 10 %, almost exclusively by female authors) could be seen as the cause for a gender stereotypical outcome. The results are also found within the traditionally 'male' genre of suspense (although half of the suspense authors are female in this corpus), and within the genre of general fiction.

Nonetheless, there are some elements to the corpus that were not considered. The most important factor not taken into account, is whether the novel has been originally written in Dutch or whether it is a translation. As noted, the general fiction category is skewed along gender lines: there are very few originally Dutch female authors.

Another, more easily overlooked factor is the existence of subgenres which might skew the outcome. Suspense and general fiction are categories that are already considerably more specific than the 'genres' (what we would call text-types) researched in the previously mentioned studies, such as fiction versus non-fiction. For instance, there is a typical subgenre in Dutch suspense novels, the so-called 'literary thriller', which has a very specific content and style (Jautze, 2013). The gender of the author—female—is part of its signature.

Readership might play a role in this as well. The percentage of readers for female and male authors, taken from the Dutch 2013 National Reader Survey (approximately 14,000 respondents) shows how gendered the division of readers is. This distribu-

LIWC category	Examples	Female		Male		effect	sign.
		mean	SD	mean	SD	size (d)	
Linguistic							
Prepositions	to, with, above	11.38	0.86	11.92	0.86	-0.63	*
Pronouns	I, them, itself	12.58	1.90	10.14	2.10	1.22	*
Negations	no, not, never	2.02	0.31	1.78	0.35	0.74	*
Article	a, an, the	8.48	1.08	9.71	1.19	-1.08	*
Numbers		0.61	0.15	0.79	0.25	-0.86	*
Psychological							
Social	mate, talk, they, child	10.81	2.00	9.54	1.73	0.68	*
Friends	buddy, friend, neighbor	0.10	0.04	0.09	0.04	0.23	
Humans		0.43	0.16	0.41	0.15	0.11	
Affect	happy, cried, abandon	2.84	0.49	2.35	0.38	1.12	*
Positive emotions	love, nice, sweet	1.38	0.34	1.13	0.23	0.86	*
Cognitive processes	cause, know, ought	5.51	0.67	5.03	0.72	0.69	*
Occupation	work, class, boss	0.54	0.15	0.67	0.20	-0.75	*
Current concerns							
Home	apartment, kitchen, family	0.42	0.13	0.34	0.14	0.57	*
Money	cash, taxes, income	0.20	0.10	0.21	0.10	-0.12	
Body	ache, breast, sleep	1.30	0.41	1.06	0.33	0.63	*

Table 1: A selection of LIWC categories with results on the Riddle corpus. The indented categories are subcategories forming a subset of the preceding category. * indicates a significant result.

tion is visualized in Figure 1, which is a Kernel Density Estimation (KDE). A KDE can be seen as a continuous (smoothed) variant of a histogram, in which the x-axis shows the variable of interest, and y-axis indicates how common instances are for a given value on the x-axis. In this case, the graph indicates the number of novels read by a given proportion of male versus female readers. Male readers barely read the female authors in our corpus, female readers read both genders; there is a selection of novels which is only read by female readers. Hence, the gender of the target reader group differs per genre as well, and this is another possible influence on author style.

In sum, there is no telling whether we are looking purely at author gender, or also at translation and/or subgenre, or even at productions of gendered perceptions of genre.

5.2 Comparison with Nominees corpus

We now consider a corpus of novels that were nominated for the two most well-known literary awards in the Netherlands, the *AKO Literatuurprijs* and *Libris Literatuur Prijs*. This corpus has less confounding variables, as these novels were all originally written in Dutch, and are all of the same genre. They are fewer, however, fifty in total. We hypothesize that there are few differences in LIWC scores between the novels by the female and male authors, as they have been nominated for a literary award, and will not be marked as overtly by a genre. All of them have passed the bar of literary quality—and

few female authors have made the cut in this period of time to begin with;[2] thus, we contend, they will be more similar to the male authors in this corpus than in the Riddle corpus containing bestsellers.

However, here we run into the problem that significance tests on this corpus of different size would not be comparable to those on the previous corpus; for example, due to the smaller size, there will be a lower chance of finding a significant effect (and indeed, repeating the procedure of the previous section yields no significant results for this corpus). Moreover, comparing only means is of limited utility. Inspection does reveal that five effect sizes increase: Negations, Positive emotions, Cognitive processes, Friends, and Money; all relate more strongly to female authors. Other effect sizes decrease, mostly mildly.

In light of these problems with the t-test in analyzing LIWC-scores, we offer an alternative. In interpretation, the first step is to note the strengths and weaknesses of the method applied. The largest problem with comparing LIWC scores among two groups with a t-test, is that it only tests means: the mean score for female authors versus the mean score for male authors in our research. A t-test to compare means is restricted to examining the groups as a whole, which, we as we argued, is un-

---

[2] Note that female authors not being nominated for literary prizes does not say anything about the relationship between gender and literary quality. Perhaps female authors are overlooked, or they write materials of lesser literary quality, or they are simply judged this way because men have set the standard and the standard is biased towards 'male' qualities.

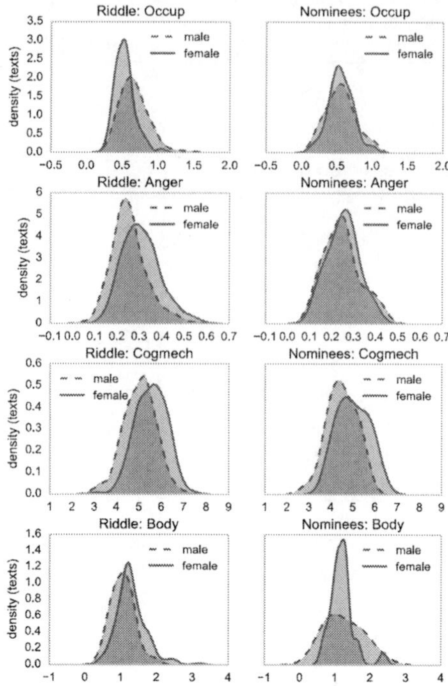

Figure 2: Kernel density estimation of four LIWC categories across the novels of the Riddle (left) and Nominees (right) corpus.

Riddle	BoW	char3grams	support
female	83.7	80.8	196
male	82.1	79.9	191
avg / total	**82.9**	80.4	387

Nominees	BoW	char3grams	support
female	63.2	57.9	24
male	77.4	74.2	26
avg / total	**70.6**	66.4	50

Table 2: Gender classification scores (F1) on the Riddle corpus (above) and the Nominees corpus (below).

sound to begin with. That is why we only use it as a means to an end. A KDE plot of scores on each category gives better insight into the distribution and differences across the novels; see Figure 2.

Occupation and Anger are two categories of which the difference in means largely disappears with the Nominees corpus, showing an effect size of $d < 0.1$. The plots demonstrate nicely how the overlap has become near perfect with the Nominees corpus, indicating that subgenre and/or translation might have indeed been factors that caused the difference in the Riddle corpus. Cognitive processes (Cogmech) is a category which increases in effect size with the Nominees corpus. We see that the overlap with female and male authors is large, but that a small portion of male authors uses the words in this category less often than other authors and a small portion of the female authors uses it more often than other authors.

While the category Body was found to have a significant difference with the Riddle corpus, in the KDE plot it looks remarkably similar, while in the Nominees corpus, there is a difference not in mean but in variance. It appears that on the one hand, there are quite some male authors who use the words *less* often than female authors, and on the other, there is a similar-sized group of male authors who—and this counters stereotypical explanations—use the words *more* often than female authors. The individual differences between authors appear to be more salient than differences between the means; contrary to what the means indicate, Body apparently is a category and topic worth looking into. This shows how careful one must be in comparing means of groups within a corpus, with respect to (author) gender or otherwise.

6 Machine Learning Experiments

In order to confirm the results in the previous section, we now apply machine learning methods that have proved most successful in previous work. Since we want to compare the two corpora, we opt for training and fitting the models on the Riddle corpus, and applying those models to both corpora.

6.1 Predictive: Classification

We replicate the setup of Argamon et al. (2009), which is to use frequencies of lemmas to train a support vector classifier. We restrict the features to the 60 % most common lemmas in the corpus and transform their counts to relative frequencies (i.e., a bag-of-words model; BoW). Because of the robust results reported with character n-grams in Sarawgi et al. (2011), we also run the experiment with character trigrams, in this case without a restriction on the features. We train on the Riddle corpus, and evaluate on both the the Riddle corpus and the Nominees corpus; for the former we use 5-fold cross-validation to ensure an out-of-sample evaluation. We leave out authors of unknown or multiple genders, since this class is too small to learn from.

See Table 2 for the results; Table 4 shows the confusion matrix with the number of correct and in-

female: toespraak, engel, energie, champagne, gehoorzaam, grendel, drug, tante, echtgenoot, vleug
speech$_{NN}$, angel, energy, champagne, docile,   lock,   drug, aunt, spouse,   tad

male: wee, datzelfde, hollen, conversatie, plak, kruimel, strijken, gelijk,   inpakken, ondergaan
woe, same,   run,   conversation, slice, crumble, iron$_{VB}$, right/just, pack,   undergo

Table 3: A sample of 10 distinctive, mid-frequency features.

Riddle	female	male
female	**170**	26
male	40	**151**
Nominees	female	male
female	**12**	12
male	2	**24**

Table 4: Confusion matrices for the SVM results with BoW. The diagonal indicates the number of correctly classified texts. The rows show the true labels, while the columns show the predictions.

correct classifications. As in the previous section, it appears that gender differences are less pronounced in the Nominees corpus, shown by the substantial difference of almost 10 F1 percentage points. We also see the effect of a different training and test corpus: the classifier reveals a bias for attributing texts to male authors with the Nominees corpus, shown by the distribution of misclassifications in Table 4. On the one hand, the success can be explained by similarities of the corpora; on the other, the male bias reveals that the model is also affected by particularities of the training corpus. Sarawgi et al. (2011) show that with actual cross-domain classification, performance drops more significantly.

A linear model[3] is in principle straightforward to interpret: features make either a positive or a negative contribution to the final prediction. However, due to the fact that thousands of features are involved, and words may be difficult to interpret without context, looking at the features with the highest weight may not give much insight; the tail may be so long that the sign of the prediction still flips multiple times after the contribution of the top 20 features has been taken into account.

Indeed, looking at the features with the highest weight does not show a clear picture: the top 20 consists mostly of pronouns and other function words. We have tried to overcome this by filter-

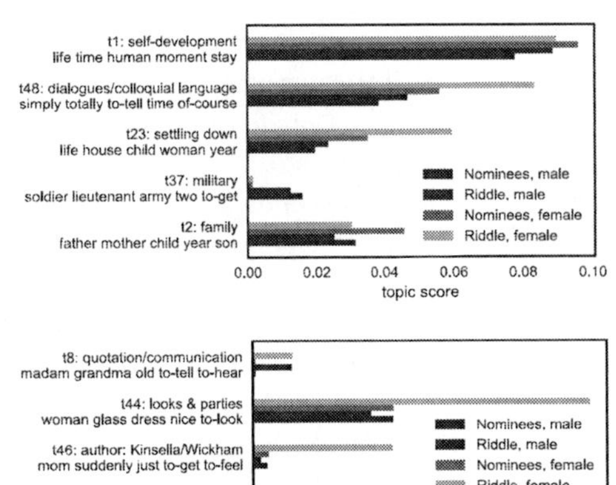

Figure 3: Comparison of mean topic weights w.r.t. gender and corpus, showing largest (above) and smallest (below) male-female differences.

ing out the most frequent words and sorting words with the largest difference in the Nominees corpus (which helps to focus on the differences that remain in the corpus other than the one on which the model has been trained). As an indication of the sort of differences the classifier exploits, Table 3 shows a selection of features; the results cannot be easily aligned with stereotypes, and it remains difficult to explain the success of the classifier from a small sample as this. We now turn to a different model to analyze the differences between the two corpora in terms of gender.

6.2 Descriptive: Topic Model

We use a topic model of the Riddle corpus presented in Jautze et al. (2016) to infer topic weights for both corpora. This model of 50 topics was derived with Latent Dirichlet Allocation (LDA), based on a lemmatized version of the Riddle corpus without function words or punctuation, divided into chunks of 1000 tokens. We compare the topic weights with respect to gender by taking the mean topic weights of the texts of each gender. From the list of 50 topics we show the top 5 with both

---

[3]Other models such as decision trees are even more amenable to interpretation. However, in the context of text categorization, bag-of-word models with large numbers of features work best, which do not work well in combination with decision trees.

the largest and the smallest (absolute) difference between the genders (with respect to the Nominees corpus);[4] see Figure 3. Note that the topic labels were assigned by hand, and other interpretations of the topic keys are possible.

The largest differences contain topics that confirm stereotypes: military (male) and settling down (female). This is not unexpected: the choice to examine the largest differences ensures these are the extreme ends of female-male differences.[5] However, the topics that are most similar for the genders in the Nominees corpus contain stereotype-confirming topics as well—i.e., they both score similarly low on 'looks and parties.'

Finally, the large difference on dialogue and colloquial language shows that speech representation forms a fruitful hypothesis for explaining at least part of the gender differences.

7 Discussion and Conclusion

Gender is not a self-explanatory variable. In this paper, we have used fairly simple, commonly applied Natural Language Processing (NLP) techniques to demonstrate how a seemingly 'neutral' corpus—one that consists of only one text-type, fiction, and with a balanced number of male and female authors—can easily be used to produce stereotype-affirming results, while in fact (at least) two other variables were not controlled for properly. Researchers need to be much more careful in selecting their data and interpreting results when performing NLP research into gender, to minimize the ethical issues discussed.

From an ethics point of view, care should be taken with NLP research into gender, due to the unavoidable ethical-theoretical issues we discussed: (1) Preemptive categorization: dividing a dataset in two preemptively invites essentialist or even stereotyping explanations; (2) The semblance of objectivity: because a computer algorithm calculates differences between genders, this lends a sense of objectivity; we are inclined to forget that the researcher has chosen to look or train for these two categories of female and male.

However, we do want to keep doing textual analysis into gender, as we argued we should, in order to analyze gender bias in cultural production. The good news is that we can take practical steps to minimize their effect. We show that we can do this by taking care to avoid two practical problems that are intertwined with the two theoretical issues: dataset bias and interpretation bias.

Dataset bias can be avoided by controlling for more variables than is generally done. We argue that apart from author variables (which we have chosen not to focus on in this paper, but which should be taken into account), text variables should be applied more restrictively. Fiction, even, is too broad as a genre; subgenres as specific as 'literary thriller' can become confounding factors as well, as we have shown in our set of Dutch bestsellers, both in the experiments with LIWC as well as the machine learning experiments.

Interpretation bias stems from considering female and male authors as groups that can be relied upon and taken for granted. We have shown with visualizations that statistically significant differences between genders can be caused by outliers on each end of the spectrum, even though the gender overlap is large on the one hand; and that possibly interesting within-group differences become confounded by solely using means over gender groups on the other hand, missing differences that might be interesting. Taking these extra visualization steps makes for a better basis for analysis that does right by authors, no matter of which gender they are.

This work has focused on standard explanatory and predictive text analysis tools. Recent developments with more advanced techniques, in particular word embeddings, appear to allow gender prejudice in word associations to be isolated, and even eliminated (Schmidt, 2015; Bolukbasi et al., 2016; Caliskan-Islam et al., 2016); applying these methods to literature is an interesting avenue for future work.

The code and results for this paper are available as a notebook at `https://github.com/andreasvc/ethnlpgender`

Acknowledgments

We thank the six (!) reviewers for their insightful and valuable comments.

---

[4]By comparing absolute differences in topic weights, rarer topics with small but nevertheless consistent differences may be overlooked; using relative differences would remove this bias, but introduces the risk of giving too much weight to rarer topics. We choose the former to focus on the more prominent and representative topics.

[5]Note that the topics were derived from the Riddle corpus, which contains romance and spy novels.

References

Gordon Willard Allport. 1979. *The nature of prejudice*. Basic books.

Shlomo Argamon, Jean-Baptiste Goulain, Russell Horton, and Mark Olsen. 2009. Vive la Différence! Text mining gender difference in French literature. *Digital Humanities Quarterly*, 3(2). http://www.digitalhumanities. org/dhq/vol/3/2/000042/000042.html.

Paul Baker. 2014. *Using corpora to analyze gender*. A&C Black.

Victoria L. Bergvall, Janet M. Bing, and Alice F. Freed, editors. 1996. *Rethinking language and gender research: theory and practice*. Longman, London.

Pauwke Berkers, Marc Verboord, and Frank Weij. 2014. Genderongelijkheid in de dagbladberichtgeving over kunst en cultuur. *Sociologie*, 10(2):124–146. Transl.: *Gender inequality in newspaper coverage of arts and culture*. https://doi.org/10. 5117/SOC2014.2.BERK.

Janet M. Bing and Victoria L. Bergvall. 1996. The question of questions: Beyond binary thinking. In Bergvall et al. (1996).

Tolga Bolukbasi, Kai-Wei Chang, James Y. Zou, Venkatesh Saligrama, and Adam T Kalai. 2016. Man is to computer programmer as woman is to homemaker? debiasing word embeddings. In *Advances in Neural Information Processing Systems*, pages 4349–4357. http://papers.nips.cc/paper/6228-man-is-to-computer-programmer-as-woman-is-to-homemaker-debiasing-word-embeddings.pdf.

Judith Butler. 2011. *Gender trouble: Feminism and the subversion of identity*. Routledge, New York, NY.

Aylin Caliskan-Islam, Joanna J. Bryson, and Arvind Narayanan. 2016. Semantics derived automatically from language corpora necessarily contain human biases. ArXiv preprint, https://arxiv.org/ abs/1608.07187.

Deborah Cameron. 1996. The language-gender interface: challenging co-optation. In Bergvall et al. (1996).

Hélène Cixous, Keith Cohen, and Paula Cohen. 1976. The laugh of the Medusa. *Signs: Journal of Women in Culture and Society*, 1(4):875–893. http://dx. doi.org/10.1086/493306.

Jacob Cohen. 1988. *Statistical power analysis for the behavioral sciences*. Routledge Academic, New York, NY.

Lucie Flekova, Jordan Carpenter, Salvatore Giorgi, Lyle Ungar, and Daniel Preoţiuc-Pietro. 2016. Analyzing biases in human perception of user age and gender from text. In *Proceedings of ACL*, pages 843–854. http://aclweb.org/anthology/ P16-1080.

Alice Freed. 1996. Language and gender research in an experimental setting. In Bergvall et al. (1996).

Susan A. Gelman. 2003. *The essential child: Origins of essentialism in everyday thought*. Oxford University Press.

Marije Groos. 2011. Wie schrijft die blijft? schrijfsters in de literaire kritiek van nu. *Tijdschrift voor Genderstudies*, 3(3):31–36. Transl.: *Who writes endures? Women writers in current literary criticism*. http://rjh.ub.rug. nl/genderstudies/article/view/1575.

David Hoover. 2013. Text analysis. In Kenneth Price and Ray Siemens, editors, *Literary Studies in the Digital Age: An Evolving Anthology*. Modern Language Association, New York.

Anna Janssen and Tamar Murachver. 2005. Readers' perceptions of author gender and literary genre. *Journal of Language and Social Psychology*, 24(2):207–219. http://dx.doi.org/10. 1177%2F0261927X05275745.

Kim Jautze. 2013. Hoe literair is de literaire thriller? Blog post. Transl.: *How literary is the literary thriller?*, http://kimjautze.blogspot. nl/2013/11/hoe-literair-is-de-literaire-thriller.html.

Kim Jautze, Andreas van Cranenburgh, and Corina Koolen. 2016. Topic modeling literary quality. In *Digital Humanities 2016: Conference Abstracts*, pages 233–237. Krákow, Poland. http: //dh2016.adho.org/abstracts/95.

Matthew L. Jockers. 2013. *Macroanalysis: Digital methods and literary history*. University of Illinois Press, Urbana, Chicago, Springfield.

Matthew L. Jockers and David Mimno. 2013. Significant themes in 19th-century literature. *Poetics*, 41(6):750–769. http://dx.doi.org/10. 1016/j.poetic.2013.08.005.

Anders Johannsen, Dirk Hovy, and Anders Søgaard. 2015. Cross-lingual syntactic variation over age and gender. In *Proceedings of CoNLL*, pages 103–112. http://aclweb.org/anthology/ K15-1011.

Moshe Koppel, Shlomo Argamon, and Anat Rachel Shimoni. 2002. Automatically categorizing written texts by author gender. *Literary and Linguistic Computing*, 17(4):401–412. http://llc.oxfordjournals.org/

content/17/4/401.abstract.

Saif Mohammad. 2011. From once upon a time to happily ever after: Tracking emotions in novels and fairy tales. In *Proceedings of the 5th Workshop on Language Technology for Cultural Heritage, Social Sciences, and Humanities*, pages 105–114. http://aclweb.org/anthology/W11-1514.

Grace Muzny, Mark Algee-Hewitt, and Dan Jurafsky. 2016. The dialogic turn and the performance of gender: the English canon 1782–2011. In *Digital Humanities 2016: Conference Abstracts*, pages 296–299. http://dh2016.adho.org/abstracts/153.

Matthew L. Newman, Carla J. Groom, Lori D. Handelman, and James W. Pennebaker. 2008. Gender differences in language use: An analysis of 14,000 text samples. *Discourse Processes*, 45(3):211–236. http://dx.doi.org/10.1080/01638530802073712.

Dong Nguyen, A. Seza Doğruö, Carolyn P. Rosé, and Franciska de Jong. 2016. Computational Sociolinguistics: A survey. *Computational Linguistics*, 42(3):537–593. http://aclweb.org/anthology/J16-3007.

Ryan Nichols, Justin Lynn, and Benjamin Grant Purzycki. 2014. Toward a science of science fiction: Applying quantitative methods to genre individuation. *Scientific Study of Literature*, 4(1):25–45. http://dx.doi.org/10.1075/ssol.4.1.02nic.

Mark Olsen. 2005. Écriture féminine: searching for an indefinable practice? *Literary and linguistic computing*, 20(Suppl. 1):147–164.

James W. Pennebaker, Roger J. Booth, and Martha E. Francis. 2007. Linguistic inquiry and word count: LIWC [computer software]. www.liwc.net.

Theo Rieder and Bernhard Röhle. 2012. Digital methods: Five challenges. In *Understanding digital humanities*, pages 67–84. Palgrave Macmillan, London.

Laurie A. Rudman and Peter Glick. 2012. *The social psychology of gender: How power and intimacy shape gender relations*. Guilford Press.

Ruchita Sarawgi, Kailash Gajulapalli, and Yejin Choi. 2011. Gender attribution: tracing stylometric evidence beyond topic and genre. In *Proceedings of CoNLL*, pages 78–86. http://aclweb.org/anthology/W11-0310.

Ben Schmidt. 2015. Rejecting the gender binary: a vector-space operation. Blog post, http://bookworm.benschmidt.org/posts/2015-10-30-rejecting-the-gender-binary.html.

Marc Verboord. 2012. Female bestsellers: A cross-national study of gender inequality and the popular–highbrow culture divide in fiction book production, 1960-2009. *European Journal of Communication*, 27(4):395–409. http://dx.doi.org/10.1177%2F0267323112459433.

Hanna Zijlstra, Henriët Van Middendorp, Tanja Van Meerveld, and Rinie Geenen. 2005. Validiteit van de Nederlandse versie van de Linguistic Inquiry and Word Count (LIWC). *Netherlands journal of psychology*, 60(3):50–58. Transl.: *Validity of the Dutch version of LIWC*. http://dx.doi.org/10.1007/BF03062342.

A Quantitative Study of Data in the NLP community

Margot Mieskes
Information Science
Darmstadt University of Applied Sciences
`margot.mieskes@h-da.de`

Abstract

We present results on a quantitative analysis of publications in the NLP domain on collecting, publishing and availability of research data. We find that a wide range of publications rely on data crawled from the web, but few give details on how potentially sensitive data was treated. Additionally, we find that while links to repositories of data are given, they often do not work even a short time after publication. We put together several suggestions on how to improve this situation based on publications from the NLP domain, but also other research areas.

1 Introduction

The Natural Language Processing (NLP) community makes extensive use of resources available on the internet. And as research in NLP attracts more attention by the general public, we have to make sure, our results are solid and reliable, similar to medicine and pharmacy. In the case of medicine, the general public is often too optimistic. In NLP this over-optimism can have a negative impact, such as in articles on automatic speech recognition[1] or personality profiling[2]. Few point out, that the algorithms are not perfect and do not solve all the problems, as on terrorism prevention[3] or sentiment analysis[4].

Therefore, important questions are, what happens to the data and how reliable are results obtained through them.

We present a quantitative analysis of how often data is being collected, how data is published, and what data types are being collected. Taken together it gives insight into issues arising from collecting data and from distributing it via channels, that do not allow for reproducing results, even after a comparably short period of time. Based on this, we open a discussion about best practices on data collection, storage and distribution in order to ensure high-quality research, that is solid and reproducable. But also to make sure, users of, i.e., social media channels are treated according to general standards concerning sensitive data.

2 Related Work

In the following we give a broad overview on re-usability of published code and data sets, but also on results of actual reproducibility studies and privacy issues from various domains.

General Guidelines "One goal of scientific publication is to share results in enough detail to allow other research teams to reproduce them and to build on them" (Iorns, 2012). But even in medical or pharmaceutical research failure to replicate results can be as high as 89% (Iorns, 2012). Journals such as Nature[5] and PLOS[6] require their authors to make relevant code available to editors and reviewers. If code cannot be shared, the editor can decline a paper from publication.[5] Additionally, they list a range of repositories that are "recognized and trusted within their respective communities" and meet accepted criteria as "trustwor-

---

[1] `https://theintercept.com/2015/05/05/nsa-speech-recognition-snowden-searchable-text/`
[2] `http://www.digitaltonto.com/2013/the-dark-side-of-technology/`
[3] `http://www.telegraph.co.uk/news/uknews/terrorism-in-the-uk/11431757/Algorithms-and-computers-wont-stop-terrorism.html`
[4] `http://www.nytimes.com/2009/08/24/technology/internet/24emotion.html?_r=1`

[5] `http://www.nature.com/authors/policies/availability.html`
[6] `http://journals.plos.org/plosone/s/data-availability`

Proceedings of the First Workshop on Ethics in Natural Language Processing, pages 23–29,
Valencia, Spain, April 4th, 2017. © 2017 Association for Computational Linguistics

thy digital repositories" for storing data[6]. This enables authors to follow best practices in their fields for the preparation, recording and storing of data.

Study on re-usability of Code Collberg et al. (2015) did an extensive study into the release and usability of code in the domain of computer science. The authors categorized published code into three categories: Projects that were obtained and built in less than 30 minutes, projects that were successfully built in more than 30 minutes and projects where the authors had to rely on the statement of the author of the published code.

Additionally, they carried out a user study, to look into reasons why code was not shared. Reasons were (among others), that the code will be available soon, that the programmer left or that the authors do not intend to release the code at all.

Their study also presents reasons why code or support is unavailable. They found that problems in building code were (among others) based on "files missing from the distribution" and "incomplete documentation". The authors also list lessons learned from their experiment, formulated as advice to the community such as: plan to release the code, plan for students to leave, create project websites and plan for longevity.

Finally, the authors present a list of suggestions to improve sharing of research artifacts, among others on how to give details about the sharing in the publications, beyond using public repositories and coding conventions.

Re-using Data Some of the findings by Collberg et al. (2015) apply to data as well. Data has to be "independently understandable", which means, that it is not necessary to consult the original provider (Peer et al., 2014). A researcher has the responsibility to publish data, code and relevant material (Hovy and Spruit, 2016). Additionally, Peer (2014) argued, that a data review process as carried out by data archives such as ICSPR[7] or ISPS[8] is feasible.

Milšutka et al. (2016) propose to store URLs as persistent identifiers to allow for future references and support long-term availability.

Francopoulo et al. (2016) looked at NLP publications and NLP resources and carried out a quantitative study into resource re-usage. The authors suggest a resource innovation impact factor to encourage the publication of data and resources.

Gratta et al. (2016) studied the types of resources published during the previous three LREC conferences. They found that more than half (58%) of the resources were corpora. They visualized collaborations between researchers on specific resources and pointed out issues concerning the meta-data provided by data publishers.

Replication Studies in NLP Experiments in reproducing results in the NLP domain such as (Fokkens et al., 2013) are still quite rare. One reason might be, that when undertaking such projects, "sometimes conflicting results are obtained by repeating a study" (Jones, 2009). Fokkens et al. (2013) found, that their experiments were difficult to carry out and to obtain meaningful results. The 4Real workshop focused on the "the topic of the reproducibility of research results and the citation of resources, and its impact on research integrity"[9]. Their call for papers[9] asked for submissions of "actual replication exercises of previous published results" (see also (Branco et al., 2016)). Results from this workshop found that reproducing experiments can give additional insights, and can therefore be beneficial for the researchers as well as for the community (Cohen et al., 2016).

Data Privacy and Ethics Another important aspect is data privacy. An overview on how to deal with data taken from, for example, social media channels can be found in (Diesner and Chin, 2016). The authors raise various issues regarding the usage of data crawled from the web. As data obtained through these channels is, strictly speaking, restricted in terms of redistribution, reproducibility is a problem.

Wu et al. (2016) present work on developing and implementing principles for creating resources based on patient data in the medical domain and working with this data.

Bleicken et al. (2016) report efforts on anonymization of video data from sign language. The authors developed a semi-automatic procedure to black relevant parts of the video, where named entities are mentioned.

Fort and Couillault (2016) report on a survey on the awareness and care NLP researchers show towards ethical issues. The authors scope also considered working conditions for crowd workers.

---

[7]http://www.icpsr.umich.edu/icpsrweb/index.jsp
[8]http://isps.yale.edu/research/data

[9]http://4real.di.fc.ul.pt/

Their results indicate that the majority (84%) consider licensing and distribution of language data during their work. Over three-quarters of the participants (77%) think that "ethics should be part of the subjects for the call for papers".

3 Research Questions

In the course of this work, we looked at various aspects of experimental work:

Collection NLP researchers collect data, often without informing the persons or entities who produced this data. These data sets are analyzed, conclusions are drawn about how people write, behave, etc. and others make use of these findings in other contexts. This gave raise to the questions:

- Has data been collected?
- If the data contains potentially sensitive data, which post-processing steps have been taken (i.e. anonymization)?
- Was the resulting data published?
- Is there enough information/is it possible to obtain the data?

Replicability/Reproducibility Often data on which these studies are based, is not published or not available anymore. This can be due to various reasons[10]. Among those are, that webpages or e-mail addresses are no longer functional after a researcher left a specific research institute, after a webpage re-design some data has not been moved to the new page, and copyright or data privacy issues could not be resolved.

This gives rise to issues, such as reproducibility of research results. Original results from these studies are published and later referred to, but they cannot be verified on the original data. In some cases, data is being re-used and extended. But often only specific parts of the original data is used. Details on how to reproduce the changed data set (e.g. code/scripts used to obtain the subset) are not published and descriptions about the procedure are insufficient. This is extends the questions:

- Was previously published data used in a different way and/or extended?

These questions target at how easy it would be to follow-up by reproducing published results and

extending the work. Our results give an indication on the availability of research data.

Specific to data taken for example from social media channels is another, additional aspect:

Personal Data Researchers present and publish their data and results of their research on conferences and workshops, often using examples taken from the actual data. And of course, they aim to look for examples that are entertaining, especially during a presentation. But we also observed that names are being used. Not just fairly common names, but real names or aliases used on social media. Which renders this person identifiable as defined by the data protection act below.

Therefore, we added the questions:

- Did the data contain sensitive data?
- Was the data anonymized?

These questions look at how researchers deal with potentially sensitive data. The results indicate how serious they take their responsibility towards their research subjects, which are either voluntarily or involuntarily taking part in a study.

What constitutes sensitive data? Related to the above presented questions, we had to define what sensitive data is. In a leaflet from the MIT Information Services and Technology sensitive data includes information about "ethnicity, race, political or religious views, memberships, physical or mental health, personal life (. . .) information on a person as consumer, client, employee, patient, student". It also includes contact information, ID, birth date, parents names, etc. (Services and Technology, 2009). The UK data protecton act contains a similar list.[11] The European Commission (Schaar, 2007) formulates personal and therefore sensitive data as "any information relating to an identified or identifiable natural person". And even anonymizing data does not solve all issues here, as "(. . .) information may be presented as aggregated data, the original sample is not sufficiently large and other pieces of information may enable the indentification of individuals".

Based on these definitions, we counted towards the *sensitive data* aspect everything that users themselves report ("user generated web content" (Diesner and Chin, 2016)), but also what is being reported about them, e.g. data gathered from

---

[10]This is based on personal experience and therefore not quantified.

[11]https://ico.org.uk/for-organisations/ guide-to-data-protection/key- definitions/

Venue	# papers	# data published	Ratio
NAACL	182	57	31.3%
ACL	231	63	27.3%
EMLNP	264	81	30.7%
Coling	337	89	26.4%
LREC	744	414	55.6%
total	1758	704	40.0%

Table 1: Results of papers reporting the usage and the publication of data.

equiment such as mobile phones which allows to identify a specific person.

4 Quantitative Analysis

Our quantitative analysis was carried out on publications from NAACL (Knight et al., 2016), ACL (Erk and Smith, 2016), EMNLP (Su et al., 2016), LREC (Calzolari et al., 2016) and Coling (Matsumoto and Prasad, 2016) from 2016. This resulted in a data set of 1758 publications, which includes long papers for ACL, long and short papers for NAACL, technical papers for Coling and full proceedings for EMNLP and LREC, but no workshop publications.

Procedure All publications were manually checked by the author. Creating an automatic method proved to be infeasible, as the descriptions on whether or not data was collected, whether it is provided to the research community, through which channel etc. is too heterogeneous across the publications. We checked the abstracts for pointers on the specific work and looked at the respective sections on procedure, data collection and looked for mentions of publication plans, link or availablility of the data. This information was collected and stored in a table for later evaluation. This analysis could have been extended by contacting the data set authors and looking at the content of the data sets. While this definitely would be a worthwhile study, this would have gone beyond the scope of the current paper, as it would have meant to contact at least over 700 authors individually. Additionally, this project was intended to raise the awareness on how data is being collected and published.

Reproducibility of Results Of the 1758 publications 704 reported to have collected or extended/changed existing data[12] (approx. 40%).

Table 1 shows the results with respect to the number of publications and the number of papers reporting data usage and/or extension. LREC saw the highest number of published papers containing collected and/or published data.

Table 2 gives details about the availability of the data sets used. 468 of the 704 publications (58%) report a link where the data can be downloaded. Another 35% report no link at all and below 1% mention that the data is proprietary and cannot be published. Out of the links given, 18% do not work at all. This includes cases where the mentioned page did not exist (anymore) or where it is inaccessible. Most cases where links did not work (15.7%) were due to incomplete or not working links to personal webpages at the respective research institutions. Therefore, we looked in more detail at the hosting methods for publishing data. We found that only about 20.7% were published on public hosting services such as `github`[13] or `bitbucket`[14]. While these services are targeted towards code and might not be appropriate for data collections, they are at least independent of personal or research institute webpages. LREC publications also mention hosting services such as metashare[15], the LRE Map[16] or that data will be provided through LDC[17] or ELRA[18] (8.9%).

Category	Percentage
Link available	65.2%
Link does not work	15.7%
No Link	31.4%
On Request	1.8%
Proprietary data	< 1%

Table 2: Detailed numbers on available and working links

Responsibility towards Research Subjects Out of 704 publications about 32.8% collected or used data from social media or otherwise sensitive data as outlined in Section 3 above. Only about 3.5% of these report the anonymization of the data. In some cases it was obvious that no anonymization has been carried out, as the discussion of the data and results mentions user names or aliases, which makes the person identifiable. The remaining publications do not mention how

---

[12]Publications used more than one data set, therefore, sums can be more than 100%.

[13]https://github.com/
[14]https://bitbucket.org/product
[15]http://www.meta-share.eu/
[16]http://www.resourcebook.eu/
[17]https://www.ldc.upenn.edu/
[18]http://catalog.elra.info/

the data was treated or processed. It is possible, that most of them anonymized their data, but it is not clearly stated. Other data collected was generally written data such as news (37%), spoken data (11%) and annotations (27%).

In LREC a considerable amount of data from the medical domain, recordings of elderly, pathological voices and data from proficiency observations, such as children or foreign language learner was reported (7%). But in only 10% of the cases anonymization was reported or became obvious through the webpage or published pictures.

5 Suggestions for future direction

From the above presented analysis, we raise several discussion points, which the NLP community should address together. The following is meant as a starting point to flesh out a *code of conduct* and potential future activities to improve the situation.

Data Collection and Usage This addresses issues such as how to collect data, how to pre-/post-process data (i.e. anonymization) and recommendations for available tools supporting these. Additionally, guidelines on how to present data in publications and presentations should enforce anonymization. This could be supported by allowing one additional page for submitted papers, where details on collections, procedures and treatement are given. A checklist both for **authors** and **reviewers** should contain at least:

- Has data been collected?
- How was this data collected and processed?
- Was previously available data used/extended – which one?
- Is a link or a contact given?
- Where does it point (private page, research institute, official repository)?

For journals the availability and usability of data (and potentially code) should be mandatory, similar to Nature and PLOS (see Section 2).

Data Distribution This addresses issues on how data should be distributed to the community, respecting data privacy issues as well. We should define standards for publications that are not tied to a specific lab or even the personal website of a researcher, similar to recommended repositories for Nature or PLOS (see Section 2), but rather provide means and guidelines to gather, work with and publish data. On publication, a defined set of meta data should be provided. These should also include information on methods and tools, which have been used to process the data. This simplifies the reproduction of experiments and results.[19] All of this could be collected in a repository, where code and data is stored. Various efforts in this direction already exist, such as LRE Map[20] or the ACL Data and Code Repository[21]. The ACL Repository currently lists only 9 resources from 2008 to 2011. The LRE Map contains over 2,000 corpora, but the newest dates from LREC 2014. So the data that was analyzed here, has not been provided there.

Adding a reproducibility section to conferences and journals in the NLP domain would support the validation of previously presented results. Studies verified by independent researchers could be raised in the awareness and given appropriate credit to both original researchers and the verification. This could be tied together with extending, encouraging, enforcing the usage of data repositories such as the ACL Repository or the LRE Map and find common interfaces between the various efforts. On the long term, virtual research environments would allow for working with sensitive data without distributing it, which would foster the collaboration across research labs.

6 Future Work

Future work includes extending this preliminary study in two directions: earlier publications and how usable are published data sets. Are various high-profile studies actually replicable and what can we learn from the results?

Additionally, the suggestions sketched in the previous section have to be fleshed out and put to action in a continious revision process.

Acknowledgments

This work was partially supported by the DFG-funded research training group "Adaptive Preparation of Information from Heterogeneous Sources" (AIPHES, GRK 1994/1). We would like to thank the reviewers for their valuable comments that helped to considerably improve the paper.

---

[19]Ideally, a labbook or experiment protocol containing all the necessary information about the experiments should be published as well.

[20]http://www.resourcebook.eu/

[21]https://www.aclweb.org/aclwiki/index.php?title=ACL_Data_and_Code_Repository

References

Julian Bleicken, Thomas Hanke, Uta Salden, and Sven Wagner. 2016. Using a Language Technology Infrastructure for German in order to Anonymize German Sign Language Corpus Data. In Nicoletta Calzolari (Conference Chair), Khalid Choukri, Thierry Declerck, Sara Goggi, Marko Grobelnik, Bente Maegaard, Joseph Mariani, Helene Mazo, Asuncion Moreno, Jan Odijk, and Stelios Piperidis, editors, *Proceedings of the Tenth International Conference on Language Resources and Evaluation (LREC 2016)*, Paris, France, May. European Language Resources Association (ELRA).

António Branco, Nicoletta Calzolari, and Khalid Choukri, editors. 2016. Portorož, Slovenia. An LREC 2016 Workshop.

Nicoletta Calzolari, Khalid Choukri, Thierry Declerck, Sara Goggi, Marko Grobelnik, Bente Maegaard, Joseph Mariani, Hlne Mazo, Asuncin Moreno, Jan Odijk, and Stelios Piperidis., editors. 2016. *Tenth International Conference on Language Resources and Evaluation (LREC 2016)*. European Language Resources Association, Portorož, Slovenia, May 23–28, 2016. published online at: http://www.lrec-conf.org/proceedings/lrec2016/index.html.

Kevin Cohen, Jingbo Xia, Christophe Roeder, and Lawrence Hunter. 2016. Reproducibility in Natural Language Processing: A Case Study of two R Libraries for Mining PubMed/MEDLINE. In *4REAL Workshop: Workshop on Research Results Reproducibility and Resources Citation in Science and Technology of Language*, pages 6–12, Portorož, Slovenia, May. An LREC 2016 Workshop.

Christian Collberg, Todd Proebsting, and Alex M. Warren. 2015. Repeatability and Benefaction in Computer Systems Research – A Study and a Modest Proposal. Technical Report TR 14-04, University of Arizona.

Jana Diesner and Chieh-Li Chin. 2016. Gratis, Libre, or Something Else? Regulations and Misassumptions Related to Working with Publicly Available Text Data. In *ETHI-CA2 2016: ETHics In Corpus Collection, Annotation & Application*, Portorož, Slovenia, May. An LREC 2016 Workshop.

Katrin Erk and Noah A. Smith, editors. 2016. *Proceedings of the 54th Annual Meeting of the Association for Computational Linguistics (Volume 1: Long Papers)*. Association for Computational Linguistics, Berlin, Germany, August.

Antske Fokkens, Marieke van Erp, Marten Postma, Ted Pedersen, Piek Vossen, and Nuno Freire. 2013. Offspring from Reproduction Problems: What Replication Failure Teaches Us. In *Proceedings of the 51st Annual Meeting of the Association for Computational Linguistics (Volume 1: Long Papers)*, pages 1691–1701, Sofia, Bulgaria, August. Association for Computational Linguistics.

Karën Fort and Alain Couillault. 2016. Yes, We Care! Results of the Ethics and Natural Language Processing Surveys. In Nicoletta Calzolari (Conference Chair), Khalid Choukri, Thierry Declerck, Sara Goggi, Marko Grobelnik, Bente Maegaard, Joseph Mariani, Helene Mazo, Asuncion Moreno, Jan Odijk, and Stelios Piperidis, editors, *Proceedings of the Tenth International Conference on Language Resources and Evaluation (LREC 2016)*, Paris, France, may. European Language Resources Association (ELRA).

Gil Francopoulo, Joseph Mariani, and Patrick Paroubek. 2016. Linking Language Resources and NLP Papers. In *4REAL Workshop: Workshop on Research Results Reproducibility and Resources Citation in Science and Technology of Language*, pages 24–32, Portorož, Slovenia, May. An LREC 2016 Workshop.

Riccardo Del Gratta, Francesca Frontini, Monica Monachini, Gabriella Pardelli, Irene Russo, Roberto Bartolini, Fahad Khan, Claudia Soria, and Nicoletta Calzolari. 2016. LREC as a Graph: People and Resources in a Network. In Nicoletta Calzolari (Conference Chair), Khalid Choukri, Thierry Declerck, Sara Goggi, Marko Grobelnik, Bente Maegaard, Joseph Mariani, Helene Mazo, Asuncion Moreno, Jan Odijk, and Stelios Piperidis, editors, *Proceedings of the Tenth International Conference on Language Resources and Evaluation (LREC 2016)*, Paris, France, May. European Language Resources Association (ELRA).

Dirk Hovy and Shannon L. Spruit. 2016. The Social Impact of Natural Language Processing. In *Proceedings of the 54th Annual Meeting of the Association for Computational Linguistics (Volume 2: Short Papers)*, pages 591–598, Berlin, Germany, August. Association for Computational Linguistics.

Elizabeth Iorns. 2012. Is medical science built on shaky foundations? `https://www.newscientist.com/article/mg21528826.000-is-medical-science-built-on-shaky-foundations/`, September.

Val Jones. 2009. Science-Based Medicine 101: Reproducibility. `https://sciencebasedmedicine.org/science-based-medicine-101-reproducibility/`, August.

Kevin Knight, Ani Nenkova, and Owen Rambow, editors. 2016. *Proceedings of the 2016 Conference of the North American Chapter of the Association for Computational Linguistics: Human Language Technologies*. Association for Computational Linguistics, San Diego, California, June.

Yuji Matsumoto and Rashmi Prasad, editors. 2016. *Proceedings of COLING 2016, the 26th International Conference on Computational Linguistics: Technical Papers*. The COLING 2016 Organizing Committee, Osaka, Japan, December.

Jozef Milšutka, Ondřej Košarko, and Amir Kamran. 2016. SHORTREF.ORG – Making URLs Easy-to-Cite. In *4REAL Workshop: Workshop on Research Results Reproducibility and Resources Citation in Science and Technology of Language*, pages 19–23, Portorož, Slovenia, May. An LREC 2016 Workshop.

Limor Peer, Ann Green, and Elizabeth Stephenson. 2014. Committing to Data Quality Review. *International Journal of Digital Curation*, 9(1):263–291.

Limor Peer. 2014. Mind the gap in data reuse: Sharing data is necessary but not sufficient for future reuse. `http://blogs.lse.ac.uk/impactofsocialsciences/2014/03/28/mind-the-gap-in-data-reuse/`, March.

Peter Schaar. 2007. Opinion 4/2007 on the concept of personal data. `http://ec.europa.eu/justice/policies/privacy/docs/wpdocs/2007/wp136_en.pdf`.

Information Services and Technology. 2009. Sensitive Data: Your Money AND Your Life. `http://web.mit.edu/infoprotect/docs/protectingdata.pdf`, January.

Jian Su, Kevin Duh, and Xavier Carreras, editors. 2016. *Proceedings of the 2016 Conference on Empirical Methods in Natural Language Processing*. Association for Computational Linguistics, Austin, Texas, November.

Stephen Wu, Tamara Timmons, Amy Yates, Meikun Wang, Steven Bedrick, William Hersh, and Hongfang Liu. 2016. On Developing Resources for Patient-level Information Retrieval. In Nicoletta Calzolari (Conference Chair), Khalid Choukri, Thierry Declerck, Sara Goggi, Marko Grobelnik, Bente Maegaard, Joseph Mariani, Helene Mazo, Asuncion Moreno, Jan Odijk, and Stelios Piperidis, editors, *Proceedings of the Tenth International Conference on Language Resources and Evaluation (LREC 2016)*, Paris, France, May. European Language Resources Association (ELRA).

Ethical by Design: Ethics Best Practices for Natural Language Processing

Jochen L. Leidner   and   **Vassilis Plachouras**
Thomson Reuters, Research & Development,
30 South Colonnade, London E14 5EP, United Kingdom.
{jochen.leidner,vassilis.plachouras}@thomsonreuters.com

Abstract

Natural Language Processing (NLP) systems analyze and/or generate human language, typically on users' behalf. One natural and necessary question that needs to be addressed in this context, both in research projects and in production settings, is the question how *ethical* the work is, both regarding the process and its outcome.

Towards this end, we articulate a set of issues, propose a set of best practices, notably a process featuring an *ethics review board*, and sketch how they could be meaningfully applied. Our main argument is that ethical outcomes ought to be achieved *by design*, i.e. by following a process aligned by ethical values. We also offer some response options for those facing ethics issues.

While a number of previous works exist that discuss ethical issues, in particular around big data and machine learning, to the authors' knowledge this is the first account of NLP and ethics from the perspective of a principled *process*.

1   Introduction

Ethics, the part of practical philosophy concerned with all things normative (moral philosophy, answering the fundamental question of *how to live one's life*) permeates all aspects of human action. Applying it to Natural language Processing (NLP), we can ask the following core questions: 1. What ethical concerns exist in the realm of NLP? 2. How should these ethical issues be addressed? At the time of writing, automation using machine learning is making great practical progress, and this includes NLP tasks, but is by no means limited to it. As more areas in life are affected by these new technologies, the practical need for clarification of ethical implications increases; in other words, we have reached the level where the topic is no longer purely academic: we need to have solutions for what a driverless car should morally do in situations that can be described as ethical dilemmas, and in language and speech-enabled system ethical questions also arise (see below). Governments and NGOs are also trying to come to grips with what machine learning, which NLP also relies on, means for policy making (Armstrong, 2015).

In this paper, a more principled way to deal with ethical questions in NLP projects is proposed, which is inspired by previous work on the more narrowly confined space of privacy, which we attempt to generalize. In doing so, we want to make sure that common pitfalls such as compartmentalization (i.e., considering one area in isolation and solving problems in a way that creates problems elsewhere), do not hinder the pursuit of ethical NLP research and development, and we shall present some possible response options for those facing non-ethical situations to stimulate discussion.

Paper Plan. The rest of this paper is structured as follows: Sec. 2 introduces the concept of "ethical by design". After reviewing some related work in Sec. 3, Sec. 4 reviews ethics issues in NLP. Sec. 5 introduces a proposed process model and some possible responses for those facing ethics dilemmas. Sec. 6 discusses the shortcomings, and Sec. 7 summarizes and concludes this paper.

2   Ethical by Design

Ann Cavoukian (2009), a Canadian privacy and information officer, has devised a set of seven principles for *privacy by design*, a sub-set of which

Proceedings of the First Workshop on Ethics in Natural Language Processing, pages 30–40,
Valencia, Spain, April 4th, 2017. © 2017 Association for Computational Linguistics

we can generalize—so that they apply to general ethics standards instead of the single issue of privacy—as follows.

1. Proactive not reactive: by planning to do things in an ethical way we avoid having to react remedially to non-ethical situations more often than without a planning approach;

2. Ethical as the default setting: by making a commitment to pursuing originally ethical paths, we create alignment within organizations towards a more streamlined set of options that comply with common values;[1]

3. Ethics embedded into the process: a process firmly inclusive of ethics at all stages and levels is less likely to create accidental harm;

4. End-to-end ethics: ethics cannot be confined to a stage; it must be an all-encompassing property of a process from basic research over product design to dissemination or delivery, i.e. the full life-cycle of a technology;

5. Visibility and transparency: a process that is published can be scrutinized, criticized and ultimately improved by a caring community;

6. Respect for user values: whatever values a research institute, university or company may hold is one thing, being user-centric means to also consider the values of the user (of a component, product) and the subjects that take part in experiments (ratings, data annotations).

How could such principles be applied to NLP, concretely? We ought to make some practical proposals how to proceed e.g. in a research project or when developing a product to avoid ethical issues. To this end, we will now look at some potential issues, review best practices that are available, and then put it all together in the form of a process recommendation and possible responses for dealing with ethical issues as they arise.

3   Related Work

Prior work on the topics of ethics in NLP can be grouped into three categories. First, there is the general body of literature covering applied ethics and moral philosophy. Second, within computer science, there are discussions around big data, data mining and machine learning and their ethical implications, often focused on privacy and bias/discrimination. Few if any of these works have mentioned issues specific to language processing, but a lot of the unspecific issues also *do* apply to NLP.[2] Third, there is a body of works on professional ethics, often talked about in the context of curriculum design for computer science teaching (didactics of computing), governance and professional conduct and legal/ethical aspects of computing (computing as a profession, continued professional development).

Moral Philosophy & Ethics. We cannot even aspire to give a survey of centuries of moral philosophy in a few sentences; instead, we briefly sketch three exemplary schools of moral philosophy to represent the fact that there is no single school of thought that settles all moral questions.[3] Aristotle's "Nicomachean Ethics" (Aristotle, 1925; Aristotle, 1934)[4], Utilitarianism (Mill, 1879) and Kant's (1785) categorical imperative are just three examples of philosophical frameworks that can be used as a frame of reference to study ethics, including the ethics of NLP and its applications. Aristotle based his system on happiness (Greek ευδαιμονìα) as the highest attainable and ultimate goal for humans, and takes a consensus-informed view starting with those moral principles that people with "good upbringing" agree on. Kant's categorical imperative posits a decision criterion to decide whether an action is moral or not, namely whether we would want to lift up our behaviour so that it may become a law of nature. Utilitarianism suggests to maximise happiness for the largest number of people, which implies a quantification- and outcome-oriented aspect; however, it also contains a severe flaw: it can be used to justify unethical behavior towards minorities as long as a majority benefits.

Information & Big Data Ethics. There is a body of work within philosophy on information ethics (Allen et al., 2005; Bynum, 2008); big data has created its own challenges, which are begin-

---

[1]There is a catch, namely different people may agree to slightly different ethical premises, or they may draw different conclusions from the same premises.

[2]An edited collection on ethics and related topics in the context of artificial companions exists (Wilks, 2010), but as Masthoff (2011) points out NLP does not feature in it.

[3]For general background reading in ethics and moral philosophy, see Gensler (2011). For computing-related ethics background there already exist many suitable entries to the literature (Brey et al., 2009; Quinn, 2016; Stahl et al., 2016; Bynum, 2008; Bynum and Rogerson, 2004; Cary et al., 2003).

[4]named after its dedication to Nicomachus, likely either Artistotle's father or son

ning to be discussed. Pasquale (2015) provides a thorough analysis of the societal impact of data collection, user profiling, data vendors and buyers, and application algorithms and the associated issues; it contains numerous real case examples. However, the exposition does not appear to include examples likely to rely on NLP. Supervised learning, clustering, data mining and recommendation methods can account for the vast majority of examples (collaborative filtering, Apriori algorithm), which raises the questions of whether there will be a second wave of more sophisticated profiling attempts relying on NLP and neural networks.

Machine Learning & Bias. Since 2014, the Fairness, Accountability, and Transparency in Machine Learning (FATML, 2014) workshop series (originally organized by S. Barocas and M. Hardt at NIPS) have been concerned with technical solutions associated with a lack of accountability, transparency and fairness in machine learning models.

NLP Application Ethics. Thieltges, Schmidt and Hegelich (2016) discuss NLP chat-bots; in particular, they focus on the dilemma they call "devil's triangle", a tension between transparency, accuracy and robustness of any proposed automatic chat-bot detection classifier. Software that interacts with humans and/or acts on humans' behalf, such as robot control code or chat-bots will need to contain embodied decisions to ensure that the software acts *as if* it was a moral agent, in other words we would expect the software to act in a way such that a human acting in the same way would be considered morally acting (Allen et al., 2005). Most recently, Hovy and Spruit (2016) provided a broad account and thought-provoking call for investigation to the NLP community to explore their impact on society. To give an example of an unethical or at least highly questionable application, Mengelkamp, Rohmann and Schumann (2016) survey (but do not advocate) practices of credit rating agencies' use of social (user-generated) content, mostly unknown and unapproved by the creators of that data. Fairfield and Shtein (2014) analyze ethics from a journalism point of view, which bears some similarity with the perspective of automatic NLP, as journalists also scrutinize textual sources and produce text, albeit not algorithmically.

NLP Methodology Ethics. Fort, Adda and Cohen (2011) provide an early account of the ethical implications of crowdsourcing, the program-controlled automation of work conducted by anonymous human subjects.

Professional Ethics. Professional ethics is the integration of codification into education and continuous professional development, and the computing profession developed the *ACM Code of Ethics and Professional Conduct* (1992), which communicates a detailed set of 22 values; however, the compliance with them has been made voluntary, there are no negative consequences to people not adhering to them; further more, insufficient detail is given with regards to where moral boundaries are on specific issues, or how they may be obtained. The current code, then, falls short of an "algorithm how to be a good professional", if that can even exist. More recently (ACM, 2017), 7 principles were postulated to promote the transparency and accountability of algorithms: 1. Awareness; 2. Access and redress; 3. Accountability; 4. Explanation; 5. Data Provenance; 6. Auditability; and 7. Validation and Testing. The Association of Internet Researchers has published ethics guidelines (Markham and Buchanan, 2012), which have seen some adoption.[5] Perhaps the most interesting *empirical* finding to date is a survey by Fort and Couillault (2016), who posed ethics-related questions to French and international audiences, respectively, in two polls. For example, over 40% of respondents said they have refused to work on a project on ethical grounds.

This work draws heavily on Cavoukian (2009)'s proposal but goes beyond in that we propose a *process model* that makes intentional and non-intentional violations harder to go unnoticed. Our process is also informed by the holistic "Resources-Product-Target" (RPT) model of Floridi (2013). As he points out (Floridi, 2013, p. 20), many models focus rather narrowly on a "ethics of information resources", "ethics of information products" or "ethics of the informational environment" view (which he calls *microethical*). His counter-proposal, the RPT model (Figure 1), in contrast, is a *macro-ethical* approach that tries to avoid dilemmas and counterproductive effects by taking too narrow a view: RPT stands for "Resources-Product-Target", because Floridi's model considers the life cycle of producing an information product (output) from and information

---

[5] e.g. by the journal PeerJ. See also AoIR (2017 to appear) for an upcoming event on ethics in Internet research.

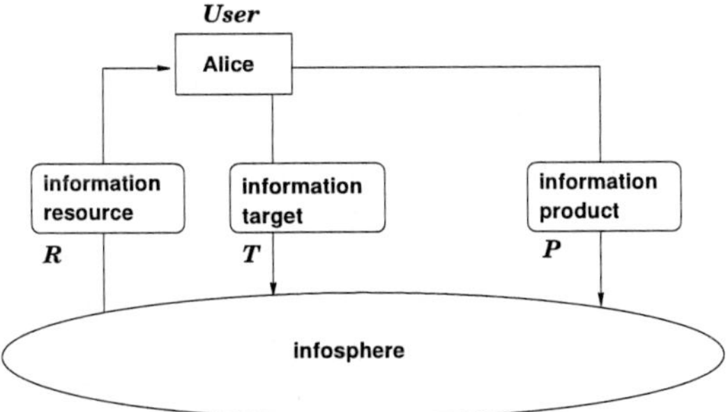

Figure 1: The Holistic Resources-Product-Target (RPT) Model after Floridi (2013).

resource (input), during which an effect on the environment (infosphere) is created (target). By considering the environment as well, compartmentalization, i.e. behaving ethically in a narrowly confined realm but not overall, can be avoided.[6] Information ethics within NLP is nascent, however there is a lot of general work that can be borrowed from, going back as far as early computer science itself (Wiener, 1954).

4 Ethical Issues in NLP

While the related work in the previous sections reviewed work on ethics including but not limited to ethics and NLP, in this section, we discuss the types of ethical issues that we are aware, and give some examples from the NLP literature. We will link each type to one or more parts of Floridi's model. An interesting question is what specifically is different in NLP with respect to ethics compared to other data-related topics or ethics in general. This question can be split into two parts: first, since it pertains to human language processing, and human language touches many parts of life, these areas also have an ethics dimension. For example, languages define linguistic communities, so inclusion and bias become relevant topics. Second, NLP is about processing by machine. This means that automation (and its impact on work) and errors (and their impact, whether intentional or not) become ethical topics. Furthermore, if NLP systems are used as (information) access mechanism, accessibility is another concern (inclusion of language-impaired users).

Unethical NLP Applications (pertains to P for Product in Floridi's RPT model). The earliest ethical issue involving NLP that the authors could find during the research for this paper surrounds the UNIX **spell(1)** command. Spell is a spell-checker: it prints out words not found in a lexicon so they can be corrected. However, in the course of its invocation, McIllroy's 1978 version (unlike Johnson's original implementation) emailed words that are not found in its lexicon to its implementer to support lexicon improvements (Bentley, 1986, p. 144); while this is technically commendable (perhaps even one of the earliest examples of log-file analysis), from a privacy point of view the author of a document may disapprove of this.[7] Youyou, Kosinski and Stillwell (2015) show that automated psychometrics—they use social media "like"s—now rivals human determination of personality traits; one interesting moral aspect is that when subjects wrote a piece of text they were likely not aware that in the future this may be possible, in the same way that many people who uploaded their photos online were not aware that one day face recognition at scale would reach maturity, which has now happened. In a similar spirit, Kosinski, Stillwell and Graepel (2013) demonstrate that other private personal traits and attributes can be computed from a user's data, including from their network of personal relationships. Thieltges, Schmidt and Hegelich (2016) describe another issue, namely that of chat-bots, which may act in a political way, such as steering or influencing a discussion or, worse, completely destroying meaningful human discourse by injecting noise: on Twitter, chat-bots made real conversation impossible for the topic channel #YaMeCance dedicated to reducing violence and corruption in Mexico, and real-life human activists were reportedly followed and threatened. It seems prudent that any bot self-identify as an automated entity, and from an ethical—if not legal—point of view, a respectful, low-traffic interaction is warranted. NLP developers should not participate in such efforts, not let themselves be instrumentalized by state actors or commercial interests, should withdraw from dubious projects, and pub-

---

[6]A famous example of compartmentalization is the cruel dictator that is loving to his children at home. In an NLP context, an example could be a friendly and caring scientist that unwittingly abuses workers using a crowdsourcing API, because he needs gold data and has a small budget.

[7]The authors of this paper do not know if all users of **spell(1)** were privy to this feature (we have not received a response from Prof. McIllroy to an email request for clarification while this paper was under review). In any case, it should be clear that the works cited here are listed to ignite the ethics discussion, not to criticize individual works or authors, whose work we greatly respect.

licize and disclose immoral practices.[8] In contrast, research into the automatic detection of such bots seems ethical, to increase transparency and reduce manipulation in a society, and this may require manipulative bots to be developed for test purposes; however, they should not be deployed, but be kept in sandboxed environments or just be implemented as simulations. Hovy and

Spruit (2016) point out the dual nature of some work: like a knife can be used to cut bread or to harm others, NLP may "have dual" use potential. There are two possible responses: either object if the non-ethical use is clearly involved in a project or product. Or alternatively, act conservatively and avoid obvious dual-use technologies entirely in favor of ethical-only use technologies (e.g. work on health-care applications instead of command-and-control software). Building an NLP application, like any other human activity that is a means to an end, can have an ethical end or not. For example, an NLP application could be an instance of an unethical application if its purpose is not consistent with ethical norms. If one adopts cherishing human life as an absolute moral value, developing a smart weapon using voice control would be an example of an application that is ethically wrong.

Davis and Patterson (2012) list identity, privacy, ownership and reputation as the four core areas of big data ethics. What is the range of potential ethical issues in NLP in specific? This paper cannot provide an exhaustive list, but we will try to give a nucleus list that serves to illustrate the breadth of topics that can be affected.

Privacy (pertains to T for target in Floridi's RPT model). Collecting linguistic data may lead to ethical questions around *privacy*[9]: Corpora such as the British National Corpus, the Collins COBUILD corpus or the Penn Treebank contain names of individuals and often substantial personal information about them; e-mail corpora to study the language of email (Klimt and Yang, 2004), or corpora of suicide notes and other sensitive psychiatric material (Pestian et al., 2012; Brew, 2016) constructed to study causes for terminating one's life are much more private still. Is the ability to construct a classifier that detects how "serious" a suicide note should be taken a good thing? It may prevent harm by directing scarce health resources in better ways, but does that justify the privacy invasion of anyone's personal good-byes, without their consent? Althoff, Clark and Leskovec (2016) describe an analysis of counseling conversations using NLP methods; here, perhaps because the patients are still alive, even stronger privacy protection is indicated. Another privacy-related issue is excessive government surveillance, which can lead to self-censoring and ultimately undermine democracy (Penney, 2016).

Fairness, Bias & Discrimination (pertains to T for target in Floridi's RPT model). Picture a spoken dialog system that is easy to use for a young male financial professional user with a London English pronunciation, but that may barely work for an elderly lady from Uddingston (near Glasgow, Scotland). As automated information systems are becoming more pervasive, they may eventually substitute human information kiosks for cost reasons, and then out-of-sample user groups could be excluded and left behind without an alternative. The internal functioning of NLP systems can raise questions of *transparency & accountability*: what if a parser does not work for particular types of inputs, and the developer does not communicate this aspect to an application developer, who wants to build a medical application that uses it. It is responsible behavior to disclose limitations of a system to its users, and NLP systems are no exception. In the context of machine learning, governments have started looking into the impact of ML on society, the need for policy guidance and regulation (Armstrong, 2015).

Abstraction & Compartmentalization (pertains to all parts of Floridi's RPT model). As mentioned earlier, Floridi's (2013) model was explicitly designed to overcome an overly narrow focus only on the input or project output. Abstracting over humans happens in crowdsourcing (see above) when work is farmed out to an API, which has individual humans behind it, but this fact can be all to easily ignored by the API's caller. If abstraction can lead to ethical ignorance in one dimension, compartmentalization can lead to the

---

[8] One reviewer has called our call for non-participation in un-ethical work "naïve"; however, we believe individuals can effect positive change through their personal choices, and especially in sought-after professions no-one has an excuse that they had to feed their family (or whatever justification one may bring forth). Also, by buying from and working for, more ethical companies, a pull towards increasing ethical behavior overall may be generated.

[9] Privacy as a concept is discussed in Westin (1967); See the recent seminal literature on big data privacy (Lane et al., 2014; Zimmer, 2010) for more in-depth discussions of data and privacy.

same in another. For example, an information extraction system that gets build without looking at the political context in which it is likely deployed may lead to unethical actions by a team of otherwise morality-oriented researchers.

Complexity (pertains to T as in target in Floridi's RPT model). Today's big data systems are cloud-based pipelines of interconnected data feeds and "black box" processes (Pasquale, 2015) combining and transforming a multitude of sources each, and these transcend individual organizational boundaries. This means that an organization offering e.g. an NLP API ceases control of how it may be used externally; this creates complex, hard-to-understand macro-ecosystems.

Un-ethical Research Methods (pertains to R as in Resource and T as in target in RPT). Doing research itself can be done in more or less ethical ways, so the discussion should not be limited to the outcome. An example for applying wrong standards could be setting up a psycholinguistic experiment about language acquisition of children in a kindergarden without briefing and getting the consent of their parents. Doing the research itself may involve hiring helpers, who should not be kept in unethical work conditions; crowdsourcing has been criticized to be a form of slavery, for instance (Fort et al., 2011). Recently, crowdsourcing has become a common element of the NLP toolbox to create gold data or to carry out cost-effective evaluations. Crowdsourcing is now ubiquitous, even indispensable for researchers in HCI, cognitive science, psycholinguistics and NLP. And it poses not just tax compliance issues (who issues tax returns for my workers that I do not know?), but also the fact that the mutual anonymity leads to a loose, non-committal relationship between researchers and crowd workers that stand against pride in the of quality of work output or a moral sense duty of care for workers.

Automation (pertains to R as in Resource and T as in target in RPT). Finally, it could be questioned whether NLP in general is unethical *per se*, based on it being an instance of *automation*: any activity that leads to, or contributes to, the loss of jobs that people use to generate their own existential support: The argument that automation destroys jobs is old (Ford, 2015; Susskind and Susskind, 2015), and traditionally, two counterarguments have been presented. Some claim automation relieves workers from menial jobs so they can pursue more interesting work thereafter. However, many may lack the qualifications or intellect, or may at least perceive stress by that perspective of being forced to taking on more and more challenging jobs. Others even see automation as "freeing humans from duty of work" completely, which would be an ethical pro-argument. In reality, most humans like to have work, and may even need it to give their lives a structure and purpose; certainly many people define who they are by what they do professionally. Therefore, taking their work from them without their consent, means taking their dignity from them. It is also often argued that NLP systems merely aim to make human analysts more productive. It is desirable to do so, and then automation would seem morally legitimate. However, in practice, many customers of applications desire automation as a tool to reduce the workforce, because they are under cost pressure.

5 Best Practices

5.1 Ethics Review Board

In order to establish ethical behavior as a default, installing a *process* likely increases the awareness; it assigns responsibility and improves consistency of procedure and outcome. An ethics review board for companies (as already implemented by universities for use in the context of the approval of experiments with human and animal subjects) included in the discussion of new products, services, or planned research experiments should be considered, very much like it already exists in university environments in an experimental natural science context; in the 21st century, experiments with data about people is a proxy for doing experiments with people, as that data affects their lives. Figure 2 shows our proposal for such a process for a hypothetical company or research institution. It shows a vetting process featuring an Ethics Review Board (ERB), which would operate as follows before and after executing research projects, before and after product development, as well as during deployment of a product or service on an ongoing basis (at regular intervals), the ERB gets to review propositions (the "what") and methods (the "how") and either gives its blessing (approve) or not (veto). Ethics stakeholders participate in research, product/service design & development, operations & customer service. Each of them could report to the Chief Informa-

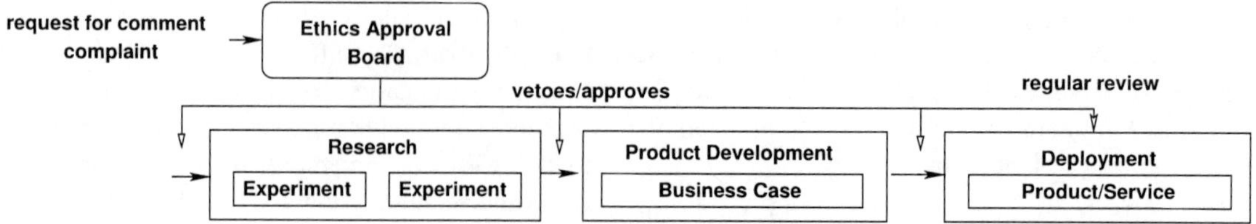

Figure 2: A Process Proposal for "Ethics by Design" in an Organization.

tion Officer via a Vice President for Governance rather than phase-specific management to give the ethics review more robustness through independence. There are associated business benefits (employee identification, reduced risk of reputation damage), however these are distinct from the ethical motive, i.e. desiring to do the right thing for its own sake. They are also distinct from legal motives, because acting legally is often not sufficient for acting ethically, especially in emerging technology areas where the law lags behind technology developments. An ERB might be too expensive to operate for smaller institutions, but it could be outsourced to independent contractors or companies that perform an external audit function ("ERB as a service"). The board would convene at well-defined points to sign off that there was an ethics conversation, documenting identified issues and recommending resolution pathways. ERB audits could benefit from check-lists that are collated in the organization based on the experience obtained in past projects (Smiley et al., 2017). In the US, Institutional Review Boards are already legally required for certain kinds of institutions and businesses (Enfield and Truwit, 2008; Pope, 2009). Our proposal is to adopt similar practices, and to customize them to accommodate particular, NLP-specific issues. An ERB should be empowered to veto new products or NLP projects on ethical grounds at the planning stage or at project launch time (earlier means less money wasted). The ERB could be installed by the board to make the company more sustainable, and more attractive to ethical investors. Note that it is not required that ERB members agree on one and the same school of ethics: a diverse ERB with voting procedures, comprising members, each of which driven by their own conscience, might converge towards wise decisions, and that may be the best way to adopt as a practical solution ("crowd wisdom"). The ethics board should ideally contain all stakeholder groups: if the organization's NLP projects are mostly pertaining to automation as an issue, worker representatives would be good to include. Moral philosophers, human rights experts and lawyers could be included as well; in general, some delegates should be independent and should have a well-developed conscience.[10] In practice, the ERB involvement incorporates elements from "value sensitive design" (Friedman et al., 2008) (thus generalizing Cavoukian's "privacy by design" idea) and works as follows: a product manager generates a document outlining a new project, or a scientist creates an idea for a new research project. At the decision point (launch or nor), the ERB is involved to give its ethics approval (in addition to other, already existing functions, e.g. finance or strategy). At this stage, the morality of the overall idea is assessed. Working at a conceptual level, the ERB needs to identify the stakeholders, both direct and indirect, as well as the values that are implicated in the proposed idea or project. Once the project is launched, detailed written specifications are usually produced. They again are brought to the ERB for review. The project plan itself is reviewed by the ERB with a view to scrutinizing research methods, understanding how the stakeholders prioritize implicated values and trade-offs between competing values, as well as how the technology supports certain values. The ERB may send documents back with additional requests to clarify particular aspects. The ERB documents permanently anything identified as unethical. Ideally, they would have a powerful veto right, but different implementations are thinkable. Much harder is the involvement in ongoing review activities, for example to decide whether or not code is ethical. It appears that a committee meeting is not well suited to ascertain moral principles are adhered to; a better way could be if the ERB was in regular informal touch

---

[10]It would definitely help to include more inexperienced and younger members, whose idealism may not have been corrupted by too much exposure to so-called "real life".

with scientists and developers in order to probe the team with the right questions. For example, a mention of the use of crowdsourcing could trigger a suggestion to pay the legal minimal hourly salary.

5.2 Responses to Ethics Dilemmas

A lot of the literature focuses on how to decide what is ethical or not. While this is obviously a core question, the discussion must not rest there: of similar relevance is an elaboration about possible remedies. Table 1 shows a set of possible responses to ethics issues. Some of these acts are about the individual's response to a situation with possible ethical implications in order to avoid becoming co- responsible/complicit, whereas others are more outcome-oriented. They are loosely oriented from least (bottom) to most (top) serious, and include internal and external activities.

6 Discussion

The privacy issue in the early UNIX **spell(1)** tool differs from the Mexican propaganda chat-bots in that the former wrongly (un-ethically) implements a particular function (if there is no on-screen warning to ensure informed consent of the user), whereas in the latter case, the chat-bot application as a whole is to be rejected on moral grounds. We can use these two situations to anecdotally test our "ethics by design" process in a thought experiment: what if both situations arose in an organization implementing the process as described above? The spell tool's hidden emails should be unearthed in the "review" stage (which could well include code reviews by independent consultants or developers in cases where questionable practices have been unearthed or suspected). And clearly, the Mexican bots should be rejected by the ERB at the planning stage. By way of self-criticism, flagging functional issues like the hidden spell email feature is perhaps less likely detectable than application-level ethical issues, since over-keen programmers may either forget, intentionally not communicate, or mis-assess the importance of the hidden-email property; nevertheless, using the process arguably makes it more likely to detect both issues than without using it. Floridi's model, which wass designed for information ethics, may have to be extended in the direction of information processing ethics (covering the software that creates or co-creates with humans the information under consideration), since the software or the process that leads to the software can itself be unethical in part or as a whole. There is also an interaction between the conversation whether AI (including NLP) can/should even aspire doing what it does, as it does, because framing of the task brings ethical baggage that some see as distraction from other (more?) important issues: as Lanier (2014) points out, the directional aspiration and framing of AI as a movement that either aims to or accidentally results in replacing humans or superseding the human race, effectively creating a post-human software-only species ("the end of human agency") is a "non-optimal" way of looking at the dangers of AI; in his view, it adds a layer of distractive arguments (e.g. ethical/religious ones about whether we should do this) that divert the discourse from other, more pressing conversations, such as over-promising (and not delivering), which leads to subsequent funding cuts ("AI winter"). We will likely be producing a world that may be likened to Brazil rather than Skynet. While Lanier has a point regarding over-selling, in our view the ethical problems need to be addressed regardless, but his argument helps to order them by immediate urgency. One could argue that our ERB proposal may slow innovation within an organization. However, it is central to protecting the organization from situations that have a significant impact on its reputations and its customers, hence, reducing the organization's risk exposure. One may also argue that, if implemented well, it could guide innovation processes towards ethical innovation.

7 Summary & Conclusion

In this paper, we have discussed some of the ethical issues associated with NLP and related techniques like machine learning. We proposed an "ethics by design" approach and we presented a new process model for ethics reviews in companies or research institutions, similar to ethics review boards that in universities must approve experiments with animal and human subjects.[11] We also presented a list of remedies that researchers can consider when facing ethical dilemmas. In future work, professional codes of conduct should be strengthened, and compliance be made mandatory for professionals.

---

[11] See also the journal *IRB: Ethics & Human Research* (currently in its 39th volume) dedicated to related topics in other disciplines.

Table 1: Remedies: Pyramid of Possible Responses to Unethical Behavior.

Demonstration	to effect a change in society by public activism
Disclosure	to document/to reveal injustice to regulators, the police, investigative journalists ("Look what they do!", "Stop what they do!")
Resignation	to distance oneself III ("I should not/cannot be part of this.')
Persuasion	to influence in order to halt non-ethical activity ("Our organization should not do this.")
Rejection	to distance oneself II; to deny participation; conscientious objection ("I can't do this.")
Escalation	raise with senior management/ethics boards ("You may not know what is going on here.")
Voicing dissent	to distance oneself I ("This project is wrong.")
Documentation	ensure all the facts, plans and potential and actual issues are preserved.

Acknowledgments. The authors would like to express their gratitude to Aaron J. Mengelkamp, Frank Schilder, Isabelle Moulinier, and Lucas Carstens for pointers and discussions, and to Khalid Al-Kofahi for supporting this work. We would also like to express our gratitude for the detailed constructive feedback from the anonymous reviewers.

References

ACM. 1992. ACM Code of Ethics and Professional Conduct. Online, cited 2016-12-27, http://bit.ly/2kbdhoD.

ACM. 2017. Principles for Algorithmic Transparency and Accountability. online, cited 2017-01-15, http://bit.ly/2jVROTx.

Colin Allen, Iva Smit, and Wendell Wallach. 2005. Artificial morality: Top-down, bottom-up, and hybrid approaches. *Ethics and Information Technology*, 7(3):149–155.

Tim Althoff, Kevin Clark, and Jure Leskovec. 2016. Large-scale analysis of counseling conversations: An application of natural language processing to mental health. *Transactions of the Association for Computational Linguistics*, 4(463–476).

Aristotle. 1925. *The Nicomachean Ethics: Translated with an Introduction.* Oxford University Press, Oxford, England, UK.

Aristotle. 1934. *Aristotle in 23 Volumes*, volume 19. Heinemann, London, England.

Harry Armstrong. 2015. Machines that learn in the wild: Machine learning capabilities, limitations and implications. Technical report, Nesta, London, England.

Association of Internet Researchers. 2017, to appear. *AoIR 2017: Networked Publics – The 18th annual meeting of the Association of Internet Researchers will be held in Tartu, Estonia, 18-21 October 2017.*

Jon Bentley. 1986. *Programming Pearls.* Addison-Wesley, Reading, MA, USA.

Chris Brew. 2016. Classifying ReachOut posts with a radial basis function SVM. In Kristy Hollingshead and Lyle H. Ungar, editors, *Proceedings of the 3rd Workshop on Computational Linguistics and Clinical Psychology, CLPsych@NAACL-HLT 2016, June 16, 2016, San Diego, California, USA*, pages 138–142. Association for Computational Linguistics.

Brey, Philip, and Johnny H. Soraker. 2009. Philosophy of computing and information technology. In Dov M. Gabbay, Antonie Neijers, and John Woods, editors, *Philosophy of Technology and Engineering Sciences*, volume 9, pages 1341–1408. North Holland, Burlington, MA, USA.

Terrell Ward Bynum and Simon Rogerson. 2004. *Computer Ethics and Professional Responsibility: Introductory Text and Readings.* Wiley-Blackwell, Malden, MA, USA.

Terell Bynum. 2008. Computer and information ethics. In *Stanford Encyclopedia of Philosophy*. Stanford University.

C. Cary, H. J. Wen, and P. Mahatanankoon. 2003. Data mining: Consumer privacy, ethical policy, and system development practices. *Human Systems Management*, 22.

Ann Cavoukian. 2009. Privacy by design. Technical report, The Office of the Information and Privacy Commissioner of Ontario, Toronto, Ontario, Canada.

Kord Davis and Doug Patterson. 2012. *Ethics of Big Data: Balancing Risk and Innovation.* O'Reilly, Sebastopol, CA, USA.

K. B. Enfield and J. D. Truwit. 2008. The purpose, composition and function of an institutional review board: Balancing priorities. *Respiratory Care*, pages 1330–1336.

Joshua Fairfield and Hannah Shtein. 2014. Big data, big problems: Emerging issues in the ethics of data science and journalism. *Journal of Mass Media Ethics*, 29(1):38–51.

FATML. 2014. Fairness, accountability, and transparency in machine learning (FATML).

Luciano Floridi. 2013. *The Ethics of Information.* Oxford University Press, Oxford, England, UK.

Martin Ford. 2015. *The Rise of the Robots: Technology and the Threat of Mass Unemployment.* Oneworld, New York, NY, USA.

Karn Fort and Alain Couillault. 2016. Yes, we care! results of the ethics and natural language processing surveys. In *10th edition of the Language Resources and Evaluation Conference, 23-28 May 2016, Portoro, Slovenia*, LREC 2016, pages 1593–1600.

K. Fort, G. Adda, and K.B. Cohen. 2011. Amazon Mechanical Turk: Gold mine or coal mine? *Computational Linguistics*, 37(2):413–420.

Batya Friedman, Peter H. Kahn Jr., and Alan Borning. 2008. Value sensitive design and information systems. In Kenneth Einar Himma and Herman T. Tavani, editors, *The Handbook of Information and Computer Ethics*, chapter 4, pages 69–101. Willey, Hoboken, NJ, USA.

Harry J. Gensler. 2011. *Ethics: A Contemporary Introduction*. Routledge Contemporary Introductions to Philosophy. Routledge, London, 2nd edition.

Dirk Hovy and Shannon L. Spruit. 2016. The social impact of natural language processing. In *Proceedings of the 54th Annual Meeting of the Association for Computational Linguistics*, pages 591–598, Berlin, Germany. Association for Computational Linguistics.

Immanuel Kant. 1785. *Grundlegung zur Metaphysik der Sitten*. J. F. Hartknoch, Riga, Latvia.

Bryan Klimt and Yiming Yang. 2004. The Enron corpus: A new dataset for email classification research. In J.-F. Boulicaut, F. Esposito, F. Giannotti, and D. Pedreschi, editors, *Machine Learning: ECML 2004, 15th European Conference on Machine Learning, Pisa, Italy, September 20-24, 2004, Proceedings*, volume 3201 of *Lecture Notes in Computer Science*, pages 217–226, Heidelberg, Germany. Springer.

Michal Kosinski, David Stillwell, and Thore Graepel. 2013. Private traits and attributes are predictable from digital records of human behavior. *Proceedings of the National Academy of Sciences*, 110(15):5802–5805.

Julia Lane, Victoria Stodden, Stefan Bender, and Helen Nissenbaum, editors. 2014. *Privacy, Big Data and the Public Good*. Cambridge University Press, New York, NY, USA.

Jason Lanier. 2014. The myth of AI: A conversation with Jaron Lanier. Online, cited 2017-01-17, https://www.edge.org/conversation/the-myth-of-ai.

Annette Markham and Elizabeth Buchanan. 2012. Ethical decision-making and Internet research: Recommendations from the AoIR ethics working committee (version 2.0). Technical report, Association of Internet Researchers.

Judith Masthoff. 2011. Review of: Close Engagements with Artificial Companions: Key Social, Psychological, Ethical, and Design Issues. *Computational Linguistics*, 37(2):399–402.

Aaron Mengelkamp, Sebastian Rohmann, and Matthias Schumann. 2016. Credit assessment based on user generated content: State of research. In Christine Bernadas and Delphine Minchella, editors, *Proceedings of the 3rd European Conference on Social Media, 12-13 July 2016*, pages 223–231, Caen, France.

John Stuart Mill. 1879. *Utilitarianism*. Floating Press, Auckland, New Zealand, 1st edition.

Frank Pasquale. 2015. *The Black Box Society: The Secret Algorithms That Control Money and Information*. Harvard University Press, Cambridge, MA, USA.

Jonathon W. Penney. 2016. Chilling effects: Online surveillance and Wikipedia use. *Berkeley Law Review*, 31(1):117–182.

John P. Pestian, Pawel Matykiewicz, and Michelle Linn-Gust. 2012. Suicide note sentiment classification: A supervised approach augmented by Web data. *Biomedical Informatics Insights*, 5 (Suppl. 1):1–6.

T. M. Pope. 2009. Multi-institutional healthcare ethics committees: The procedurally fair internal dispute resolution mechanism. *Campbell Law Review*, 31:257–331.

Michael J. Quinn. 2016. *Ethics for the Information Age*. Pearson, 7th edition.

Charese Smiley, Frank Schilder, Vassilis Plachouras, and Jochen L. Leidner. 2017. Say the right thing right: Ethics issues in natural language generation systems. In *Proceedings of the Workshop on Ethics & NLP held at the EACL Conference, April 3-7, 2017*, Valencia, Spain. ACL.

Bernd Carsten Stahl, Job Timmmermans, and Brent Daniel Mittelstadt. 2016. The ethics of computing: A survey of the computing-oriented literature. *ACM Computing Survey*, 48(4):55:1–55:38.

Richard Susskind and Daniel Susskind. 2015. *The Future of the Professions: How Technology Will Transform the Work of Human Experts Hardcover*. Oxford University Press, New York, NY, USA.

Andree Thieltges, Florian Schmidt, and Simon Hegelich. 2016. The devils triangle: Ethical considerations on developing bot detection methods. In *Proc. 2016 AAAI Spring Symposium, Stanford University, March 2123, 2016*, pages 253–257. AAAI.

Alan F. Westin. 1967. *Privacy and Freedom*. Atheneum, New York, NY, USA, 1st edition.

Norbert Wiener. 1954. *The Human Use of Human Beings*. Houghton Mifflin, Boston, MA, USA.

Yorick Wilks, editor. 2010. *Close Engagements with Artificial Companions: Key Social, Psychological, Ethical, and Design Issues*. John Benjamins, Amsterdam, The Netherlands.

Wu Youyou, Michal Kosinski, and David Stillwell. 2015. Computer-based personality judgments are more accurate than those made by humans. *Proceedings of the National Academy of Sciences*, 112(4):1036–1040.

M. Zimmer. 2010. 'but the data is already public': On the ethics of research in Facebook. *Ethics and Information Technology*, 12(4):313–325.

Building Better Open-Source Tools to Support Fairness in Automated Scoring

Nitin Madnani[1], Anastassia Loukina[1], Alina von Davier[2], Jill Burstein[1] and Aoife Cahill[1]

[1]Educational Testing Service, Princeton, NJ
[2]ACT, Iowa City, IA
[1]{nmadnani,aloukina,jburstein,acahill}@ets.org
[2]Alina.vonDavier@act.org

Abstract

Automated scoring of written and spoken responses is an NLP application that can significantly impact lives especially when deployed as part of high-stakes tests such as the GRE® and the TOEFL®. Ethical considerations require that automated scoring algorithms treat *all* test-takers *fairly*. The educational measurement community has done significant research on fairness in assessments and automated scoring systems must incorporate their recommendations. The best way to do that is by making available automated, *non-proprietary* tools to NLP researchers that directly incorporate these recommendations and generate the analyses needed to help identify and resolve biases in their scoring systems. In this paper, we attempt to provide such a solution.

1 Introduction

Natural Language Processing (NLP) applications now form a large part of our everyday lives. As researchers who build such applications, we have a responsibility to ensure that we prioritize the ideas of fairness and transparency and not just blindly pursue better algorithmic performance.

In this paper, we discuss the ethical considerations pertaining to automated scoring of written or spoken test responses, referred to as "constructed responses". Automated scoring is an NLP application which aims to automatically predict a score for such responses. We focus on automated systems designed to score open-ended constructed response questions. Such systems generally use text and speech processing techniques to extract a set of features from responses which are then combined into a scoring model to predict the fi-

nal score assigned by a human rater (Page, 1966; Burstein et al., 1998; Zechner et al., 2009; Bernstein et al., 2010).

Test scores whether assigned by human raters or computers can have a significant effect on people's lives and, therefore, must be fair to all test takers. Automated scoring systems may offer some advantages over human raters, e.g., higher score consistency (Williamson et al., 2012). Yet, like any other machine learning algorithm, models used for score prediction may inadvertently encode discrimination into their decisions due to biases or other imperfections in the training data, spurious correlations, and other factors (Romei and Ruggieri, 2013b; von Davier, 2016).[1]

The paper has the following structure. We first draw awareness to the psychometric research and recommendations on quantifying potential biases in automated scoring and how it relates to the ideas of fairness, accountability, and transparency in machine learning (FATML). The second half of the paper presents an open-source tool called *RSMTool*[2] for developers of automated scoring models which *directly* integrates these psychometric recommendations. Since such developers are likely to be NLP or machine learning researchers, the tool provides an important bridge from the educational measurement side to the NLP side. Next, we discuss further challenges related to fairness in automated scoring that are not currently addressed by *RSMTool* as well as methods for *avoiding* bias in automated scoring rather than just detecting it. The paper concludes with a discussion of how these tools and methodologies may, in fact, be ap-

---

[1]Some of these problems were recently discussed at a panel focused on Fairness in Machine learning in Educational Measurement that was held at the annual meeting of National Council for Educational Measurement (von Davier and Burstein, 2016).

[2]http://github.com/
EducationalTestingService/rsmtool

Proceedings of the First Workshop on Ethics in Natural Language Processing, pages 41–52,
Valencia, Spain, April 4th, 2017. © 2017 Association for Computational Linguistics

plicable to other NLP applications beyond automated scoring.

2 Ethics and Fairness in Constructed Response Scoring

At this point in the paper, we believe it is important
to define exactly what we refer to as *fairness* for
the field of scoring constructed responses, whether
it is done manually by humans or automatically by
NLP systems.

A key concept here is the idea of a "construct"
which is defined as a set of related knowledge,
skills, and other abilities that a test is designed to
measure. Examples of possible constructs include
logical reasoning, language proficiency, reading
comprehension etc. A fair test is one where differences in test scores between the test-takers are
due *only* to differences in skills which are part of
the construct. Any consistent differences in scores
between different groups of test takers that result
from other factors *not* immediately related to the
construct (i.e., "construct-irrelevant") — e.g., test-
taker gender — may indicate that the test is unfair.
Specifically, for a test to be fair, the non-random
effects of construct-irrelevant factors need to be
minimized during the four major phases of a test:
test development, test administration, test scoring,
and score interpretation (Xi, 2010; Zieky, 2016):

1. **Test development.** All tests must be free
   of bias, i.e., no questions on a test should
   include any content that may advantage or
   disadvantage any specific subgroup of test-
   takers in ways that are unrelated to the construct the test is designed to assess. The subgroups in this case are defined based on factors that include test-taker personal information such as gender, race, or disability, but
   may also go beyond the standard protected
   properties. For example, Xi (2010) discusses
   how familiarity with the subject matter in an
   English language proficiency test may impact
   test performance and, thus, would require an
   explicit analysis of fairness for a group defined by test-taker fields of study. Additionally, on the same test, test-takers whose native languages use the Roman alphabet will
   have an advantage over test-takers with native
   languages based on other alphabets. However, this advantage is allowable because it is
   relevant to the construct of English comprehension. To ensure bias-free questions, the
   developers of the test conduct both qualitative and quantitative reviews of each question
   (Angoff, 2012; Duong and von Davier, 2013;
   Oliveri and von Davier, 2016; Zieky, 2016).

2. **Test administration.** All test-takers must
   be provided with comparable opportunities to
   demonstrate the abilities being measured by
   the test. This includes considerations such as
   the location and number of test centers across
   the world, and whether the testing conditions
   in each test center are standardized and secure. For example, Bridgeman et al. (2003)
   showed that, at least for some tests, exami-
   nee test scores may be affected by screen resolution of the monitors used to administer the
   test. This means that for such tests to be fair,
   it is necessary to ensure that all test-takers use
   monitors with a similar configuration.

3. **Test scoring.** There should also be no bias
   in the test scores irrespective of whether they
   are produced by human raters or by automated scoring models. The unequal distribution of social, economic, and educational resources means that some differences in performance across subgroups are to be ex-
   pected. However, differences large enough to
   have practical consequences must be investigated to ensure that they are not caused by
   construct-irrelevant factors (AERA, 1999).

4. **Score interpretation** Finally, while most
   tests tend to have a constant structure, the
   actual questions change regularly. Sometimes several different versions of a test ("test
   forms") exist in parallel. Even if two test-
   takers take different versions of a test, their
   test scores should still be comparable. To
   achieve this, a separate statistical process
   process called "test equating" is often used to
   adjust for unintended differences in the difficulty of the test forms (Lee and von Davier,
   2013; Liu and Dorans, 2016). This process
   itself must also be investigated for fairness to
   ensure that it does not introduce bias against
   any group of test-takers.

In this paper, we focus on the third phase: the
fairness of test scores as measured by the impact
of construct-irrelevant factors. As Xi (2010) discusses in detail, unfair decisions based on scores
assigned to test-takers from oft-disadvantaged

groups are likely to have profound consequences: they may be denied career opportunities and access to resources that they deserve. Therefore, it is important to ensure — among other things — that construct-irrelevant factors *do not* introduce systematic biases in test scores, irrespective of whether they are produced by human raters or by an automated scoring system.

Over the last few years, there has been a significant amount of work done on ensuring fairness, accountability, and transparency for machine learned models from what is now referred to as the FATML community (Kamiran and Calders, 2009; Kamishima et al., 2012; Luong et al., 2011; Zemel et al., 2013). More recently, Friedler et al. (2016) proposed a formal framework for conceptualizing the idea of fairness. Within that framework, the authors define the idea of "structural bias": the unequal treatment of subgroups when there is no clear mapping between the features that are easily observable for those subgroups (e.g., largely irrelevant, culturally and historically defined characteristics) and the true features on which algorithmic decisions should actually be based (the "construct"). Our conceptualization of fairness for automated scoring models in this paper — avoiding systematic biases in test scores across subgroups due to construct-irrelevant factors — fits perfectly in this framework.

3   Detecting Biases in Automated Scoring

Human scoring of constructed responses is a subjective process. Among the factors that can impact the assigned scores are rater fatigue (Ling et al., 2014), differences between novice and experienced raters (Davis, 2015), and the effect of raters' linguistic background on their evaluation of the language skill being measured (Carey et al., 2011). Furthermore, the same response can sometimes receive different scores from different raters. To guard against such rater inconsistencies, responses for high-stakes tests are often scored by multiple raters (Wang and von Davier, 2014; Penfield, 2016). Automated scoring of constructed responses can overcome many of these issues inherent to human scoring: computers do not get tired, do not have personal biases, and can be configured to always assign the *same* score to a given response.

However, recent studies in machine learning have highlighted that algorithms often introduce their own biases (Feldman et al., 2015) either due to an existing bias in the training data or due to a minority group being inadequately represented in the training data. Automated scoring is certainly not immune to such biases and, in fact, several studies have documented differing performance of automated scoring models for test-takers with different native languages or with disabilities (Burstein and Chodorow, 1999; Bridgeman et al., 2012; Wang and von Davier, 2014; Wang et al., 2016; An et al., 2016; Loukina and Buzick, In print).

Biases can also arise because of techniques used to develop new features for automated scoring models. The automated score may be based on features which are construct-irrelevant despite being highly correlated with the human scores in the training data. As an example, consider that more proficient writers tend to write longer responses. Therefore, one almost always observes a consistent positive correlation between essay length and human proficiency score (Perelman, 2014; Shermis, 2014b). This is acceptable since verbal fluency — a correlate of response length — is considered an important part of the writing proficiency. Yet, longer essays should not *automatically* receive higher scores. Therefore, without proper model validation to consider the *relative* impact of such features, decisions might be made that are unfair to test-takers.

On this basis, the psychometric guidelines require that if automated scoring models are to be used for making high-stakes decisions for college admissions or employment, the NLP researchers developing those models should perform model validation to ensure that demographic and construct-irrelevant factors are not causing their models to produce significant differences in scores across different subgroups of test-takers (Yang et al., 2002; Clauser et al., 2002; Williamson et al., 2012). This is exactly what *fairness* – as we define it in this paper – purports to measure.

However, it is not easy for an NLP or machine learning researcher to perform comprehensive model validation since they may be unfamiliar with the required psychometric and statistical checks. The solution we propose is a tool that incorporates *both* the standard machine learning pipeline necessary for building an automated scoring model *and* a set of psychometric and statistical analyses aimed at detecting possible bias in engine performance. We believe that such a tool should be open-source and non-proprietary so that the automated scoring community can not only audit the source code of the already available analyses to ensure their compliance with fairness standards but also contribute new analyses.

We describe the design of such a tool in the rest of the paper. Specifically, our tool provides the following model validation functionality to NLP/ML researchers working on automated scoring: (a) defining custom subgroups and examining differences in the performance of the automated scoring model across these groups; (b) examining the effect of construct-irrelevant factors on automated scores; and (c) comparing the effects of such factors in two different versions of the same scoring model, e.g., a version with a new feature added to the model and a version without the same feature.

4 *RSMTool*

In this section, we present an open-source Python tool called *RSMTool* developed by two of the authors for building and evaluating automated scoring models. The tool is intended for NLP researchers who have already extracted features from the responses and need to choose a learner function and evaluate the performance as well as the fairness of the *entire* scoring pipeline (the training data, the features, and the learner function).

Once the responses have been represented as a set of features, automated scoring essentially becomes a machine learning problem and NLP researchers are free to use any of the large number of existing machine learning toolkits. However, most of those toolkits are general-purpose and do not provide the aforementioned fairness analyses. Instead, we leverage one such toolkit — *scikit-learn* (Pedregosa et al., 2011) — to build a tool that integrates these fairness analyses *directly* into the machine learning pipeline and researchers then get them automatically in the form of a comprehensive HTML report.

Note that the automated scoring pipeline built into the tool provides functionality for *each* step of the process of building and evaluating automated scoring models: (a) feature transformation, (b) manual and automatic feature selection, and (c) access to linear and non-linear learners from *scikit-learn* as well as the custom linear learners we have implemented. In this paper, we will fo-

cus solely on the fairness-driven evaluation capabilities of the tool that are directly relevant to the issues we have discussed so far. Readers interested in other parts of the *RSMTool* are referred to the comprehensive documentation available at `http://rsmtool.readthedocs.org`.

Before we describe the fairness analyses implemented in the tool, we want to acknowledge that there are many different ways in which researchers might approach building as well as evaluating scoring models (Chen and He, 2013; Shermis, 2014a). The list of learners and fairness analyses the tool provides is not, and cannot be, exhaustive. In fact, later in the paper, we discuss some analyses that could be implemented in future versions of the tool since one of the core characteristics of the tool is its flexible architecture. See §4.4 for more details.

In the next section, we present in detail the analyses incorporated into *RSMTool* aimed at detecting the various sources of biases we introduced earlier. As it is easier to show the analyses in the context of an actual example, we use data from the Hewlett Foundation Automated Student Assessment Prize (ASAP) competition on automated essay scoring (Shermis, 2014a).[3] As our scoring model, we use ordinary linear regression with features extracted from the text of the essay; see Attali and Burstein (2006) for details of the features. Note that since the original ASAP data does not contain any demographic information, we simulate an L1 attribute (the test-taker's native language) for illustration purposes.[4] The complete report automatically generated by *RSMTool* is available at: `http://bit.ly/fair-tool`. The report contains links to the raw data used to generate it and to other input files needed to run *RSMTool*. We focus on specific sections of the report below.

4.1 Differential Feature Functioning

In order to evaluate the fairness of a machine learning algorithm, Feldman et al. (2015) recommend preventive auditing of the training data to determine if the resulting decisions will be fair, irrespective of the machine learning model learned from that training data. *RSMTool* incorporates sev-

---

[3]`https://www.kaggle.com/c/asap-aes/data/`

[4]We believe it is more transparent to use a publicly available dataset with simulated demographics, rather than a proprietary dataset with real demographics that cannot be shared publicly. The value added by the fairness analyses comes through in either case.

eral such auditing approaches borrowed from previous research in both educational measurement and machine learning.

The first step in evaluating the fairness of an automated scoring model is to ensure that the performance of each feature is not primarily determined by construct-irrelevant factors. The traditional way to approach this is to have an expert review the features and ensure that their description and method of computation are in line with the definition of the specific set of skills that the given test purports to measure (Deane, 2013). However, features incorporated into a modern automated scoring system often rely on multiple underlying NLP components such as part-of-speech taggers and syntactic parsers as well as complex computational algorithms and, therefore, a qualitative review may not be sufficient. Furthermore, some aspects of spoken or written text can *only* be measured indirectly given the current state of NLP technologies (Somasundaran et al., 2014).

RSMTool allows the user to explore the quantitative effect of two types of construct-irrelevant factors that may affect feature performance: categorical and continuous.

4.1.1 Categorical Factors

This group of factors generally includes variables that can take on one of a fixed number of possible values, e.g., test-takers' demographic characteristics, different versions of the same test question, or various testing conditions. We refer to these factors as "subgroups" though they are not always limited to demographic subgroups.

When this information is available for all or some of the responses, *RSMTool* allows the user to compare the feature distributions for different subgroups using box-plots and other distributional statistics such as mean and standard deviations. However, feature distributions depend on the scores which may differ across subgroups and, therefore, differences in a feature's distribution across subgroups may not always indicate that the feature is biased. To address this, *RSMTool* also includes *Differential feature functioning* (DFF) analysis (Penfield, 2016; Zhang et al., In print). This approach compares the mean values of a given feature for test-takers with the same score but belonging to different subgroups. These differences can be described and reviewed directly using DFF line plots. Figure 1(a) shows a box-plot for the distribution of the GRAMMAR feature by test-taker L1 subgroups in our sample dataset; Figure 1(b) shows a DFF line plot for the same feature. These plots indicate that the values for the GRAMMAR feature are consistently lower for one of the test-taker subgroups (L1=Hindi) across all score levels. If such a pattern were observed in real data, it would warrant further investigation to establish the reasons for such behavior.

4.1.2 Continuous Factors

This type of construct-irrelevant factors includes continuous covariates which despite being correlated with human scores are either *not* directly relevant to the construct measured by the test or, even if they are, should *not* be the primary contributor to the model's predictions. Response length, as previously discussed, is an example of such covariates. Even though it provides an important indication of verbal fluency, a model which predominantly relies on length will not generate fair scores. To explore the impact of such factors, *RSMTool* computes two types of correlations: (a) the marginal correlation between each feature and the covariate, and (b) the "partial" correlation between each feature and the human score, with the effects of the covariate removed (Cramér, 1947). This helps to clearly bring out the contribution of a feature above and beyond being a proxy for the identified covariate. The marginal and partial correlation coefficients for our example are shown in Figure 1(c). It shows that although all features in our simulated dataset contribute information beyond response length, for some features, length accounts for a substantial part of their performance.

4.2 Bias in Model Performance

Not all types of machine learning algorithms lend themselves easily to the differential feature functioning analysis. Furthermore, the sheer number of features in some models may make the results of such analyses difficult to interpret. Therefore, a second set of fairness analyses included into *RSMTool* considers how well the automated scores agree with the human scores (or another, user-specified gold standard criterion) and whether this agreement is consistent across different groups of test-takers.

RSMTool computes all the standard evaluation metrics generally used for regression-based machine learning models such as Pearson's correlation coefficient (r), coefficient of determination

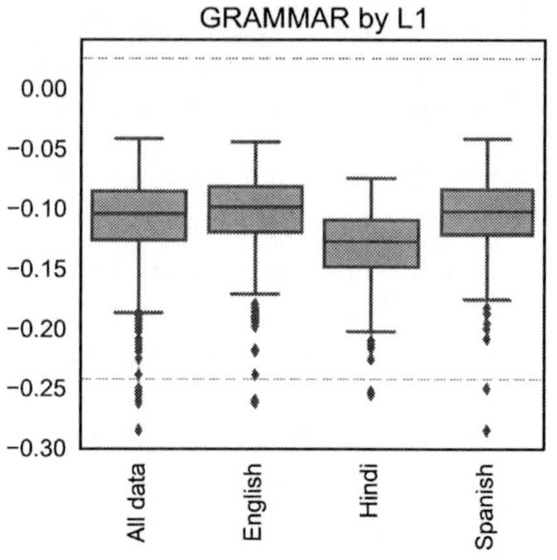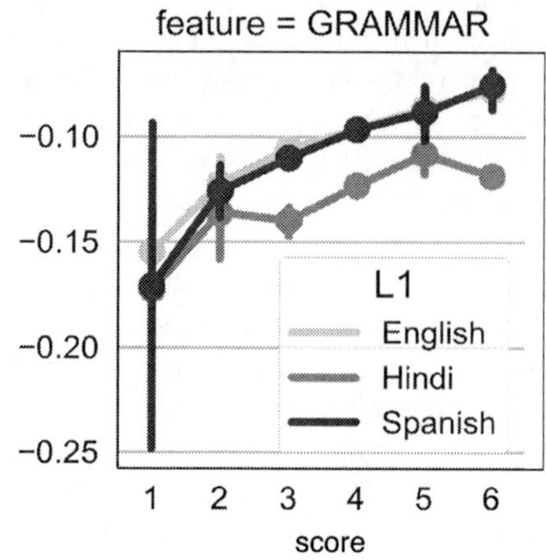

(a) Box-plots showing the distribution of standardized GRAMMAR feature values by test-taker native language (L1). The dotted red lines represent the thresholds for outlier truncation computed as the mean feature value $\pm$ 4 standard deviations.

(b) A differential feature functioning (DFF) plot for the GRAMMAR feature. Each line represents an L1; each point shows the mean and 95% confidence intervals of the feature values computed for test-takers with that L1 and that assigned score.

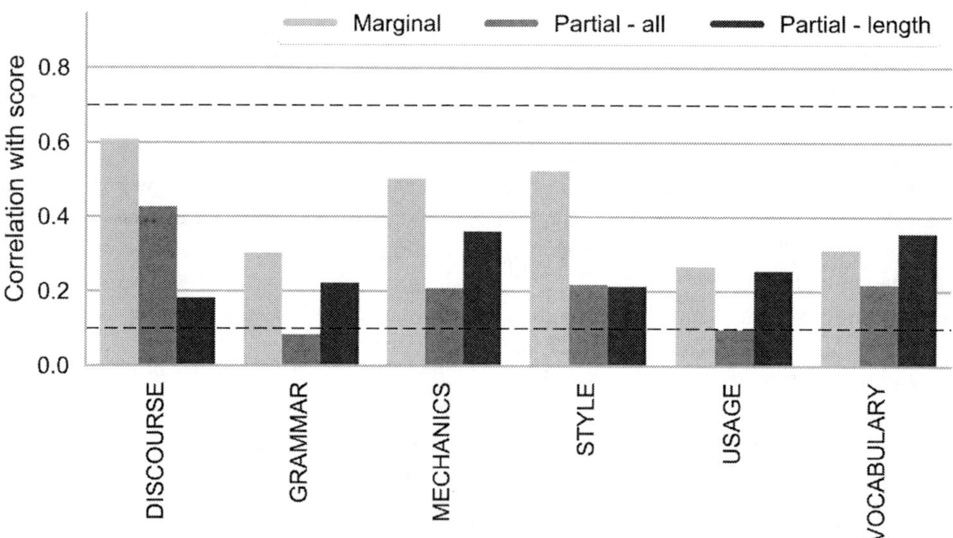

(c) Pearson's correlation coefficients (r) between features and human scores: (a) **Marginal**: marginal correlation of each feature with human score (b) **Partial – all**: correlation of each feature with human score with the effects of all other features removed, and (c) **Partial – length**: the correlation of each feature with human score with the effect of response length removed. The two dotted lines represent correlations thresholds recommended by Williamson et al. (2012).

Figure 1: Examples of *RSMTool* fairness analyses for categorical and continuous factors.

(R^2), and root mean squared error ($RMSE$). In addition, it also computes other measures that are *specifically* recommended in psychometric literature for evaluating automated scoring models: quadratically-weighted kappa, percentage agreement with human scores, and the standardized mean difference (SMD) between human and automated scores (Williamson et al., 2012; Ramineni and Williamson, 2013). These metrics are computed for the whole evaluation set as well as for each subgroup separately in order to evaluate whether the accuracy of automated scores is consistent across different groups of test-takers. Figure 2 shows a plot illustrating how the model R^2 computed on the evaluation set varies across the different test-taker L1 subgroups.

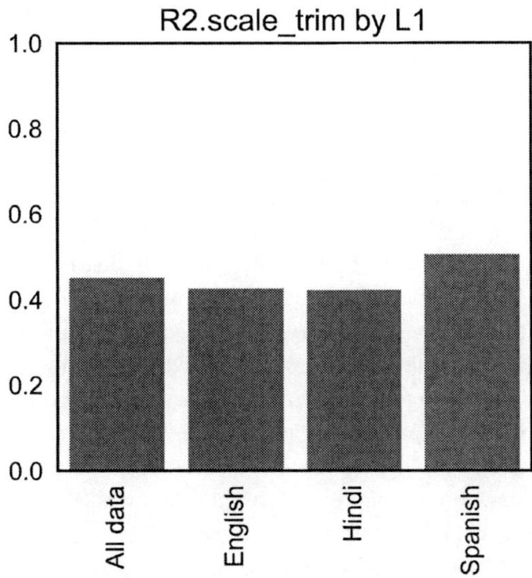

Figure 2: The performance of our scoring model (R^2) for different subgroups of test-takers as defined by their native language (L1). Before computing the R^2, the predictions of the model are trimmed and then re-scaled to match the human score distribution in the training data.

4.3 Model comparison

Like any other software, automated scoring systems are updated on a regular basis as researchers develop new features or identify better machine learning algorithms. Even in scenarios where new features or algorithms are not needed, changes in external dependencies used by the scoring pipeline might necessitate new releases. Automated scoring models may also be regularly re-trained to avoid population drift which can occur when the test-taker population used to train the model no longer matches the population *currently* evaluated by this model.

When updating an automated scoring system for one of the above reasons, one should not only conduct a fairness analysis for the new version of the model, but also a comprehensive comparison of the old and the new version. For example, a change in the percentage of existing test-takers who have passed a particular test resulting from the update would need to be explained not only to the test-takers but also to the people making decisions based on test scores (von Davier, 2016).

RSMTool includes the functionality to conduct a comprehensive comparison of two different versions of a scoring system and produce a report which includes fairness analyses for each of the versions as well as how these analyses differ between the two versions. As an example, we compare two versions of our example scoring model — one that uses all features and another that does not include the GRAMMAR feature. The comparison report can be be seen here: `http://bit.ly/fair-tool-compare`.

4.4 Customizing *RSMTool*

The measurement guidelines currently implemented in *RSMTool* follow the psychometric framework suggested by Williamson et al. (2012). It was developed for the evaluation of *e-rater*, an automated system designed to score English writing proficiency (Attali and Burstein, 2006), but is generalizable to other applications of automated scoring. This framework was chosen because it offers a comprehensive set of criteria for both the accuracy as well as the fairness of the predicted scores. Note that not all of these recommendations are universally accepted by the automated scoring community. For example, Yannakoudakis and Cummins (2015) recently proposed a different set of metrics for evaluating the accuracy of automated scoring models.

Furthermore, the machine learning community has recently developed various analyses aimed at detecting bias in algorithm performance that could be applied in the context of automated scoring. For example, in addition to reviewing individual features, one could also attempt to predict the subgroup membership from the features used to score the responses (Feldman et al., 2015). If this prediction is generally accurate, then there is a risk that subgroup membership could be implicitly used by the scoring model and lead to unfair scores. However, if the subgroup prediction has high error over all models generated from the features, then the scores assigned by a model trained on this data are likely to be fair.

RSMTool has been designed to make it easy for the user to add new evaluations and analyses of these types. The evaluation and report-generation components of *RSMTool* (including the fairness analyses) can be run on predictions from *any* external learner, not just the ones that are provided by the tool itself. Each section of its report is implemented as a separate Jupyter/IPython notebook (Kluyver et al., 2016). The user can choose which sections should be included into the final HTML report and in which order. Furthermore, NLP researchers who want to use different evaluation metrics or custom fairness analyses can provide them in the form of new Jupyter notebooks; these analyses are dynamically executed and incorporated into the final report along with the existing analyses or even in their place, if so desired, without modifying a single line of code.

Finally, for those who want to make more substantive changes, the tool is written entirely in Python, is open-source with an Apache 2.0 license, and has extensive online documentation. We also provide a well-documented API which allows users to integrate various components of *RSMTool* into their own applications.

4.5 Model Transparency & Interpretability

The analyses produced by *RSMTool* only suggest a *potential* bias and flag individual subgroups or features for further consideration. As we indicated earlier, the presence of differences across subgroups does not automatically imply that the model is unfair; further review is required to establish the source of such differences. One of the first steps in such a review usually involves examining each feature separately as well as the individual contribution of each feature to the final score. It is important to note here that unfairness may also be introduced by what is *not* in the model. An automated scoring system may not cover a particular aspect of the construct which can be evaluated by humans. If the performance across subgroups differs on this aspect of the construct, the difference may be due to "construct under-representation"

rather than due to construct-irrelevant factors.

The automated scoring models used in systems such as *e-rater* for assessing writing proficiency in English (Attali and Burstein, 2006) or *SpeechRater* for spoken proficiency (Zechner et al., 2009) have traditionally been linear models with a small number of interpretable features because such models lend themselves more easily to a detailed fairness review and allow decision-makers to understand how, and to what extent, different parts of the test-takers' skill set are being covered by the features in the model (Loukina et al., 2015). For such linear models, *RSMTool* displays a detailed model description including the model fit (R^2) computed on the training set as well as the contribution of each feature to the final score (via raw, standardized, and relative coefficients).

At the same time, recent studies (Heilman and Madnani, 2015; Madnani et al., 2016) on scoring actual content rather than just language proficiency suggest that it is possible to achieve higher performance, as measured by agreement with human raters, by employing many low-level features and more sophisticated machine learning algorithms such as support vector machines or random forests. Generally, these models are built using sparse feature types such as word n-grams, often resulting in hundreds of thousands of predominantly binary features. Using models with such a large feature space means that it is no longer clear how to map the individual features and their weights to various parts of the test-takers' skill set, and, therefore, difficult to identify whether any differences in the model performance stem from the effects of construct-irrelevant factors.

One way to increase the interpretability of such models is to group multiple features by feature type (e.g. "syntactic relationships") and build a stacked model (Wolpert, 1992) containing simpler models for each feature type. These stacked models can then be combined in a final linear model which can be examined in the usual manner for fairness considerations (Madnani and Cahill, 2016). The idea of making complex machine-learned models more interpretable to users and stakeholders has been investigated more thoroughly in recent years and several promising solutions have been proposed that could also be used for content-scoring models (Kim et al., 2016; Wilson et al., 2016).

5 Mitigating Bias in Automated Scoring

So far we have primarily discussed techniques for *detecting* potential biases in automated scoring models. We showed that there are multiple sources of possible bias which makes it unlikely that there would be a single "silver bullet" that can make test scores completely bias-free. The approach currently favored in the educational measurement community is to try and reduce susceptibility to construct-irrelevant factors by design. This includes an expert review of each feature before it is added to the model to ensure that it is theoretically and practically consistent with the skill set being measured by the test. These features are then combined in an easily interpretable model (usually linear regression) which is trained on a representative sample of test-taker population.

However, simpler scoring models may not always be the right solution. For one, as we discussed in §3, several studies have shown that even such simple models may still exhibit bias. In addition, recent studies on scoring test-takers' knowledge of content rather than proficiency have shown that using more sophisticated — and hence, less transparent — models yields non-trivial gains in the accuracy of the predicted scores. Therefore, ensuring completely fair automated scoring at large requires more complex solutions.

The machine learning community has identified several broad approaches to deal with discrimination that could, in theory, be used for automated scoring models, especially those using more complex non-linear algorithms: the training data can be modified (Feldman et al., 2015; Kamiran and Calders, 2012; Hajian and Domingo-Ferrer, 2013; Mancuhan and Clifton, 2014), the algorithm itself can be changed so that it optimizes for fairness as well as the selection criteria (Kamishima et al., 2012; Zemel et al., 2013; Calders and Verwer, 2010), and the output decisions can be changed after-the-fact (Kamiran et al., 2012). A survey of such approaches is provided by Romei and Ruggieri (2013a). Future work in automated scoring could explore whether these methods can address some of the known biases.

Of course, it is also important to note that such bias-mitigating approaches often lead to a decline in the overall model performance and, therefore, one needs to balance model fairness and accuracy which likely depends on the stakes for which the model is going to be used.

6 Conclusion

In this paper, we discussed considerations that go into developing fairer automated scoring models for constructed responses. We also presented *RSMTool*, an open-source tool to help NLP researchers detect potential biases in their scoring models. We described the analyses currently incorporated into the tool for evaluating the impact of construct-irrelevant categorical and continuous factors. We also showed that the tool is designed in a flexible manner which allows users to easily add their own custom fairness analyses and showed some examples of such analyses.

While *RSMTool* has been designed for automated scoring research (some terminology in the tool and the report is specific to automated scoring), its flexible nature and well-documented API allow it to be easily adapted for *any* machine learning task in which the numeric prediction is generated by regressing on a set of non-sparse, numeric features. Furthermore, the evaluation component can be used separately which allows users to evaluate the performance and fairness of *any* model that generates numeric predictions.

Acknowledgments

We would like to thank the anonymous reviewers for their valuable comments and suggestions. We would also like to thank Lei Chen, Sorelle Friedler, Brent Bridgeman, Vikram Ramanarayanan, and Keelan Evanini for their contributions and comments.

References

AERA. 1999. *Standards for Educational and Psychological Testing*. American Educational Research Association.

Ji An, Vincent Kieftenbeld, and Raghuveer Kanneganti. 2016. Fairness in Automated Scoring: Screening Features for Subgroup Differences. Presented at the Annual Meeting of the National Council on Measurement in Education, Washington DC.

William H. Angoff. 2012. Perspectives on Differential Item Functioning Methodology. In P.W. Holland and H. Wainer, editors, *Differential Item Functioning*, pages 3–23. Taylor & Francis.

Yigal Attali and Jill Burstein. 2006. Automated Essay Scoring with e-rater V. 2. *The Journal of Technology, Learning and Assessment*, 4(3):1–30.

Jared Bernstein, A. Van Moere, and Jian Cheng. 2010. Validating Automated Speaking Tests. *Language Testing*, 27(3):355–377.

Brent Bridgeman, Mary Lou Lennon, and Altamese Jackenthal. 2003. Effects of Screen Size, Screen Resolution, and Display Rate on Computer-Based Test Performance. *Applied Measurement in Education*, 16(3):191–205.

Brent Bridgeman, Catherine Trapani, and Yigal Attali. 2012. Comparison of Human and Machine Scoring of Essays: Differences by Gender, Ethnicity, and Country. *Applied Measurement in Education*, 25(1):27–40.

Jill Burstein and Martin Chodorow. 1999. Automated essay scoring for nonnative english speakers. In *Proceedings of a Symposium on Computer Mediated Language Assessment and Evaluation in Natural Language Processing*, pages 68–75, Stroudsburg, PA, USA.

Jill Burstein, Karen Kukich, Susanne Wolff, Chi Lu, Martin Chodorow, Lisa Braden-Harder, and Mary Dee Harris. 1998. Automated Scoring Using A Hybrid Feature Identification Technique. In *Proceedings of the 36th Annual Meeting of the Association for Computational Linguistics and 17th International Conference on Computational Linguistics, Volume 1*, pages 206–210, Montreal, Quebec, Canada, August. Association for Computational Linguistics.

Toon Calders and Sicco Verwer. 2010. Three Naive Bayes Approaches for Discrimination-Free Classification. *Data Mining journal; special issue with selected papers from ECML/PKDD*.

M. D. Carey, R. H. Mannell, and P. K. Dunn. 2011. Does a Rater's Familiarity with a Candidate's Pronunciation Affect the Rating in Oral Proficiency Interviews? *Language Testing*, 28(2):201–219.

Hongbo Chen and Ben He. 2013. Automated Essay Scoring by Maximizing Human-Machine Agreement. In *Proceedings of the 2013 Conference on Empirical Methods in Natural Language Processing*, pages 1741–1752, Seattle, Washington, USA, October. Association for Computational Linguistics.

Brian E. Clauser, Michael T. Kane, and David B. Swanson. 2002. Validity Issues for Performance-Based Tests Scored With Computer-Automated Scoring Systems. *Applied Measurement in Education*, 15(4):413–432.

Harald Cramér. 1947. *Mathematical Methods of Statistics*. Princeton University Press.

Larry Davis. 2015. The Influence of Training and Experience on Rater Performance in Scoring Spoken Language. *Language Testing*, 33:117–135.

Paul Deane. 2013. On the Relation between Automated Essay Scoring and Modern Views of the Writing Construct. *Assessing Writing*, 18(1):7–24.

Minh Q. Duong and Alina von Davier. 2013. Heterogeneous Populations and Multistage Test Design. In Roger E. Millsap, L. Andries van der Ark, Daniel M. Bolt, and Carol M. Woods, editors, *New Developments in Quantitative Psychology: Presentations from the 77th Annual Psychometric Society Meeting*, pages 151–170. Springer New York.

Michael Feldman, Sorelle A. Friedler, John Moeller, Carlos Scheidegger, and Suresh Venkatasubramanian. 2015. Certifying and Removing Disparate Impact. *Proceedings of the 21th ACM SIGKDD International Conference on Knowledge Discovery and Data Mining*, pages 259–268.

Sorelle A. Friedler, Carlos Scheidegger, and Suresh Venkatasubramanian. 2016. On the (Im)possibility of Fairness. *CoRR*, abs/1609.07236.

Sara Hajian and Josep Domingo-Ferrer. 2013. A Methodology for Direct and Indirect Discrimination Prevention in Data Mining. *IEEE Transactions on Knowledge and Data Engineering*, 25(7):1445 – 1459.

Michael Heilman and Nitin Madnani. 2015. The Impact of Training Data on Automated Short Answer Scoring Performance. In *Proceedings of the Tenth Workshop on Innovative Use of NLP for Building Educational Applications*, pages 81–85, Denver, Colorado, June. Association for Computational Linguistics.

Faisal Kamiran and Toon Calders. 2009. Classifying without Discriminating. In *Proceedings of the IEEE International Conference on Computer, Control and Communication*, pages 1–6.

Faisal Kamiran and Toon Calders. 2012. Data Preprocessing Techniques for Classification Without Discrimination. *Knowledge and Information Systems*, 33(1):1 – 33.

Faisal Kamiran, Asad Karim, and Xiangliang Zhang. 2012. Decision Theory for Discrimination-aware Classification. In *International Conference on Data Mining (ICDM)*.

Toshihiro Kamishima, Shotaro Akaho, Hideki Asoh, and Jun Sakuma. 2012. Fairness-aware Classifier with Prejudice Remover Regularizer. In *Proceedings of the Joint European Conference on Machine Learning and Knowledge Discovery in Databases*, pages 35–50.

Been Kim, Dmitry Malioutov, and Kush Varshney, editors. 2016. *Proceedings of the ICML Workshop on Human Interpretability in Machine Learning*.

Thomas Kluyver, Benjamin Ragan-Kelley, Fernando Prez, Brian Granger, Matthias Bussonnier, Jonathan Frederic, Kyle Kelley, Jessica Hamrick, Jason Grout, Sylvain Corlay, Paul Ivanov, Damin Avila,

Safia Abdalla, Carol Willing, and Jupyter Development Team. 2016. Jupyter Notebooks — A Publishing Format for Reproducible Computational Workflows. In *Proceedings of the 20th International Conference on Electronic Publishing*. IOS Press.

Yi-Hsuan Lee and Alina von Davier. 2013. Monitoring Scale Scores over Time via Quality Control Charts, Model-Based Approaches, and Time Series Techniques. *Psychometrika*, 78(3):557–575.

G. Ling, P. Mollaun, and X. Xi. 2014. A Study on the Impact of Fatigue on Human Raters when Scoring Speaking Responses. *Language Testing*, 31:479–499.

Jinghua Liu and Neil J. Dorans. 2016. Fairness in Score Interpretation. In Neil J. Dorans and Linda L. Cook, editors, *Fairness in educational assessment and measurement*, pages 77–96. Routledge.

Anastassia Loukina and Heather Buzick. In print. Automated Scoring of Speakers with Speech Impairments. *ETS Research Report Series*, In print.

Anastassia Loukina, Klaus Zechner, Lei Chen, and Michael Heilman. 2015. Feature Selection for Automated Speech Scoring. In *Proceedings of the Tenth Workshop on Innovative Use of NLP for Building Educational Applications*, pages 12–19, Denver, Colorado, June. Association for Computational Linguistics.

Binh Thanh Luong, Salvatore Ruggieri, and Franco Turini. 2011. k-NN as an Implementation of Situation Testing for Discrimination Discovery and Prevention. In *Proceedings of the 17th ACM SIGKDD international conference on Knowledge discovery and data mining*, pages 502–510.

Nitin Madnani and Aoife Cahill. 2016. Automated Scoring of Content. Presented at the panel on Fairness and Machine Learning for Educational Practice, Annual Meeting of the National Council on Measurement in Education, Washington DC.

Nitin Madnani, Aoife Cahill, and Brian Riordan. 2016. Automatically Scoring Tests of Proficiency in Music Instruction. In *Proceedings of the 11th Workshop on Innovative Use of NLP for Building Educational Applications*, pages 217–222, San Diego, CA, June. Association for Computational Linguistics.

Koray Mancuhan and Chris Clifton. 2014. Combating Discrimination Using Bayesian Networks. *Artif. Intell. Law*, 22(2):211–238.

Mara Elena Oliveri and Alina von Davier. 2016. Psychometrics in Support of a Valid Assessment of Linguistic Minorities: Implications for the Test and Sampling Designs. *International Journal of Testing*, 16(3):220–239.

Ellis B. Page. 1966. The Imminence of ... Grading Essays by Computer. *The Phi Delta Kappan*, 47(5):238–243.

Fabian Pedregosa, Gal Varoquaux, Alexandre Gramfort, Vincent Michel, Bertrand Thirion, Olivier Grisel, Mathieu Blondel, Peter Prettenhofer, Ron Weiss, Vincent Dubourg, Jake Vanderplas, Alexandre Passos, David Cournapeau, Matthieu Brucher, Matthieu Perrot, and douard Duchesnay. 2011. Scikit-learn: Machine learning in Python. *Journal of Machine Learning Research*, 12:2825–2830.

Randall D. Penfield. 2016. Fairness in Test Scoring. In Neil J. Dorans and Linda L. Cook, editors, *Fairness in Educational Assessment and Measurement*, pages 55–76. Routledge.

Les Perelman. 2014. When the state of the art is Counting Words. *Assessing Writing*, 21:104–111.

Chaitanya Ramineni and David M. Williamson. 2013. Automated Essay Scoring: Psychometric Guidelines and Practices. *Assessing Writing*, 18(1):25–39.

Andrea Romei and Salvatore Ruggieri. 2013a. A Multidisciplinary Survey on Discrimination Analysis. *The Knowledge Engineering Review*, pages 1–57.

Andrea Romei and Salvatore Ruggieri. 2013b. Discrimination Data Analysis: A Multi-disciplinary Bibliography. In Bart Custers, Toon Calders, Bart Schermer, and Tal Zarsky, editors, *Discrimination and Privacy in the Information Society: Data Mining and Profiling in Large Databases*, pages 109–135. Springer Berlin Heidelberg.

Mark D. Shermis. 2014a. State-of-the-art Automated Essay Scoring: Competition, Results, and Future Directions from a United States demonstration. *Assessing Writing*, 20:53–76.

Mark D. Shermis. 2014b. The Challenges of Emulating Human Behavior in Writing Assessment. *Assessing Writing*, 22:91–99.

Swapna Somasundaran, Jill Burstein, and Martin Chodorow. 2014. Lexical Chaining for Measuring Discourse Coherence Quality in Test-taker Essays. In *Proceedings of COLING 2014, the 25th International Conference on Computational Linguistics: Technical Papers*, pages 950–961, Dublin, Ireland, August. Dublin City University and Association for Computational Linguistics.

Alina von Davier and Jill Burstein. 2016. Fairness and Machine Learning for Educational Practice. Coordinated Session, Annual meeting of the National Council on Measurement in Education, Washington DC.

Alina von Davier. 2016. Fairness Concerns in Computational Psychometrics. Presented at the panel on Fairness and Machine Learning for Educational Practice, Annual Meeting of the National Council on Measurement in Education, Washington DC.

Zhen Wang and Alina von Davier. 2014. Monitoring of scoring using the e-rater automated scoring system and human raters on a writing test. *ETS Research Report Series*, 2014(1):1–21.

Zhen Wang, Klaus Zechner, and Yu Sun. 2016. Monitoring the Performance of Human and Automated Scores for Spoken Responses. *Language Testing*, pages 1–20.

David M. Williamson, Xiaoming Xi, and F. Jay Breyer. 2012. A Framework for Evaluation and Use of Automated Scoring. *Educational Measurement: Issues and Practice*, 31(1):2–13.

Andrew Gordon Wilson, Been Kim, and William Herlands, editors. 2016. *Proceedings of the NIPS Workshop on Interpretable Machine Learning for Complex Systems*.

David H. Wolpert. 1992. Stacked Generalization. *Neural Networks*, 5:241–259.

Xiaoming Xi. 2010. How do we go about Investigating Test Fairness? *Language Testing*, 27(2):147–170.

Yongwei Yang, Chad W. Buckendahl, Piotr J. Juszkiewicz, and Dennison S. Bhola. 2002. A Review of Strategies for Validating Computer-Automated Scoring. *Applied Measurement in Education*, 15(4):391–412, oct.

Helen Yannakoudakis and Ronan Cummins. 2015. Evaluating the Performance of Automated Text Scoring systems. In *Proceedings of the Tenth Workshop on Innovative Use of NLP for Building Educational Applications*, pages 213–223, Denver, Colorado, June. Association for Computational Linguistics.

Klaus Zechner, Derrick Higgins, Xiaoming Xi, and David M. Williamson. 2009. Automatic Scoring of Non-native Spontaneous Speech in Tests of Spoken English. *Speech Communication*, 51(10):883–895.

Richard S Zemel, Yu Wu, Kevin Swersky, Toniann Pitassi, and Cynthia Dwork. 2013. Learning fair representations. In *Proceedings of ICML*, pages 325–333.

Mo Zhang, Neil J. Dorans, Chen Li, and Andre A. Rupp. In print. Differential feature functioning in automated essay scoring. In H. Jiao and R.W. Lissitz, editors, *Test fairness in the new generation of large-scale assessment*.

Michael J. Zieky. 2016. Fairness in Test Design and Development. In Neil J. Dorans and Linda L. Cook, editors, *Fairness in Educational Assessment and Measurement*, pages 9–32. Routledge.

Gender and Dialect Bias in YouTube's Automatic Captions

Rachael Tatman
Department of Lingusitics
University of Washington
`rctatman@uw.edu`

Abstract

This project evaluates the accuracy of YouTube's automatically-generated captions across two genders and five dialects of English. Speakers' dialect and gender was controlled for by using videos uploaded as part of the "accent tag challenge", where speakers explicitly identify their language background. The results show robust differences in accuracy across both gender and dialect, with lower accuracy for 1) women and 2) speakers from Scotland. This finding builds on earlier research finding that speaker's sociolinguistic identity may negatively impact their ability to use automatic speech recognition, and demonstrates the need for sociolinguistically-stratified validation of systems.

1 Introduction

The overall accuracy of automatic speech recognition (ASR) has increased substantially over the past decade: a decade ago it was not uncommon to report a ASR error rates of 27% (Sha and Saul, 2007), while a recent Microsoft system achieved a word error rate (WER) of just 6.3% on the Switchboard corpus (Xiong et al., 2016). Have these strong gains benefited all speakers evenly? Previous work, briefly discussed below, has found systematic bias both by dialect and gender. This paper provides additional evidence that sociolinguistic variation continues to provide a source of avoidable error by showing that the WER is robustly different for male and female native English speakers from different dialect regions.

It is well established in the field of sociolinguistics that there is quantifiable variation in language use between social groups. Gender-based varia-tion in language use, for example, has been extensively studied (Trudgill, 1972; Eckert, 1989, among many others). There is also robust variation in language use by native speakers across dialect regions. For instance, English varies dramatically between the United States (Cassidy and others, 1985), New Zealand (Hay et al., 2008) and Scotland (Milroy and Milroy, 2014).

Sociolinguistic variation has historically been a source of error for natural language processing. Differences across genders in automatic speech recognition accuracy have been previously reported, with better recognition rates reported for both men (Ali et al., 2007) and women (Goldwater et al., 2010; Sawalha and Abu Shariah, 2013). Previous work has also found evidence of dialectal bias in speech recognition in both English (Wheatley and Picone, 1991) and Arabic (Droua-Hamdani et al., 2012). In addition, there are many anecdotal accounts of bias against dialect in speech recognition. For example, in 2010 Microsoft's Kinect was released and, while it shipped with Spanish voice recognition, it did not recognize Castilian Spanish (Plunkett, 2010). This study investigates whether YouTube's automatic captions have different WER for native English speakers across two genders and five dialect regions.

2 Method

Data for this project was collected by hand checking YouTube's automatic captions (Harrenstien, 2009) on the word list portion of accent tag videos. Annotation was done by a phonetically-trained listener familiar with the dialects in the study. YouTube's automatic captions were chosen for three reasons. The first is that they're backed by Google's speech recognition software, which is both very popular and among the more accurate

Proceedings of the First Workshop on Ethics in Natural Language Processing, pages 53–59,
Valencia, Spain, April 4th, 2017. © 2017 Association for Computational Linguistics

proprietary ASR systems (Liao et al., 2013). The second is the fact that the accuracy of YouTube's automatic captions specifically are an area of immediate concern to the Deaf community and is a frequent topic of (frustrated) discussion: they are often referred to as "autocraptions" (Lockrey, 2015) due to their low accuracy and the fact that content creators will often rely on them instead of providing accurate captions. Finally, YouTube's large, diverse userbase allowed for the direct comparison of speakers from a range of demographic backgrounds.

2.1 Accent tag

The accent tag, developed by Bert Vaux and based on the Harvard dialect survey (Vaux and Golder, 2003), has become a popular and sustained internet phenomenon. Though it was designed to elicit differences between dialect regions in the United States, it has achieved wide popularity across the English-speaking world. Variously called the "accent tag", "dialect meme", "accent challenge" or "Tumblr/Twitter/YouTube accent challenge", videos in this genre follow the same basic outline. First, speakers introduce themselves and describe their linguistic background, with a focus on regional dialect. Then speakers read a list of words designed to elicit phonological dialect differences. Finally, speakers read and then answer a list of questions designed to elicit lexical variation. For example, one question asks "What do you call gym shoes?", which speakers variously answered "sneakers", "tennis shoes", "gym shoes" or whatever the preferred term is in thier dialect.

This study focuses on only the word list portion of the accent tag. Over time, the word list has been changed and appended, most notably with terms commonly used in on-line communities such as "GPOY" (gratuitous picture of yourself) or "gif" (graphics interchange format, a popular digital image format). Even with these variations, all videos discussed here used some subset of the word-list shown in Table 1.

It should be noted that this is a particularly difficult ASR task. First, words are presented in isolation rather than within a frame sentence, which means that ASR systems cannot benefit from the use of language models. Second, the word-list portion of the accent tag challenge was intentionally constructed to only include words with multiple possible pronunciations and that serve as di-

Again	Envelope	Potato
Alabama	Figure	Probably
Aluminum	Fire	Quarter
Arizona	Florida	Roof
Ask	Gif	Route
Atlantic	GPOY	Ruin
Attitude	Guarantee	Salmon
Aunt	Halloween	Sandwich
Auto	Image	Saw
Avocado	Iron	Spitting
Bandanna	Lawyer	Sure
Both	Marriage	Syrup
Car	Mayonnaise	Theater
Caramel	Muslim	Three
Catch	Naturally	Tomato
Caught	New Orleans	Twenty
Cool Whip	Officer	Waffle
Coupon	Oil	Wagon
Crayon	Oregon	Wash
Data	Pajamas	Water
Eleven	Pecan	

Table 1: Word list for accent tag videos.

alect markers. "Lawyer", for example, is generally pronounced [lɔɪ.jɚ] in New England and California, but [lɔ.jɚ] in Georgia (Vaux and Golder, 2003). These facts do place the ASR system used to generate the automatic captions at a disadvtange, and may help to explain the high error rates.

2.2 Speakers

A total of eighty speakers were sampled for this project. Videos for eight men and eight women from each dialect region were included. The dialect regions were California, Georgia, New England (Maine and New Hampshire), New Zealand and Scotland. These regions were chosen based on their high degree of geographic separation from each other, distinct local regional dialects and (relatively) comparable populations. Of these regions, California has the largest population, with approximately 38.8 million residents, and New England the smallest, with Maine and New Hampshire having a combined population of approximately 2.6 million (although the United States census bureau estimates the population of New England as a region at over 14 million as of 2010 (Bogue et al., 2010)).

Sampling was done by searching YouTube using the exact term "accent challenge" or "accent tag" and the name of the geographical region. Only videos which had automatic captions were included in this study. For each speaker, the word error rate (WER) was calculated separately. Data and code used for analysis is available online[1].

3   Results

The effect of dialect and gender on WER was evaluated using liner mixed-effects regression. Both speaker and year were included as random effects. Speaker was included to control for both individual variability in speech clarity and also recording quality, since only one recording per speaker was used. Year was included to control for improvements in ASR over time. Automatic captions are generated just after the video is uploaded to YouTube, and the recordings used were uploaded over a five year period, so it was important to account for overall improvements in speech recognition.

A model which included both gender and dialect as fixed effects more closely fit the data (i.e. had a lower Akaike information criterion) than nested models without gender (χ^2 (5, N= 80) = 31 p $<$0.01), without dialect (χ^2 (5, N= 80) = 14, p $<$0.01) or without either (χ^2 (5, N= 80) = 31, p $<$0.01). In terms of dialect, speakers from Scotland had reliably worse performance than speakers from the United States or New Zealand, as can be seen in Figure 1. The lower level of accuracy for Scottish English can not be explained by, for example, a small number of speakers of that variety. The population of New Zealand, the dialect which had the second-lowest WER, is roughly 80% that of Scotland. Nor is it factor of wealth. Scotland and New Zealand have a GDP *per capita* that falls within one hundred US dollars of each other.

There was also a significant effect of gender: the word error rate was higher for women than men (t(78) = -3.5, p $<$0.01). This is shown in Figure 2. This is somewhat surprising given earlier studies which found the opposite result (Goldwater et al., 2010; Sawalha and Abu Shariah, 2013).

In addition, there was an interaction between gender and dialect. Adding an interaction term between gender and dialect to the model above significantly improved model fit (χ^2 (5, N= 80) = 16, p $<$0.01). As can be seen in Figure 3, the effect of gender was not equal across dialects. Differences between genders were largest for speakers

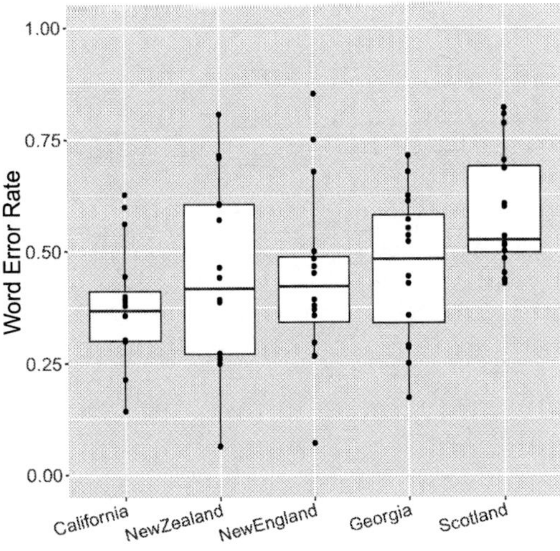

Figure 1: YouTube automatic caption word error rate by speaker's dialect region. Points indicate individual speakers.

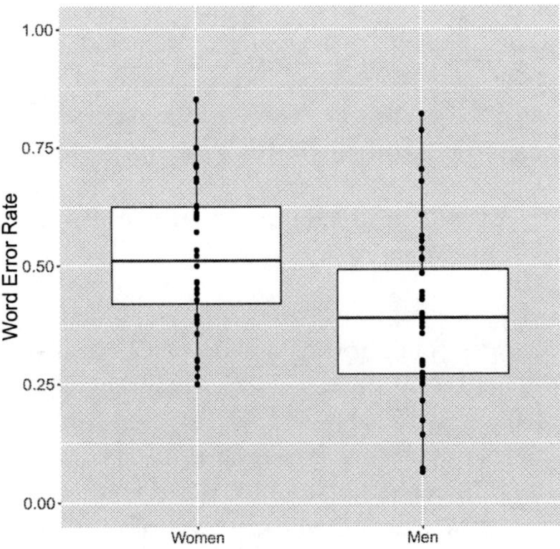

Figure 2: YouTube automatic caption word error rate by speaker's gender. Points indicate individual speakers.

---

[1]https://github.com/rctatman/youtubeDialectAccuracy

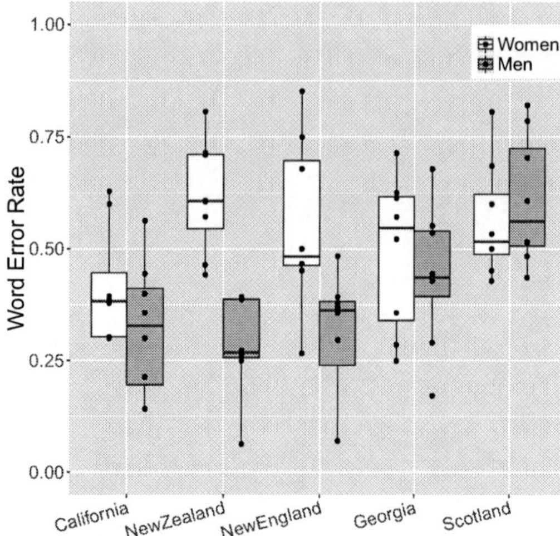

Figure 3: Interaction of gender and dialect. The difference in Word Error Rates between genders was largest for speakers from New Zealand and New England. In no dialect was accuracy reliably better for women than men.

from New Zealand and New England.

Given the nature of this project, there is limited access to other demographic information about speakers which might be important, such as age, level of education, socioeconomic status, race or ethnicity[2]. The last is of particular concern given recent findings that automatic natural language processing tools, including language identifiers and parsers struggle with African American English (Blodgett et al., 2016).

4 Effects of pitch on YouTube automatic captions

One potential explanation for the different error rates found for male and female speakers is differences in pitch. Pitch differences are one of the most reliable and well-studied perceptual markers of gender in speech (Wu and Childers, 1991; Gelfer and Mikos, 2005) and speech with a high fundamental frequency (typical of women's speech) has also been found to be more difficult for automatic speech recognizers (Hirschberg et al., 2004; Goldwater et al., 2010). A small experiment was carried out to determine whether pitch

differences were indeed underlying the differing word error rates for male and female speakers.

First, a female speaker of standardized American English was recorded clearly reading the word list shown in Table 1. In order to better approximate the environment of the recordings in the accent tag videos, the recording was made using a consumer-grade headset microphone in a quiet environment, rather than using a professional-grade microphone in a sound-attenuated booth. The original recording had a mean pitch of 192 Hz and a median of 183 Hz, which is slightly lower than average for a female speaker of American English (Pépiot, 2014). The pitch of the original recording was artificially scaled both up and down 60 Hz in 20 Hz intervals using Praat (Boersma and others, 2002). This resulted in a total of seven recordings: the original, three progressively lower pitched and three progressively higher pitched. These resulting sound-files were then uploaded to YouTube and automatic captions were generated. The video, and captions, can be viewed on YouTube[3].

Overall, the automatic captions for the word list were very accurate; there were a total of 9 errors across all 434 tokens, for a WER of .002. Though it may be due to ceiling effects, there was no significant effect of pitch on accuracy. The much higher accuracy of this set of captions may be due to improvement in the algorithms underlying the automatic captions or the nature of the speech in the recording, which was clear, careful and slow. More investigation with a larger sample of voices is necessary to determine if pitch differences, or perhaps another factor such as intensity, are what is underlying the differences in WER for male and female speakers. That said, even if gender-based differences in accuracy between genders can be attributed to acoustic differences associated with gender, that would not account for the strong effect of dialect region.

5 Discussion

The results presented above show that there are differences in WER between dialect areas and genders, and that manipulating one speaker's pitch was not sufficient to affect WER for that speaker. While the latter needs additional data to form a robust generalization, the size of the effect for the former is deeply disturbing. Why do these

---

[2]Speakers in this sample did not self-report their race or ethnicity and, given the complex nature of race and ethnicity in both New Zealand and the US, the researcher opted not to guess at speaker' race and ethnicity.

[3]https://www.YouTube.com/watch?v=eUgrizlV-R4

differences exist? From a linguistics standpoint, no dialect is inherently more or less intelligible. The main factor which determines how well a listener understands a dialect is the amount of exposure they have had to it (Clarke and Garrett, 2004; Sumner and Samuel, 2009); with sufficient exposure, any human listener can learn any language variety. In addition, earlier research that found lower WER for female speakers shows that creating such ASR systems is possible (Goldwater et al., 2010; Sawalha and Abu Shariah, 2013). Given that there is also a difference between dialects, these differences are most likely due to something besides the inherent qualities of the signal.

One candidate for the cause of these differences is imbalances in the training dataset. Any bias in the training data will be embedded in a system trained on it (Torralba and Efros, 2011; Bock and Shamir, 2015). While the system behind YouTube's automatic captions is propriety and it is thus impossible to validate this supposition, there is room for improvement in the social stratification of many speech corpora. Librevox, for example, is a popular open-source speech data set that "suffers from major gender and per speaker duration imbalances" (Panayotov et al., 2015). TIMIT, the most-distributed corpora available through the linguistic data consortium, is balanced for speaker dialect but approximately 69% of the speech in it comes from male speakers (Garofolo et al., 1993). Switchboard (Godfrey et al., 1992) undersamples women, Southerns and non-college-educated speakers. Many other popular speech corpora such as the Numbers corpus (Cole et al., 1995) or the AMI meeting corpus (McCowan et al., 2005) don't include information on speaker gender or dialect background. Taken together, these observations suggest that socially stratified sampling of spekaers has historically not been the priority during corpus construction for computational applications.

One solution to imbalanced training sets to focus on collecting unbiased socially stratified samples, or at the very least documenting the ways in which samples are unbalanced, for future speech corpora. This is already being addressed in the data collection of some new corpora such as the Automatic Tagging and Recognition of Stance (ATAROS) corpus (Freeman et al., 2014).

This does not help to address existing imbalances in training data, however. One way of doing this is to include information about speaker's social identity, such as the geographic location of the speaker (Ye et al., 2016) or using gender-dependent speech recognition models (Konig and Morgan, 1992; Abdulla and Kasabov, 2001).

Regardless of the method used to correct biases, it is imperative that the NLP community work to do so. Robust differences in accuracy of automatic speech recognition based on a speaker's social identity is an ethical issue (Hovy and Spruit, 2016). In particular, if NLP and ASR systems consistently preform worse for users from disadvantaged groups than they do for users from privileged groups, this exacerbates existing inequalities. The ideal would be for systems to preform equally well for users regardless of their sociolinguistic backgrounds.

Differences in performance derived from speakers' social identity is particularly concerning given the increasing use of speech-analysis algorithms during the hiring process (Shahani, 2015; Morrison, 2017). Given the evidence that speech analysis tools preform more poorly on some speakers who are members of protected classes, this could legally be discrimination (Ajunwa et al., 2016). Error analyses that compare performance across sociolinguistic-active social groups, like the one presented in this paper, can help ensure that this is not the case and highlight any imbalances that might exist.

Acknowledgments

The author would like to thank Richard Wright, Gina-Anne Levow, Alicia Beckford Wassink, Emily M. Bender, the University of Washington Computational Linguistics Laboratory and the reviewers for their helpful comments and support. Any remaining errors are mine. This work has been supported by supported by National Science Foundation grant DGE-1256082.

References

Waleed H. Abdulla and Nikola K. Kasabov. 2001. Improving speech recognition performance through gender separation. *changes*, 9:10.

Ifeoma Ajunwa, Sorelle Friedler, Carlos Scheidegger, and Suresh Venkatasubramanian. 2016. Hiring by algorithm: predicting and preventing disparate impact. *Available at SSRN*.

S. Ali, K. Siddiqui, N. Safdar, K. Juluru, W. Kim, and E. Siegel. 2007. Affect of gender on speech recognition accuracy. In *American Journal of Roentgenology*, volume 188. American Roentgen Ray Society.

Su Lin Blodgett, Lisa Green, and Brendan O'Connor. 2016. Demographic Dialectal Variation in Social Media: A Case Study of African-American English. *arXiv preprint arXiv:1608.08868*.

Benjamin Bock and Lior Shamir. 2015. Assessing the efficacy of benchmarks for automatic speech accent recognition. In *Proceedings of the 8th International Conference on Mobile Multimedia Communications*, pages 133–136. ICST (Institute for Computer Sciences, Social-Informatics and Telecommunications Engineering).

Paul Boersma et al. 2002. Praat, a system for doing phonetics by computer. *Glot international*, 5(9/10):341–345.

Donald J. Bogue, Douglas L. Anderton, and Richard E. Barrett. 2010. *The population of the United States*. Simon and Schuster.

Frederic Gomes Cassidy et al. 1985. *Dictionary of American Regional English*. Belknap Press of Harvard University Press.

Constance M. Clarke and Merrill F. Garrett. 2004. Rapid adaptation to foreign-accented English. *The Journal of the Acoustical Society of America*, 116(6):3647–3658.

Ronald A. Cole, Mike Noel, Terri Lander, and Terry Durham. 1995. New telephone speech corpora at CSLU. In *Eurospeech*. Citeseer.

Ghania Droua-Hamdani, Sid-Ahmed Selouani, and Malika Boudraa. 2012. Speaker-independent asr for modern standard arabic: effect of regional accents. *International Journal of Speech Technology*, 15(4):487–493.

Penelope Eckert. 1989. The whole woman: Sex and gender differences in variation. *Language variation and change*, 1(03):245–267.

Valerie Freeman, Julian Chan, Gina-Anne Levow, Richard Wright, Mari Ostendorf, Victoria Zayats, Yi Luan, Heather Morrison, Lauren Fox, Maria Antoniak, et al. 2014. ATAROS Technical Report 1: Corpus collection and initial task validation. *U. Washington Linguistic Phonetics Lab*.

John S. Garofolo, Lori F. Lamel, William M. Fisher, Jonathan G. Fiscus, David S. Pallett, Nancy L. Dahlgren, and Victor Zue. 1993. TIMIT acoustic-phonetic continuous speech corpus. *Linguistic data consortium, Philadelphia*, 33.

Marylou Pausewang Gelfer and Victoria A. Mikos. 2005. The relative contributions of speaking fundamental frequency and formant frequencies to gender identification based on isolated vowels. *Journal of Voice*, 19(4):544–554.

John J. Godfrey, Edward C. Holliman, and Jane McDaniel. 1992. Switchboard: Telephone speech corpus for research and development. In *Acoustics, Speech, and Signal Processing, 1992. ICASSP-92., 1992 IEEE International Conference on*, volume 1, pages 517–520. IEEE.

Sharon Goldwater, Dan Jurafsky, and Christopher D. Manning. 2010. Which words are hard to recognize? prosodic, lexical, and disfluency factors that increase speech recognition error rates. *Speech Communication*, 52(3):181–200.

Ken Harrenstien. 2009. Automatic captions in YouTube. *The Official Google Blog*, 11.

Jennifer Hay, Margaret Maclagan, and Elizabeth Gordon. 2008. *New Zealand English*. Edinburgh University Press.

Julia Hirschberg, Diane Litman, and Marc Swerts. 2004. Prosodic and other cues to speech recognition failures. *Speech Communication*, 43(1):155–175.

Dirk Hovy and Shannon L. Spruit. 2016. The social impact of natural language processing. In *Proceedings of the 54th Annual Meeting of the Association for Computational Linguistics*, volume 2, pages 591–598.

Yochai Konig and Nelson Morgan. 1992. Gdnn: A gender-dependent neural network for continuous speech recognition. In *Neural Networks, 1992. IJCNN., International Joint Conference on*, volume 2, pages 332–337. IEEE.

Hank Liao, Erik McDermott, and Andrew Senior. 2013. Large scale deep neural network acoustic modeling with semi-supervised training data for YouTube video transcription. In *Automatic Speech Recognition and Understanding (ASRU), 2013 IEEE Workshop on*, pages 368–373. IEEE.

Michael Lockrey. 2015. YouTube automatic craptions score an incredible 95% accuracy rate! *medium.com*, July. [Online; posted 25-July-2015].

Iain McCowan, Jean Carletta, W. Kraaij, S. Ashby, S. Bourban, M. Flynn, M. Guillemot, T. Hain, J. Kadlec, V. Karaiskos, et al. 2005. The AMI meeting corpus. In *Proceedings of the 5th International Conference on Methods and Techniques in Behavioral Research*, volume 88.

James Milroy and Lesley Milroy. 2014. *Real English: the grammar of English dialects in the British Isles*. Routledge.

Lennox Morrison. 2017. Speech analysis could now land you a promotion. *BBC News*, Jan.

Vassil Panayotov, Guoguo Chen, Daniel Povey, and Sanjeev Khudanpur. 2015. Librispeech: an ASR corpus based on public domain audio books. In *2015 IEEE International Conference on Acoustics, Speech and Signal Processing (ICASSP)*, pages 5206–5210. IEEE.

Erwan Pépiot. 2014. Male and female speech: a study of mean f0, f0 range, phonation type and speech rate in Parisian French and American English speakers. In *Speech Prosody 7*, pages 305–309.

Luke Plunkett. 2010. Report: Kinect Doesn't Speak Spanish (It Speaks Mexican). September.

M. Sawalha and M. Abu Shariah. 2013. The effects of speakers' gender, age, and region on overall performance of Arabic automatic speech recognition systems using the phonetically rich and balanced Modern Standard Arabic speech corpus. In *Proceedings of the 2nd Workshop of Arabic Corpus Linguistics WACL-2*. Leeds.

Fei Sha and Lawrence K. Saul. 2007. Large margin hidden Markov models for automatic speech recognition. *Advances in neural information processing systems*, 19:1249.

Aarti Shahani. 2015. Now algorithms are deciding whom to hire, based on voice. *All Tech Considered: Tech, culture and connection*, March.

Meghan Sumner and Arthur G. Samuel. 2009. The effect of experience on the perception and representation of dialect variants. *Journal of Memory and Language*, 60(4):487–501.

Antonio Torralba and Alexei A. Efros. 2011. Unbiased look at dataset bias. In *Computer Vision and Pattern Recognition (CVPR), 2011 IEEE Conference on*, pages 1521–1528. IEEE.

Peter Trudgill. 1972. Sex, covert prestige and linguistic change in the urban British English of Norwich. *Language in society*, 1(02):179–195.

Bert Vaux and Scott Golder. 2003. The Harvard dialect survey. *Cambridge, MA: Harvard University Linguistics Department*.

Barbara Wheatley and Joseph Picone. 1991. Voice Across America: Toward robust speaker-independent speech recognition for telecommunications applications. *Digital Signal Processing*, 1(2):45–63.

Ke Wu and Donald G. Childers. 1991. Gender recognition from speech. part i: Coarse analysis. *The journal of the Acoustical society of America*, 90(4):1828–1840.

W. Xiong, J. Droppo, X. Huang, F. Seide, M. Seltzer, A. Stolcke, D. Yu, and G. Zweig. 2016. The Microsoft 2016 Conversational Speech Recognition System. *arXiv preprint arXiv:1609.03528*.

Guoli Ye, Chaojun Liu, and Yifan Gong. 2016. Geolocation dependent deep neural network acoustic model for speech recognition. In *2016 IEEE International Conference on Acoustics, Speech and Signal Processing (ICASSP)*, pages 5870–5874. IEEE.

Integrating the Management of Personal Data Protection and Open Science with Research Ethics

David Lewis
ADAPT Centre
Trinity College Dublin
Ireland
`dave.lewis`
`@adaptcentre.ie`

Joss Moorkens
ADAPT Centre/SALIS
Dublin City University
Ireland
`joss.moorkens`
`@dcu.ie`

Kaniz Fatema
ADAPT Centre
Trinity College Dublin
Ireland
`kaniz.fatema`
`@scss.tcd.ie`

Abstract

This paper examines the impact of the EU General Data Protection Regulation, in the context of the requirement from many research funders to provide open access research data, on current practices in Language Technology Research. We analyse the challenges that arise and the opportunities to address many of them through the use of existing open data practices for sharing language research data. We discuss the impact of this also on current practice in academic and industrial research ethics.

1 Introduction

Language Technology (LT) research is facing an unprecedented confluence of issues in the management of experimental data. The EU's adoption of the General Data Protection Regulation (GDPR) (European Parliament and Council of the European Union, 2016) imposes new requirements for tracking informed consent for the usage of personal data that may impact all European LT research significantly. National guidelines now need to be established on how GDPR applies to scientific data, and given the large penalties involved, this uncertainty presents significant institutional risk for those undertaking research with the unanonymised or unanonymisable data often needed in LT research.

In addition, the European Commission (EC) and other research funding bodies increasingly encourage open science practices. The aim is to publish research data alongside research papers in order to reduce the cost of obtaining research data and improve the repeatability, replicability and reproducibility of research. While this is a positive move for the quality and integrity of LT research, it must respect the needs of data protection legislation, including different EU member states' implementation of GDPR, and the data protection regimes in jurisdictions outside the EU. These may greatly complicate and delay the benefits of open science policies. This paper reviews these trends and aims to distil the issues that researcher institutes as well as national and transnational research bodies need to face in the coming years to effectively manage research data amid these parallel and sometime conflicting needs. In particular, we highlight the interdependency between these issues and how those who manage research ethics will need to react.

2 GDPR and LT Research Data

As Hovy and Spruit (2016) point out, language data contains latent characteristics of the person producing it, and language technology therefore has the inherent potential to expose personal characteristics of the individual. Coulthard (2000) notes that identification of authors is very difficult from linguistic data alone, but has been successful when accompanied by metadata "information which massively restricts the number of possible authors". This presents a distinct data protection challenge for the sharing and reuse of language resources as they are difficult to reliably anonymise and in some cases can already be used as a biometric.

As the sharing of language resources is an established feature of LT research internationally we must carefully examine the provisions coming into force in the EU with the introduction of GDPR. As an example we can consider research conducted into the productivity changes to translator practice resulting from the use of LT. Translation memory (TM) data is often used for MT training, although identifying metadata is almost always re-

Proceedings of the First Workshop on Ethics in Natural Language Processing, pages 60–65,
Valencia, Spain, April 4th, 2017. © 2017 Association for Computational Linguistics

moved beforehand. Measures to retain the metadata in order to strengthen copyright claims in respect of translators, as suggested by Moorkens et al. (2016), would create a risk of data breach under the terms of GDPR. This means that one possibility for extending human translator earnings will almost definitely become an impossibility for creators of MT systems. Machine translation (MT) is another popular LT technique use in translation practice. The impact of MT is being increasingly assessed through detailed analyses of keystroke logs of translators making corrections to such translations. These logs may also be published to accompany such studies (Carl, 2012), but are known at the level of keystroke timings to possess biometric signals that can identify the translator. Another growing practice is translation dictation using automated speech translation. Here, repeatable studies may involve the sharing of recordings and transcripts of spoken translation, where again speech recording could be used to identify the speaker.

2.1 What is the GDPR?

The GDPR is an EU Regulation, adopted in April 2016 and due to come into force in May 2018. It addresses protection of people with regard to the processing and free movement of personal data, replacing the 1995 Data Protection Directive. The GDPR (Article 4) defines Personal Data as "information relating to an identified or identifiable natural person", who it refers to as a Data Subject. An identifier for the Data Subject may be a name, an identification number, location data, an online identifier or "one or more factors specific to the physical, physiological, genetic, mental, economic, cultural or social identity" of the Data Subject. It is these latter factors that perhaps lie latent in language resources and data that is increasingly subject to analysis by language technologies, such as samples of utterances from specific data subjects.

The organisation that collects and uses personal information is the Data Controller, and bears the primary responsibility for implementing the provisions of GDPR. This role would be conducted by research institute which will be responsible for GDPR on many forms of personal data (e.g. student, staff and alumni records) beyond that generated by research. Other organisations in receipt of personal data from a controller is known as a Data Processor, and in LT research this would correspond to other research organisations receiving and reusing research data from the controller. The potential penalties for a data breach fall within two categories with differing maximum fines. A fine of up to 20 million or 4% of turnover (whichever is greater) may be imposed for failure to adhere to basic principles for processing, including conditions for consent (Articles 5, 6, 7 and 9), infringing on the rights of Data Subjects (Articles 20, 21, 22), or improper international data transfers (Articles 44-49). Other failures to comply, such as by failing to obtain proper consent for childrens' data, to keep sufficient records, or to apply proper safeguards, may result in a fine of up to 10 million or 2% of turnover (whichever is greater). Both Data Controllers and Data Processors may be considered liable for the security of personal data, and any data breach must be reported within 72 hours.

The GDPR explicitly encompasses pseudonymised data, which would require additional information (stored separately) to identify the Data Subject. This would include, for example, TM data with a translation unit ID that can be attributed to an individual. Personal data should be retained for a period no longer than is necessary to accomplish the purpose for which it was collected. However long-term archiving is permitted if this is in the public interest for scientific and historical research purposes, or statistical purposes, providing that there are some safeguards. These exemptions for research aim to reconcile privacy with data-driven innovation and the public good that may result. The GDPR states that the designation of scientific research should be "interpreted in a broad manner" including technological development, fundamental research, applied research and privately funded research. Importantly, therefore, consideration of GDPR exemptions for LT research may have widespread implications for industry as well as for academia. GDPR might not apply to data processing where the focus is not on "personal data, but aggregate data" and is statistical rather than referring to a particular individual. Where personal data is processed however, separate consents are required for different processing activities. However, providing that safeguards are implemented, secondary processing and processing of sensitive categories of data may be permitted for research purposes where data has been collected lawfully. Article 89, which addresses exemptions for scientific research that, states these safeguards should include technical and organisational measures to protect data, following the principle of data minimisation, and may include pseudonymisation or anonymisation where possible or appropriate. As discussed above however, these mechanisms may not be adequate for protecting data subject identity in the sharing and reuse of language resources. Significantly, the precise nature of the safeguard required by Article 89 are left for EU member states to legislate on (Beth Thompson, 2016). So while this enables interpretation of GDPR that aligns with existing national standards for research data, different interpretations may impede efforts to share and reuse experimental data internationally if differing GDPR enforcement regimes emerge.

3 Requirements of Open Science

The requirement for open access research publication of the results of publicly funded research has become common practice in recent years. However the central importance of data in all empirical research, in addition to the growth of big data research approaches, has heightened the call for common policies on publishing and sharing research data associated with a publication (of European Research Universities, 2013).

Major research funders, including the EC, have widened their guidelines on open science to now address open research data (European Commission, 2016). The aim in doing so is to make it easier for researchers to: build on previous research and improve the quality of research results; collaborate and avoid duplication of effort to improve the efficiency of publicly funded research; accelerate progress to market in order to realise economic and social benefits; and involve citizens and society. It is anticipated that EC-funded projects will transition from optional involvement in open data pilots to working under a stronger obligation to provide open access to research data. This however has to be provided within the constraints of EU and national data regulations, now including GDPR. Initiatives such as the Open Access Infrastructure for Research in Europe (OpenAIRE)[1] provide additional information and support on linking publications to underlying research data, and is developing open interfaces for exchange between research data repositories. However, for such open access to work at scale, improved level of interoperability will be required for the meta-data associated with data sets made availalbe through different institutional research data repositories. Such meta-data interoperability is needed to support the aggregation, indexing and searching of experimental data from different repositories so that researchers can find suitable data with less effort. Further, reflecting data protection and research ethics properties in such meta-data will also reduce the effort required to ensure that reusing experimental data from another source does not incur data protection compliance risks.

3.1 Open Data for Open Science

In parallel to other initiatives, Linked Open Data based on open data standards of the World Wide Web Consortium is being adopted as a common means for sharing all types of data between organisations, with strong uptake reported in the public sector. Linked Open Data is based upon the principle of interlinking resources and data with standardised Resource Description Framework (RDF) and Uniform Resource Identifiers (URIs) that can be read and queried by machines through powerful standardised querying mechanisms (Bizer et al., 2009).

Open RDF-based data vocabularies such as DCAT [2] help in expressing authorship of research data sets, while ODRL vocabulary[3] can express usage rights and licensing. The provenance of an experiment, in terms of which people and programmes performed which actions on which resources at what time, can be captured and modelled using the PROV[4] family of data vocabularies. Garijo et al. (2014) build on these standards to propose an open data format for recording both the sequence of experimental steps and the data resources passing between them. This would allow the publication and discovery of experimental descriptions with specific metadata (such as usage rights or data subject consent) associated with specific data elements.

Experiential description using these open vocabularies can be collected or aggregated to form linked repositories such as those supported by OpenAire and Linghub[5], which are being piloted

---

[1] https://www.openaire.eu/

[2] http://www.w3.org/TR/vocab-dcat/

[3] http://www.w3.org/TR/odrl/

[4] http://www.w3.org/TR/prov-0/

[5] http://linghub.lider-project.eu

for language resources. Existing research for these standard vocabularies has provided best practice for publishing data sets' metadata as linked open data (Brummer et al., 2014). The machine readable nature of metadata can make it easy for an automated system to verify the correctness of the data, or perform other operations such as checking of data formats, completeness of metadata and the provenance of data used (Freudenberg et al., 2016). This approach is amenable to extension with domain-specific experimental metadata, such as the machine learning metadata proposed in the MEX vocabulary (Esteves et al., 2015). The LT research community has already developed a schema, termed META-SHARE (Piperidis, 2012), for language resource metadata that shares many characteristics with the OpenAire scheme. The META-SHARE schema has also been mapped onto RDF with relevant attributes mapped to specific properties from the standard vocabularies previously mentioned, and is used by LingHub as an aggregation source (McCrae et al., 2015).

4 Discussion

Combining the emerging imperative of GDPR compliance and data science poses the following challenges for organisations undertaking LT research and concerned with research ethics. Firstly the encouragement by funders for researchers to provide open access to experimental data must be tempered by the overriding legal requirements of GDPR compliance. While GDPR offers derogation of certain rights when dealing with personal data for the purposes of scientific research, this does not remove the obligation for research performing organisations in the EU to demonstrate their conformance to GDPR, to conduct data protection impact assessments, and to ensure that the appropriate safeguards for the derogation are in place, especially in cases where anonymisation of experimental data is not possible.

In GDPR terms, a data processor receiving data from an LT experiment will need to know the terms of consent agreed to by the data subject in giving the primary data collector permission to use their personal data for a stated purpose. This will enable the receiving party to assess whether the purpose to which they now intend to put the data is compatible with that consent. Given that information, the receiving data processor would also need to give an undertaking that it will only perform processing of that data for purposes that are compatible with that consent.

This will mean therefore that exchange of LT research data with latent personal features cannot proceed without an appropriate contract on the usage of this data being signed and recorded for GDPR compliance purposes. It should also include an undertaking by the data processor not to attempt the identification of natural persons from the data, including through analysis in aggregation with other data. This goes beyond the standard form license agreements already in place for reuse of language resources, e.g. the META-SHARE licences [6], which focus mostly on issues of copyright ownership and usage conditions related to attribution or, in some cases, to compensation. To avoid GDPR unduly impeding the sharing and reuse of experimental data, we recommend that bodies such as the EC and ELRA develop standard form contract terms for the reuse of research data that the LT research community can use in documenting this aspect of GDPR compliance.

GDPR, in Recital 33, acknowledges that it "is often not possible to fully identify the purpose of personal data processing for scientific research purposes at the time of collection". It allows data subjects to provide consent to only specific parts of a research activity "when in keeping with recognised ethical standards for scientific research". This highlights the fact that good practice in research ethics *already* incorporates many features now formalised in GDPR, i.e. the need for a clear explanation of the data collection and processing purposes; the explicit gathering of informed consent and the option of the data subject to withdraw from any part of the research activity at any time. If EU proposals for ePrivacy (European Parliament and Council of the European Union, 2017) move on to become a regulation, the data subject will have more control over whether data may be repurposed by being offered "the option to prevent third parties from storing information on the terminal equipment of an end user or processing information already stored on that equipment" (Article 10). Key to data subjects exercising such control over the processing of personal data is their full understanding of the scientific research purposes to which their data will be subject.

Further research is required to assess the comprehensibility of plain language descriptions of

---

[6]http://wizard.elda.org/

purpose typically used by researchers for data subjects. The META-SHARE schema, for example, supports a 'purpose' attribute, but it is populated with names of different areas of LT research that are unlikely to be accessible to data subjects. Further, more applied research, perhaps conducted by industry, may be conducted with the known intention of supporting new service features, e.g. personalisation, targeted marketing, or differential pricing. As these are of direct concern to the data subject, such intentions should not be concealed by statements of purpose related to the broader generation of knowledge when seeking informed consent. From such research, the LT community and research institutes should seek to find classifications of purpose that are both accessible to data subjects and convey the differences in purpose of basic and applied research. Current rules and practices on academic research ethics tend to vary from institution to institution, with the intention of protecting participants and researchers by making clear the purpose of data collection, and requesting explicit consent to use personal data for that purpose. Researchers may have to make an undertaking with regard to data protection, but there is rarely any follow-up to ascertain whether the data has been stored or destroyed as promised. In contrast, GDPR compliance will require rigorous organisational and technical systems for record keeping and tracking the use to which data is put by data processors, including data transfer to processors in other institutes and other jurisdictions. Further, much LT research data processing involves secondary processing of industrial data, such as TMs or glossaries. As these are not collected from directly from experimental data subjects but via industrial processes, this data is collected, stored, retained, and shared without a reliable trace of research ethics clearance. Further, as LT research is increasingly undertaken by large companies with access to vast data-sets of customer information, the resulting experimental data is typically not subject to the *a priori* scrutiny of institutional review boards or ethics committees as is common with publicly funded research. This disparity between public and private norms for undertaking research ethics may create barriers to research collaboration and impede the progression of reproducable research results into the public domain. An opportunity therefore exists for the LT research community to better leverage open data standards tracking the transfer and use of personal data in a way that can support GDPR compliance checking. Use of open data standards that capture the detail of data processing workflows may be annotated to better record the processes by which: informed consent is gathered from individual data subjects; their individual objections to specific uses of personal data is handled and the purposes to which personal data is put is audited. Consent must be first collected, then stored and processed for checking compliance with data processing.

Consent can be modified. The modification can be initiated by the data subject or due to change of context the controller can re-solicit for consent that can lead to modification of consent. Consent can be revoked. After revocation, the data may be archived for the time necessary for research result verification and finally destroyed. Further research is needed on how to annotate open experimental workflow provenance records with details of consent management and its impact on the lifecycle management of the subject's data. A possible benefit of an open data approach, is that it may allow individual institutes to publish the attributes of their differing ethics review processes, allowing collection and analysis of variations that may assist in normalising standards. This will also allow those reusing others' data to be reassured that it was collected under ethical standards with which they are familiar. Ultimately this could result is a simple badge system, similar to that employed for creative commons, that could simplify the selection of LT research data according to the compatibility of research ethics and data protection protocols under which it was produced with those sought by the research hoping to use that data. Design of such a seal for reuse of experimental data could benefit from the work already underway in developing data protection seals [7] given the overlap between research ethics protocols and the informed consent requirements of GDPR.

Acknowledgements

Supported by the ADAPT Centre for Digital Content Technology which is funded under the SFI Research Centres Programme (Grant 13/RC/2106) and is co-funded under the European Regional Development Fund.

---

[7]https://ico.org.uk/for-organisations/improve-your-practices/privacy-seals/

References

Beth Thompson. 2016. Analysis: Research and the general data protection regulation. Technical report, July.

Chris Bizer, Tom Heath, and Martin Hepp. 2009. Special issue on linked data. *International Journal on Semantic Web and Information Systems*, 5(3):1–22.

Martin Brummer, Ciro Baron, Ivan Ermilov, Markus Freudenberg, Dimitris Kontokostas, and Sebastian Hellmann. 2014. Dataid: Towards semantically rich metadata for complex datasets. In *Proceedings of the 10th International Conference on Semantic Systems (SEM'14)*, New York, USA. ACM.

Michael Carl. 2012. Translog-ii: a program for recording user activity data for empirical reading and writing research. In *Proceedings of the Eight International Conference on Language Resources and Evaluation (LREC'12)*, Istanbul, Turkey, may. European Language Resources Association (ELRA).

Malcolm Coulthard. 2000. Whose text is it? on the linguistic investigation of authorship. In Srikant Sarangi and Malcolm Coulthard, editor, *Discourse and Social Life*, chapter 15, pages 270–288. Routledge, London.

Diego Esteves, Diego Moussallem, Ciro Baron Neto, Tommaso Soru, Ricardo Usbeck, Markus Ackermann, and Jens Lehmann. 2015. Mex vocabulary: A lightweight interchange format for machine learning experiments. In *Proceedings of the 11th International Conference on Semantic Systems*, SEMANTICS '15, pages 169–176, New York, NY, USA. ACM.

European Commission. 2016. Guidelines on open access to scientific publications and research data in horizon 2020. Technical report, February.

European Parliament and Council of the European Union. 2016. Regulation (eu) 2016/679 of the european parliament and of the council (GDPR). *Official Journal of the European Union*, 119(1):1–88.

European Parliament and Council of the European Union. 2017. Proposal for a regulation concerning the respect for private life and the protection of personal data in electronic communications.

Markus Freudenberg, Martin Brummer, Jessika Rucknagel, Robert Ulrich, Thomas Eckart, Dimitris Kontokostas, and Sebastian Hellmann. 2016. The metadata ecosystem of dataid. In *Special Track on Metadata & Semantics for Open Repositories at 10th International Conference on Metadata and Semantics Research*.

Daniel Garijo, Yolanda Gil, and Oscar Corcho. 2014. Ninth workshop on workflows in support of large-scale science (works). In *Ninth Workshop on Workflows in Support of Large-Scale Science (WORKS)*,, New Orleans, USA, Nov. IEEE.

Dirk Hovy and Shannon L. Spruit. 2016. The social impact of natural language processing. In *Proceedings of the 54th Annual Meeting of the Association of Computational Linguistics*, pages 591–598, August.

John P. McCrae, Penny Labropoulou, Jorge Gracia, Marta Villegas, Víctor Rodríguez-Doncel, and Philipp Cimiano, 2015. *One Ontology to Bind Them All: The META-SHARE OWL Ontology for the Interoperability of Linguistic Datasets on the Web*, pages 271–282. Springer International Publishing, Cham.

Joss Moorkens, David Lewis, Wessel Reijers, Eva Vanmassenhove, and Andy Way. 2016. Translation resources and translator disempowerment. In *ETHICA 2016: Workshop on ETHics In Corpus Collection, Annotation and Application*, Portoroz, Slovenia, May.

League of European Research Universities. 2013. Leru roadmap for research data. Technical report, Dec.

Stelios Piperidis. 2012. The meta-share language resources sharing infrastructure: Principles, challenges, solutions. In *Proceedings of the Eight International Conference on Language Resources and Evaluation (LREC'12)*, Istanbul, Turkey, may. European Language Resources Association (ELRA).

Ethical Considerations in NLP Shared Tasks

Carla Parra Escartín[1], Wessel Reijers[2], Teresa Lynn[2], Joss Moorkens[1],
Andy Way[2] and Chao-Hong Liu[2]

[1]ADAPT Centre, SALIS, Dublin City University, Ireland
[2]ADAPT Centre, School of Computing, Dublin City University, Ireland
`{carla.parra,wessel.reijers,teresa.lynn,joss.moorkens,andy.way,chaohong.liu}`
`@adaptcentre.ie`

Abstract

Shared tasks are increasingly common in our field, and new challenges are suggested at almost every conference and workshop. However, as this has become an established way of pushing research forward, it is important to discuss how we researchers organise and participate in shared tasks, and make that information available to the community to allow further research improvements. In this paper, we present a number of ethical issues along with other areas of concern that are related to the competitive nature of shared tasks. As such issues could potentially impact on research ethics in the Natural Language Processing community, we also propose the development of a framework for the organisation of and participation in shared tasks that can help mitigate against these issues arising.

1 Introduction

Shared tasks are competitions to which researchers or teams of researchers submit systems that address specific, predefined challenges. The competitive nature of shared tasks arises from the publication of a system ranking in which the authors of the systems achieving the highest scores obtain public acknowledgement of their work. In this paper, we discuss a number of ethical issues and various other areas of concern that relate to the competitive nature of shared tasks. We then move to propose the creation of a common framework for shared tasks that could help in overcoming these issues.

The primary goal of shared tasks is to encourage wider international participation in solving particular tasks at hand. A second objective is to learn from the competing systems so that research can move forward from one year to the next, or to establish best practices as to how to tackle a particular challenge.

Over the past few years, the organisation of and participation in shared tasks has become more popular in Natural Language Processing (NLP), speech and image processing. In the field of NLP study, researchers now have an array of annual tasks in which they can participate. For example, several shared tasks are organised at the Conference on Natural Language Learning (CoNLL),[1] the Conference and Labs of the Evaluation Forum (CLEF),[2] or the International Workshop on Semantic Evaluation (SEMEVAL).[3] For those working on a topic that proves to be particularly challenging, it has also become a trend to propose a new shared task co-located at a related conference or workshop in order to encourage contributions from the wider community to address the problem at hand. The NLP community has seen a rapid increase in the number of shared tasks recently, with many repeated periodically while others have been organised only once. During all collocated workshops at ACL 2016 alone, a total of 9 **new** shared tasks were proposed, along with others held annually. The 2016 Conference on Machine Translation (WMT16), for instance, offered 6 shared tasks already held in previous years along with 4 new ones.[4]

A distinctive feature of shared tasks is their integral competitive nature. In the field of research ethics, the factor of competition in research projects has been shown to have potentially negative ethical consequences for upholding research

---

[1]`http://www.signll.org/conll`
[2]`http://www.clef-initiative.eu/`
[3]`http://alt.qcri.org/semeval2016/`
[4]`http://www.statmt.org/wmt16/`

Proceedings of the First Workshop on Ethics in Natural Language Processing, pages 66–73,
Valencia, Spain, April 4th, 2017. © 2017 Association for Computational Linguistics

integrity and the open character of scientific research. For instance, McCain (1991) has argued that increased competition for funding and publications in the field of genetics has resulted in undesirable 'secretive' behaviour of scientists, of refusal to provide access to data sets or conflicts about ownership of experimental materials. Additionally, Mumford and Helton (2001) argued that the negative perception among researchers of the intentions of their competitors might invoke unethical behaviour. These are serious consequences of elements of competition on the work of researchers. However, to date, little attention seems to have been paid to preventing these problems from arising in the organisation of shared tasks in NLP research.

With the experience gathered in our community thanks to the organisation of shared tasks over the past 30 years, we believe the time is right to initiate an open discussion on a common ethical framework for the organisation of shared tasks, in order to reduce the potential negative ethical consequences of their competitive character. Such discussions should be held in the spirit of trying to globally establish – as a research community – which ethical issues should be tackled and considered across *all* shared tasks; the purpose of this paper is not to criticise how any particular shared task is or has been organised thus far in the field.

The remainder of this paper is organised as follows: Section 2 is devoted to an overview of the role of shared tasks in NLP, including their definition, importance as well as particular issues in the existing shared tasks in our field. Section 3 is devoted to a discussion on the potential negative ethical impacts of the factor of competition that is insufficiently regulated, and finally Section 4 proposes steps towards the creation of a common framework for the organisation of shared tasks in NLP that assists at overcoming the ethical issues we identify.

2   Shared Tasks in NLP

As mentioned in Section 1, shared tasks are competitions to which researchers or teams of researchers submit systems that address a particular challenge. In the field of NLP, the first shared tasks were initiated in the United States by NIST in collaboration with DARPA (Mariani et al., 2014). Paroubek et al. (2007) report that the first shared tasks – then called evaluation campaigns – focused on speech processing and started in 1987.[5]

In 1992, new initiatives focused on the field of text understanding under the umbrella of the DARPA TIPSTER Program (Harman, 1992). Since then, researchers in NLP have experienced how this type of benchmarking for NLP tools and systems has become a tradition in many sub-areas. In fact, some of the current annual shared tasks date all the way back to 1998 and 1999 when the first SEMEVAL (then called SENSEVAL-1)[6] and CONLL[7] were organised.

Typically, shared tasks consist of 4 distinct phases (Paroubek et al., 2007):

1. Training phase,

2. Dry-run phase,

3. Evaluation phase, and

4. Adjudication phase.

During the training phase, participants are provided with data to calibrate and train their systems. Such systems are subsequently used to process a blind test set during the dry-run phase, and their results are evaluated against a 'gold standard' previously prepared by the shared task organisers. In the adjudication phase, participants are asked to raise any issues observed during the evaluation and validate the obtained results.

2.1   Why are shared tasks important in our field?

Shared tasks are important because they help boost the pace of development in our field and encourage a culture of improving upon the state-of-the-art. Shared tasks have an additional advantage: by using the same data, all systems can be evaluated objectively and comparisons across systems could be made easier.

At the same time, some best practices and *de facto* standards have evolved from shared tasks, e.g. the widely used CoNLL format used in parsing and many other NLP tasks, and the splitting of German compounds in MT proposed by Koehn and Knight (2003).

A by-product of these shared tasks are the new datasets that are made available for use by the

---

[5] See Pallett (2003) for an overview of these first shared tasks and the role that NIST played in them.

[6] http://www.senseval.org/

[7] http://www.cnts.ua.ac.be/conll99/npb/

wider research community. Shared tasks encourage the development of new resources and also encourage innovative approaches to data collection. Moreover, provided the data is made available, any researcher can measure the performance of their system against past shared task data. It is also possible for any researcher outside one shared task (possibly investigating different topics) to use the publicly available shared task data after the event to benchmark new systems or applications, and allow for replication of experiments, e.g. Mate Tools development reported evaluations based on datasets from the CoNLL 2009 Shared Task (Bohnet, 2010).

Shared tasks with a large number of participants can also indicate the need to tackle a particular problem, or point to challenges that are particularly attractive for the NLP research community. The participation of industry-based teams in shared tasks shows that some of them are relevant beyond the academic research community.

Taken together, shared tasks have proven themselves to be very effective in incentivising research in specialised areas, but they come at a cost: organisers need to prepare the datasets well in advance, define the evaluation criteria, gather enough interest for participation, rank the submitted systems, and so on. At the same time, there is little information sharing among shared tasks that would allow organisers to benefit from the experience of others. As a result, shared tasks vary greatly in the way they are organised, how the datasets are shared, and the type of information (and data) which is available to participants and the research community both before, during, and after the evaluation.

2.2 Variability across shared tasks

Depending on the task at hand, shared tasks are organised in different ways. In some cases (such as the MT shared tasks), no annotated data is needed, and thus only aligned bilingual data is used.

In others, prior to the shared task, the organisers create annotated data that will be distributed to all participating teams to allow them to prepare their systems for the task. Such annotated data is used with two main aims: (i) adjusting to the format required for submissions, and (ii) allowing researchers to explore the data to develop automatic systems, either rule-based or machine-learning based, so that they are able to perform the

task on unseen data.

In some cases, the shared task organisers will distinguish between two different tracks for the same shared task depending on the source of the data being used to train the systems. In most cases, all teams in an evaluation test their systems on the same datasets to allow for easier across-the-board comparisons ('closed' track). Other shared tasks allow for the inclusion of additional data by individual teams ('open' track). In these 'open' tracks, the inclusion of other data is not necessarily verified and based on a trust system. It is worth noting that, to date, this system has worked well and, to the best of our knowledge, there have been no known issues of mistrust in NLP shared tasks.

Depending on the type of shared tasks, different evaluation methodologies will be used, ranging from purely automatic metrics, such as precision and recall for many of the shared tasks focusing on Information Retrieval, to human evaluation, such as the ranking of MT outputs or automatically generated text.[8]

3 Potential ethical issues concerning the competitive nature of shared tasks

As we have seen in the previous section, there is currently a great variability and a lack of standardisation in the organisation of shared tasks. Because shared tasks have become an important part of the scientific research in NLP, a certain level of standardisation is nonetheless required in order to safeguard satisfactory levels of scientific integrity and openness of scientific research. This standardisation in the organisation of shared tasks is needed specifically to mitigate potential negative ethical impacts of their competitive character. With a view to proposing a standard approach to shared task organisation, in this section, we discuss the potential negative ethical impacts of competition in scientific research and subsequently illustrate this by addressing potentially problematic aspects of the organisation of shared tasks in NLP.

3.1 Ethical issues arising from competition in scientific research

Competition is a factor in scientific research that is not limited to the field of NLP. In the organisation of contemporary science, competitive schemes for

---

[8]Paroubek et al. (2007) offer a good overview of the organisation of shared tasks and the different types of evaluation that one may come across.

scientific positions, publication possibilities or research funding are increasingly influential. However, shared tasks are distinctive from traditional forms of research, such as the writing of individual research papers or the organisation of experiments in a closed research project, because the element of competition is integral to the research activity. In other words, shared tasks not only take place within a competitive context, they are competitions *per se*.

For this reason, the effects of competition on the conduct of researchers should be taken seriously. As Anderson et al. (2007, p. 439) argue: "the relationship between competition and academic misconduct is a serious concern". A number of negative ethical impacts of competition in scientific research are discussed in the literature on research ethics. We suggest that the NLP community could draw on previous experiences and studies in the wider scientific community. We present three of the most important ones:

- **Secretive behaviour.** This effect of competition results from the tendency of researchers to give themselves an unfair competitive advantage in terms of knowledge concerning the research challenge at hand. McCain (1991) suggests that this behaviour can have several concrete forms, such as the unwillingness to publish research results in a timely fashion, refusal to provide access to data sets and conflicts concerning the 'ownership' of experimental materials.

- **Overlooking the relevance of ethical concerns.** Another effect of competition is the tendency of the teams competing to overlook the relevance of ethical concerns in their research. As Mumford and Helton (2001) explain, this might have the form of disregarding ethical concerns in general, or specifically with regard to one's own work while anticipating the potential ethical misconduct of others ("if they can do it, why shouldn't we?"). This can lead to careless – or questionable – research conduct.

- **Relations with other scientists.** Because the stakes in competitions can be very high (they might result in further or decreased research funding, or in opening up or closing off of future career paths), competitions might have negative impacts on the relations between peers (Anderson et al., 2007). This might lead researchers to have the tendency to behave unethically with regards to their peers in order to preserve or strengthen their reputation.

3.2 Potential negative effects of competition in shared tasks in NLP

The motivation for involvement in shared tasks has evolved somewhat over the recent past. Many researchers in MT, for example, will participate in the annual shared tasks organised at WMT, where there is a ranking of the best systems for a proposed task. Participation and success in tasks such as these are often used to demonstrate research excellence to funding agencies. At the same time, performance of the systems may also have a greater impact on the funding for a complete research area (not only for individual teams or institutions). We only need to look back to the notorious ALPAC report (Pierce and Carroll, 1966), whose consequences for research funding in the US for MT were devastating for a considerable period. Such funding-related motivation can in turn lead to increased competitiveness.

When we revisit the shared tasks within NLP, the potential negative ethical impacts of competition identified in the literature on research ethics can also be found in this field. Here, we discuss the main issues identified which require mechanisms to be established by our community to prevent them from happening.

- **Secretiveness.** Competitiveness can sometimes lead to secretiveness with respect to the specific features used to tune a system to ensure that the best methods and/or approaches stay in the same institution/team. Participants usually submit their system descriptions to the shared task, in the form of presentations and research papers. However, the way in which such systems are described may vary greatly, as one can always choose a more abstract higher-level description to avoid 'spilling the beans' about the methodology applied, and retaining the knowledge rather than sharing it.

- **Unconscious overlooking of ethical concerns.** Leading on from the secretiveness issue raised above, teams may unintentionally be vague in reporting details of their systems' parameters and functionality solely on the basis that other teams have also previously reported in this way. Such practice can simply arise from the existence of convention in the absence of guidelines or standards.

- **Potential conflicts of interest.** Finally, another potential ethical issue is related to organisers or annotators being allowed to participate in the shared task in which they are involved. Again, while some find it unethical to participate in their own shared task, others disagree, and the community trusts that in such cases the organisers trained their systems under the same conditions as the rest of the participants, i.e. they did not take advantage of prior access to data and did not train their systems for a longer period of time, or have a sneak peak at – or hand-select for optimal performance – the test data to improve their system's performance and cause it to be highly ranked. Both points of view are perfectly valid, and in some cases even justified, e.g. teams working on (usually low-resourced) languages for which they themselves are one of the few potential participants for those languages. While the overlap of organisers, annotators and participants has not yet revealed itself to be a major issue in our field, and the goodwill and ethical conduct of all involved is generally trusted, it is worth considering the establishment of methods for minimising the risk of this happening in the future. One such measure could be for the organisers to explicitly state whether the overlap is likely to happen.[9]

Subsequently, we have identified a number of other potential conflicts with the objectivity and integrity of research that may arise from the competitive nature of shared tasks in NLP. Whether intentional or unintentional, these issues are worth considering when developing a common framework for the organisation of and participation in shared tasks:

- **Lack of description of negative results.** The fact that negative results are also informative is something that no researcher will deny.

However, as shown by Fanelli (2010), researchers have a tendency to report only positive results. He claims that this may be because they "attract more interest and are cited more often", adding that there is a belief that "journal editors and peer reviewers might tend to favour them, which will further increase the desirability of a positive outcome to researchers".

Furthermore, with PhD students being pressed to publish in the top conferences in their fields, they may be reluctant to submit systems that do not report on positive results. As a result, while we always discover what worked for a particular task, we are not usually told what did *not* work, although that may be of equal or (even) greater importance than the methodology that worked, as it would help others to avoid repeating the same mistake in the future. In fact, it may be the case that the same approach has been tested by different institutions with no success and that we are incurring a hidden redundancy that does not help us to move forward as a field. In order to prevent these issues from occurring, we should design mechanisms that incentivise the publication of negative results and more thorough error analysis of systems

Similarly, it may be the case that although it is highly desirable that industry-based teams participate in a shared task, some may be reluctant to do so on the basis of the negative impact that this may have for their product if it does not end up among the first ranked. Thus, rather than strengthening the academia-industry relationship and learning from each other, we risk making the gap between the two bigger rather than bridging it. Should we not address this and establish mechanisms that encourage industrial teams to participate in shared tasks without such associated risks?

- **Withdrawal from competition.** Some teams may prefer to withdraw from the competition rather than participate if they fear that their performance may have a negative impact in their future funding: how could research excellence on a particular topic be argued if one's team came last in a competition? Again, mechanisms could be de-

---

[9]This type of overlap was highlighted by the organisers of the PARSEME shared task at the 13th Workshop on Multiword Expressions (MWE 2017): `http://bit.ly/2jPsu2n`.

signed with the aim of discouraging this type of withdrawal. For example, one possible solution would be to only report on the upper 50% of the ranked systems.

- **Potential 'gaming the system'.** Another concern is the impact of the results of the shared task beyond the shared task itself (e.g. real-world applications, end-users). Shared tasks are evaluated against a common test set under the auspices of a 'fair' comparison among systems. However, as the ultimate goal of most participating teams is to obtain the highest positions in the ranking, there is a risk of focusing on winning, rather than on the task itself. Of course, accurate evaluation is crucial when reporting results of NLP tasks (e.g. Summarisation (Mackie et al., 2014); MT (Graham, 2015)). As evaluation metrics play a crucial role in determining who is the winner of a shared task, many participating teams will tune their systems so that they achieve the highest possible score for the objective function at hand, as opposed to focusing on whether this approach is actually the best way to solve the problem. This, in turn, impacts directly on the real-world applications for which solving that challenge is particularly relevant, as it may be the case that the 'winning' systems are not necessarily the best ones to be used in practice.

As discussed previously, some shared tasks allow for 'closed' and 'open' variants, i.e. in the 'closed' sub-task, participants use only the data provided by the shared task organisers, such that the playing field really is level (we ignore for now the question as to whether the leading system really is the 'best' system for the task at hand, or (merely) has the best pre-preprocessing component, for instance). By contrast, in the 'open' challenge, teams are permitted to add extra data such that true comparison of the merits of the competing systems is much harder to bring about.

- **Redundancy and replicability in the field.** Another important issue is that, although this should be the overriding goal, we typically find that for any new data set – even for the same language pair – optimal parameter settings established in a previous shared task do not necessarily carry over to the new, albeit related challenge. This is a *real* problem, as if this is the case, we should ask ourselves what we as a field are really learning. At the same time, our field experiences a lot of redundancy, as we try to reimplement others' algorithms against which we test our own systems. This is the case particularly when systems participating in a shared task are not subsequently released to the community.[10]

- **Unequal playing field.** Another potential risk is the fact that larger teams at institutions with greater processing power (e.g. better funded research centres or large multinationals) may have a clear unfair advantage in developing better performing systems, rendering the 'competition' as an unequal playing field for researchers in general. This could be mitigated against by establishing, beforehand, the conditions under which systems are trained and tested for the task.

In this section, we have identified several potential ethical concerns related to the organization and participation in shared tasks. As observed, the three issues discussed in the academic literature on competition in research (cf. Section 3.1) appear to be important considerations for shared tasks in NLP. In addition, we have highlighted some other areas of potential ethical consideration in our field with respect to shared tasks. In the next section, we discuss potential paths to tackle the ethical concerns raised here.

4 Future directions

The great value of shared tasks is there for all to see, and there is no doubt that they will continue to be a major venue for many researchers in NLP in the future. Nonetheless, we have pointed out several ethical concerns that we believe should be addressed by the NLP community, and mechanisms created to prevent them should be also agreed upon. At the same time, there may be other ethical considerations that the authors have omitted due to lack of knowledge about *all* shared tasks

---

[10]The existence of initiatives such as CLARIN[11] or the recent efforts made by ELDA to try to standardize even various versions of the 'same' dataset, evaluation metric, or even a particular run of an experiment show that we are shifting to a new research paradigm where open data, research transparency, reproducibility of results and a collaborative approach to advancements in science are advocated (Pedersen, 2008; Perovšek et al., 2015).

in NLP, or simply because they arose within participation in specific shared tasks and have never been shared with the community. Thus, we see that a first step towards determining potential ethical issues related to the organisation of and participation in shared tasks is to conduct a survey in our community to ensure broad contribution. Such a survey – to be launched shortly after discussions at the 2017 Ethics in NLP workshop – consists of two parts. The first tries to gauge the varying requirements of shared tasks, and the second one aims at assessing what people feel are important factors for consideration when drawing up a common framework for shared tasks in NLP. This common framework will ensure greater transparency and understanding of shared tasks in our community, and prevent us from encountering the potential negative impact of the ethical concerns raised here.

Questions regarding past experiences related to shared tasks (either as organisers, annotators or participants) are included in the survey to gather information regarding (i) best practices used in specific shared tasks that could be extrapolated to new ones, (ii) the type of information that is available to participants before, during and after the shared task, (iii) potential ethical concerns encountered in the past and how they were tackled, (iv) other causes for concern from the NLP community and (v) good experiences that we should aim at replicating.

Besides recommendations on best practice, we envisage the creation of shared task checklists based on the questions in the survey and their replies. These checklists would target the organisers, annotators and participating teams in shared tasks, and would be used to state any relevant information required in each case. By subsequently making them publicly available to the community (e.g. at the shared task website), any participating team or researcher interested in the shared task topic would know how specific topics were addressed in the shared task, and what information was or will be available to them. What follows is a non-exhaustive list of some of the items that we foresee including in the checklist (subject to discussion and amendment):

- Participation of organisers in the shared task;

- Participation of annotators or people who had prior access to the data in the shared task;

- Public release of the results of the participating systems after the shared task, under an agreed license;

- Declaration of the list of contributors to a certain system at submission time;

- Anonymisation of the lower (50% ?) of systems evaluated to be referred to by name in published results;

- ...

5   Conclusion

In this paper we have discussed a number of potential ethical issues in the organisation and participation of shared tasks that NLP scientists should address to prevent them from arising as problems in the future. Besides taking into account the particular features of shared tasks, we investigated the potential ethical issues of competition in scientific research and extrapolated such issues to the potential problems that may arise in our own field. In addition, as we believe this should be tackled by the NLP community as a whole, we have proposed the launch of a survey to gather further information about shared tasks in NLP that will help in the development of a common framework in the near future. This would include current best practice, a series of recommendations and checklists as to what issues should be taken into account, as well as what information is provided to participants, depending on the type of shared tasks in question.

Finally, shared tasks in our field play an essential role in NLP. They have undoubtedly helped improve the quality of the systems we develop across a range of NLP sub-fields, to a point where many of them comprise essential components of professional workflows. The system as such is not irretrievably broken, so there may be a temptation to not fix the issues outlined in this paper. However, we firmly believe that the field of NLP has reached a level of maturity where some reflection on the practices that we currently take for granted is merited, such that our shared tasks become ever more reliable and consistent across our discipline, and further strides are made to the benefit of the field as a whole as well as to the wider community.

Acknowledgements

The authors wish to thank the anonymous reviewers for their valuable feedback. This research is supported by Science Foundation Ireland in the ADAPT Centre (Grant 13/RC/2106) (www.adaptcentre.ie) at Dublin City University.

References

Melissa S. Anderson, Emily A. Ronning, Raymond de Vries, and Brian C. Martinson. 2007. The perverse effects of competition on scientists' work and relationships. *Science and Engineering Ethics*, 13(4):437–461.

Bernd Bohnet. 2010. Very high accuracy and fast dependency parsing is not a contradiction. In *Proceedings of the 23rd International Conference on Computational Linguistics*, COLING '10, pages 89–97, Stroudsburg, PA, USA. Association for Computational Linguistics.

Daniele Fanelli. 2010. Do pressures to publish increase scientists' bias? an empirical support from us states data. *PLoS ONE*, 5(4):e10271, 04.

Yvette Graham. 2015. Improving evaluation of machine translation quality estimation. In *Proceedings of the 53rd Annual Meeting of the Association for Computational Linguistics and the 7th International Joint Conference on Natural Language Processing (Volume 1: Long Papers)*, pages 1804–1813, Beijing, China, July. Association for Computational Linguistics.

Donna Harman. 1992. The darpa tipster project. *SIGIR Forum*, 26(2):26–28, October.

Philipp Koehn and Kevin Knight. 2003. Empirical Methods for Compound splitting. In *Proceedings of the Tenth Conference of the European Chapter of the Association for Computational Linguistics*, pages 187–193, Stroudsburg, PA, USA. Association for Computational Linguistics.

Stuart Mackie, Richard McCreadie, Craig Macdonald, and Iadh Ounis. 2014. On choosing an effective automatic evaluation metric for microblog summarisation. In *Proceedings of the 5th Information Interaction in Context Symposium*, pages 115–124. ACM.

Joseph Mariani, Patrick Paroubek, Gil Francopoulo, and Olivier Hamon. 2014. Rediscovering 15 years of discoveries in language resources and evaluation: The lrec anthology analysis. In *Proceedings of the Ninth International Conference on Language Resources and Evaluation (LREC'14)*, Reykjavik, Iceland, may. European Language Resources Association (ELRA).

Katherine W. McCain. 1991. Communication, competition, and secrecy: The production and dissemination of research-related information in genetics. *Science, Technology & Human Values*, 16(4):491–516.

Michael D. Mumford and Whitney B. Helton. 2001. Organizational influences on scientific integrity. In Nicholas Steneck and Mary Scheetz, editors, *Investigating research integrity: Proceedings of the first ORI research conference on research integrity*, volume 5583, pages 73–90.

David S. Pallett. 2003. A look at nist's benchmark asr tests: past, present, and future. In *2003 IEEE Workshop on Automatic Speech Recognition and Understanding (IEEE Cat. No.03EX721)*, pages 483–488, Nov.

Patrick Paroubek, Stéphane Chaudiron, and Lynette Hirschman. 2007. Principles of Evaluation in Natural Language Processing. *Traitement Automatique des Langues*, 48(1):7–31, May.

Ted Pedersen. 2008. Empiricism is not a matter of faith. *Computational Linguistics*, 34(3):465–470.

Matic Perovšek, Vid Podpečan, Janez Kranjc, Tomaž Erjavec, Senja Pollak, Quynh Ngoc Thi Do, Xiao Liu, Cameron Smith, Mark Cavazza, and Nada Lavrač. 2015. Text mining platform for nlp workflow design, replication and reuse. In *Proceedings of the Workshop on Replicability and Reproducibility in Natural Language Processing: adaptive methods, resources and software at IJCAI 2015*.

John R. Pierce and John B. Carroll. 1966. *Language and Machines: Computers in Translation and Linguistics*. National Academy of Sciences/National Research Council, Washington, DC, USA.

Social Bias in Elicited Natural Language Inferences

Rachel Rudinger*
Johns Hopkins University
`rudinger@jhu.edu`

Chandler May*
Johns Hopkins University
`cjmay@jhu.edu`

Benjamin Van Durme
Johns Hopkins University
`vandurme@cs.jhu.edu`

Abstract

We analyze the Stanford Natural Language Inference (SNLI) corpus in an investigation of bias and stereotyping in NLP data. The human-elicitation protocol employed in the construction of the SNLI makes it prone to amplifying bias and stereotypical associations, which we demonstrate statistically (using pointwise mutual information) and with qualitative examples.

1 Introduction

Since the statistical revolution in Artificial Intelligence (AI), it is standard in areas such as natural language processing and computer vision to train models on large amounts of empirical data. This "big data" approach popularly connotes objectivity; however, as a cultural, political, and economic phenomenon in addition to a technological one, big data carries subjective aspects (Crawford et al., 2014). The data mining process involves defining a target variable and evaluation criteria, collecting a dataset, selecting a manner in which to represent the data, and sometimes eliciting annotations: bias, whether or implicit or explicit, may be introduced in the performance of each of these tasks (Barocas and Selbst, 2016).

We focus on the problem of *overgeneralization*, in which a data mining model extrapolates excessively from observed patterns, leading to *bias confirmation* among the model's users (Hovy and Spruit, 2016). High-profile cases of overgeneralization in the public sphere abound (Crawford, 2013; Crawford, 2016; Barocas and Selbst, 2016).

Research on the measurement and correction of overgeneralization in NLP in particular is nascent.

Stock word embeddings have been shown to exhibit gender bias, leading to proposed *debiasing* algorithms (Bolukbasi et al., 2016). Word embeddings have been shown to reproduce harmful implicit associations exhibited by human subjects in implicit association tests (Caliskan-Islam et al., 2016). Gender bias in sports journalism has been studied via language modeling, confirming that male athletes receive questions more focused on the game than female athletes (Fu et al., 2016). In guessing the gender, age, and education level of the authors of Tweets, crowdworkers found to exaggerate stereotypes (Carpenter et al., 2017).

A prerequisite to resolving the above issues is basic awareness among NLP researchers and practitioners of where systematic bias in datasets exists, and how it may arise. In service of this goal, we offer a case study of bias in the Stanford Natural Language Inference (SNLI) dataset. SNLI is a recent but popular NLP dataset for textual inference, the largest of its kind by two orders of magnitude, offering the potential to substantially advance research in Natural Language Understanding (NLU). We select this dataset because (1) we predict that natural language inference as a NLP task may be generally susceptible to emulating human cognitive biases like social stereotyping, and (2) we are interested in how eliciting written inferences from humans with minimal provided context may encourage stereotyped responses.

Using the statistical measure of pointwise mutual information along with qualitative examples, we demonstrate the existence of stereotypes of various forms in the elicited hypotheses of SNLI.

2 The SNLI Dataset

Bowman et al. (2015) introduce the Stanford Natural Language Inference corpus. The corpus was generated by presenting crowdworkers with

---

* denotes equal contribution.

74

Proceedings of the First Workshop on Ethics in Natural Language Processing, pages 74–79,
Valencia, Spain, April 4th, 2017. © 2017 Association for Computational Linguistics

a photo caption (but not the corresponding photo) from the Flickr30k corpus (Young et al., 2014) and instructing them to write a new alternate caption for the unseen photo under one of the following specifications: The new caption must either be [1] "definitely a true description of the photo," [2] "might be a true description of the photo," or [3] "definitely a false description of the photo." Thus, in the parlance of Natural Language Inference, the original caption and the newly elicited caption form a sentence pair consisting of a *premise* (the original caption) and a *hypothesis* (the newly elicited sentence). The pair is labeled with one of three entailment relation types (ENTAILMENT, NEUTRAL, or CONTRADICTION), corresponding to conditions [1–3] above. The dataset contains 570K such pairs in total.

Given the construction of this dataset, we identify two possible sources of social bias: **caption bias**,[1] already present in the premises from the Flickr30k corpus (van Miltenburg, 2016), and **(inference) elicitation bias**, resulting from the SNLI protocol of eliciting possible inferences from humans provided an image caption. Though we recognize these sources of bias may not be as tidy and independent as their names suggest, it is a useful conceptual shorthand: In this paper, we are primarily interested in detecting elicitation bias.

3   Methodology

We are ultimately concerned with the impact of a dataset's biases on the models and applications that are trained on it. To avoid dependence on a particular model or model family, we evaluate the SNLI dataset in a model-agnostic fashion using the pointwise mutual information (PMI) measure of association (Church and Hanks, 1990) and likelihood ratio tests of independence (Dunning, 1993) between lexical units.

Given categorical random variables W_1 and W_2 representing word occurrences in a corpus, for each word type (or bigram) w_1 in the range of W_1 and for each word type (or bigram) w_2 in the range

---

[1]Note that what we call caption bias may be due either to the Flickr30k caption writing procedure, or the underlying distribution of images themselves. Distilling these two sources of bias is outside the scope of this paper, as the SNLI corpus makes no direct use of the images themselves. Put another way, because SNLI annotators did not see images, the elicited hypotheses are independent of the Flickr images, conditioned on the premises.

of W_2, PMI is defined as

$$\text{PMI}(w_1, w_2) = \log \frac{P(W_1 = w_1, W_2 = w_2)}{P(W_1 = w_1)P(W_2 = w_2)}.$$

To compute PMI from corpus statistics, we plug in maximum-likelihood estimates of the joint and marginal probabilities:

$$\hat{P}(W_1 = w_1, W_2 = w_2) = C(w_1, w_2)/C(*, *),$$
$$\hat{P}(W_1 = w_1) = C(w_1, *)/C(*, *),$$
$$\hat{P}(W_2 = w_2) = C(*, w_2)/C(*, *),$$

where $C(w_1, w_2)$ represents the co-occurrence count of $W_1 = w_1$ and $W_2 = w_2$ in the corpus and $*$ denotes marginalization (summation) over the corresponding variable. We wish to focus on the bias introduced in the hypothesis elicitation process, so we count co-occurrences between words (or bigrams) w_1 in a premise and words (or bigrams) w_2 in a corresponding hypothesis.

For each pair of word types (or bigrams) w_1 and w_2, we can check the independence between the indicator variables $X_{w_1} = I_{\{W_1 = w_1\}}$ and $Y_{w_2} = I_{\{W_2 = w_2\}}$ with a likelihood ratio test. (Hereafter we omit subscripts w_1 and w_2 for ease of notation.) Denote the observed counts of X and Y over the corpus by $C'(x, y)$ for $x, y \in \{0, 1\}$.[2] The test statistic is

$$\Lambda(C') = \frac{\sum_{x,y} \left(\hat{P}(X = x)\hat{P}(Y = y) \right)^{C'(x,y)}}{\sum_{x,y} \hat{P}(X = x, Y = y)^{C'(x,y)}}.$$

where $\hat{P}$ is the maximum likelihood estimator (using C'), the summations range over $x, y \in \{0, 1\}$, and we have dropped the subscripts w_1 and w_2 for ease of notation. The quantity $-2 \log \Lambda(C')$ is χ^2-distributed with one degree of freedom, so we can use it to test rejection of the null hypothesis (independence between X and Y) for significance. That quantity is also equal to a factor of $2C'(*, *)$ times the mutual information between X and Y, and the PMI between W_1 and W_2 (on which X and Y are defined) is a (scaled) component of the mutual information. Noting this relationship between PMI (which we use to sort all candidate word pairs) and the likelihood ratio test statistic (which we use to test for independence of the top word

---

[2]For example, note $C'(1, 1) = C(w_1, w_2)$ and $C'(1, 0) = C(w_1, *) - C(w_1, w_2)$; the other counts $C'(0, 1)$ and $C'(0, 0)$ can also be computed in this manner.

		GENDER		
woman	hairdresser‡ fairground grieving receptionist widow	**man**	rock-climbing videoing armband tatooes gent	
women	actresses† husbands‡ womens‡ gossip‡ wemon‡	**men**	gypsies supervisors contractors mens‡ cds	
girl	schoolgirl piata cindy pigtails‡ gril	**boy**	misbehaving see-saw timmy lad‡ sprained	
girls	fifteen‡ slumber sking‡ jumprope† ballerinas‡	**boys**	giggle‡ youths‡ sons‡ brothers‡ skip	
mother	kissed‡ parent‡ mom‡ feeds daughters	**father**	fathers‡ dad‡ sons† daughters plant	

		AGE		
old	ferret‡ quilts‡ knits‡ grandpa‡ elderly‡	**young**	giggle cds youthful‡ tidal amusing	
old woman	knits‡ grandmother‡ scarf† elderly‡ lady‡	**young woman**	salon† attractive blow blowing feeds	
old man	ferret‡ grandpa‡ wrapping‡ grandfather‡ elderly‡	**young man**	boarder disabled rollerblades graduation skate‡	

		RACE/ETHNICITY/NATIONALITY		
indian	indians‡ india‡ native‡ traditional‡ pouring†	**caucasian**	blond white‡ american asian blonde	
indian woman	cooking† clothes lady using making	**american**	patriotic‡ canadian‡ americans‡ reenactment‡ america‡	
indian man	food couple a‡ sleeping sitting	**american woman**	women‡ black white front her‡	
asian	kimonos‡ asians‡ asain‡ oriental‡ chinatown‡	**american man**	speaking‡ money‡ black‡ white‡ music	
asians	asian‡ food people‡ eating friends	**black woman**	african‡ american asian white‡ giving	
asian woman	oriental‡ indian† chinese‡ listens† customers	**black man**	african‡ american white‡ roller face	
asian man	shrimp† rice† chinese‡ businessman cooks†	**native american**	americans‡ music‡ dressed they woman	
white woman	protesting‡ lady‡ looks women‡ was	**african american**	caucasian asian‡ speaking‡ black‡ white‡	
white man	pancakes‡ caucasian‡ class black† concert	**african**	africans‡ africa‡ pots† receives† village†	

Table 1: Top five words in hypothesis by PMI with specified words in premise, filtered to co-occurrences with a unigram with count at least five. Queries in bold. Significance of a likelihood ratio test for independence denoted by † ($\alpha = 0.01$) and ‡ ($\alpha = 0.001$).

pairs), we control for the family-wise error rate using the Holm-Bonferroni procedure (Holm, 1979) on all candidate word pairs. The procedure is applied separately within each view of the corpus that we analyze: the all–inference-type view, ENTAILMENT-only view, NEUTRAL-only view, and CONTRADICTION-only view.

The U.S. Equal Employment Opportunity Commission (EEOC) characterizes discrimination by type, where types of discrimination include age, disability, national origin, pregnancy, race/color, religion, and sex.[3] To test for the existence of harmful stereotypes in the SNLI dataset we pick words and bigrams used to describe people labeled as belonging to each of these categories, such as *Asian* or *woman*, and list the top five or ten co-occurrences with each of those query terms in the SNLI dataset, sorted by PMI.[4] We omit co-occurrences with a count of less than five. We include both broad and specific query words; for example, we include adjectives describing nationalities as well as those describing regions and races. We also include query bigrams describing people labeled as belonging to more than one category, such as *Asian woman*. Due to space constraints, we report a subset of the top-five lists exhibiting harmful stereotypes. The code and query list used in our analysis are available online, facilitating further analysis of the complete results.[5]

Preliminary results contained many bigrams in the top-five lists that overlapped with the query— exactly or by lemma—along with a stop word. To mitigate this redundancy we filter the query results to unigrams before sorting and truncating.

4 Results

We analyze bias in the SNLI dataset using both PMI as a statistical measure of association (Sec. 4.1) and with demonstrative examples (Sec. 4.2).

4.1 Top Associated Terms by PMI

For each social identifier of interest (for example, "woman," "man," "Asian," "African American," etc.) we query for the top 5 or 10 unigrams in the dataset that share the highest PMI with the identifier. In Table 1, the results are broken down by gender-, age-, and race/ethnicity/nationality-based query terms, though some query terms combine more than one type of identifier (for example, gender and race). Table 2 shows the results for the same gender-based queries run over different portions of SNLI, as partitioned by entailment type (ENTAILMENT, NEUTRAL, and CONTRADICTION). As described in Sec. 3, the pairwise counts used to estimate PMI are between a word in the premise and a word in the hypothesis; thus, query terms correspond with SNLI premises, and the results of the query correspond with hypotheses. A discussion of these results follows in Sec. 5.

[3] https://www.eeoc.gov/laws/types/

[4] We use the provided Stanford tokenization of the SNLI dataset, converting all words to lowercase before counting co-occurrences.

[5] https://github.com/cjmay/snli-ethics

ENTAILMENT	**women**	scarves† ladies‡ womens‡ wemon‡ females‡ woman‡ affection dressing chat smile†
	men	mens‡ guys‡ guitars cowboys† remove dock dudes workers‡ computers‡ boxers
	girls	cheerleaders‡ females‡ girl‡ dancers children‡ smile practice dance‡ outfits laughing
	boys	males‡ children‡ boy‡ kids‡ four‡ fighting† exercise play‡ pose fun
NEUTRAL	**women**	actresses‡ gossip‡ husbands‡ womens‡ nuns† bridesmaids† gossiping‡ ladies‡ strippers purses
	men	lumberjacks mens‡ supervisors thieves‡ homosexual roofers reminisce† contractors groomsmen engineers‡
	girls	fifteen‡ slumber† gymnasts‡ cheerleading‡ bikinis† sisters‡ cheerleaders‡ daughters‡ selfies† teenage‡
	boys	skip† sons‡ brothers‡ twins‡ muddy trunks† males† league‡ cards recess†
CONTRADICTION	**women**	womens† wemon bikinis‡ ladies‡ towels females‡ politics dresses‡ discussing men‡
	men	dudes mens‡ motel‡ gossip surfboards wives caps sailors floors helmets
	girls	sking‡ boys‡ 50 brothers sisters dolls† pose opposite phones hopscotch
	boys	girls‡ sisters‡ sons bunk homework† males coats beds† guns professional

Table 2: Top-ten words in hypothesis by PMI with gender-related query words in premise, filtered to co-occurrences with a unigram with count of at least five, sorted by inference type (ENTAILMENT, NEUTRAL, or CONTRADICTION). Queries in bold. Significance of a likelihood ratio test for independence denoted by † ($\alpha = 0.01$) and ‡ ($\alpha = 0.001$).

4.2 Qualitative Examples

Some forms of bias in a dataset may only be detectable with aggregate statistics such as PMI. Other, more explicit forms of bias may be apparent from individual data points. Here we present some example sentence pairs from SNLI that outwardly exhibit harmful stereotypes (labeled HS) or the use of pejorative language or slurs (labeled PL).[6] Note that in these examples, the identifiable biases have been introduced as a result of the SNLI inference elicitation protocol, that is, they arise in the hypothesis.

> PREMISE: An African American man looking at some butchered meat that is hanging from a rack outside a building.
> HYPOTHESIS (CONTRA.): A black man is in jail [HS]

> PREMISE: New sport is being played to show appreciation to the kids who can not walk.
> HYPOTHESIS (ENTAIL.): People are playing a sport in honor of crippled people. [PL]

> PREMISE: Several people, including a shirtless man and a woman in purple shorts which say "P.I.N.K." on the back, are walking through a crowded outdoor area.
> HYPOTHESIS (ENTAIL.): The woman is wearing slutty shorts. [PL]

> PREMISE: adult with red boots and purse walking down the street next to a brink wall.
> HYPOTHESIS (NEUTR.): A whore looking for clients. [PL, HS]

> PREMISE: Several Muslim worshipers march towards Mecca.
> HYPOTHESIS (NEUTR.): The Muslims are terrorists. [HS]

> PREMISE: A man dressed as a woman and other people stand around tables with checkered tablecloths and a ladder.
> HYPOTHESIS (NEUTR.): The man is a transvestite. [PL]

---

[6]The authors recognize the partially subjective nature of applying these labels.

Explicit introduction of harmful stereotypes or pejorative language by crowdworkers (such as that presented here) is a form of elicitation bias; it may be a result of many factors, including the crowdworker's personal experiences, cultural identities, native English dialect, political ideology, socioeconomic status, anonymity (and hence relative impunity), and lack of awareness of their responses' potential impact. As one reviewer suggested, in the case of CONTRADICTION elicitation, some crowdworkers may even have "viewed their role as being not just contradictory, but outrageously so." While these explanations are speculative, the harmful language and stereotypes observed in these examples are not.

5 Discussion of Results

From the top associated terms by PMI, as reported in Tables 1 and 2, the clearest stereotypical patterns emerge for gender categories. Stereotypical associations evoked for women (but not men) include: expectations of emotional labor (*smile, kissed*), "pink collar" jobs (*hairdresser*), sexualization and emphasis on physical appearance (*bikinis*), talkativeness (*gossip, gossiping*), and being defined in relation to men (*men, husbands*). Conversely, stereotypical views of men are also evoked: performance of physical labor (*cowboys, workers*), and professionals in technical jobs (*computers, engineers*).

Gender-based stereotypes in the corpus cut across age, as well. Girls are associated with particular sports (*ballerinas, cheerleaders, cheerleading, dance, gymnasts*), games and toys (*jumprope, dolls*), outward appearances (*pigtails, bikinis*), and activities (*slumber [parties], selfies*). Boys, meanwhile, are stereotyped as troublemakers (*fighting*) and active outdoors (*recess, league, play*).

Though gender stereotypes appear in all three entailment categories in Table 2, those under the NEUTRAL label appear especially strong. We hypothesize this is a result of the less constrained nature of eliciting inferences that are neither "definitely true" nor "definitely false": Eliciting inferences that merely "might be true" may actually encourage stereotyped responses. Formally, neutral inferences may or may not be true, so those expressing stereotypes could be assumed to have no negative impact on the downstream model. However, if the model assumes neutral inferences are equally likely to be true or false *a priori*, that assumption's impact may be greater on minority groups subject to harmful negative stereotypes.

As represented by top-k PMI lists, individual terms for race, ethnicity, and nationality appear to have less strongly stereotyped associations than gender terms, but some biased associations are still observed. Words associated with Asians in this dataset, for example, appear to center around food and eating; the problematic term "Oriental" is also highly associated (another example of pejorative language, as discussed in Sec. 4.2). For many race, ethnicity, and nationality descriptors, some of the top-5 results by PMI are terms for *other* races, ethnicities, or nationalities. This is in large part a result of an apparent SNLI annotator tactic for CONTRADICTION examples: If the race, ethnicity, or nationality of a person in the premise is specified, simply replace it with a different one.

6 Conclusion

We used a simple and interpretable association measure, namely pointwise mutual information, to test the SNLI corpus for elicitation bias, noting that bias at the level of word co-occurrences is likely to lead to overgeneralization in a large family of downstream models. We found evidence that the elicited hypotheses introduced substantial gender stereotypes as well as varying degrees of racial, religious, and age-based stereotypes. We caution that our results do not imply the latter stereotypes are not present: rather, the prominence of gender stereotypes may be due to the relatively visual expression of gender, and the absence of other stereotypes in our results may be due to sparsity. We also note that our analysis reflects our own experiences, beliefs, and biases, inevitably influencing our results.

Future work may find more comprehensive evidence of stereotypes, including stereotypes of intersectional identities, by merging the counts of semantically related terms (or, conversely, by decoupling the counts of homonyms). It could also be fruitful to infer dependency parses and compute co-occurrences between dependency paths rather than individual words to facilitate interpretation of the results (Lin and Pantel, 2001; Chambers and Jurafsky, 2009), if sparsity can be controlled.

We have focused on the identities and accompanying biases present in the SNLI dataset, in particular those created in the hypothesis elicitation process; one complement to our study would measure the demographic bias in the corpus. Correlations introduced at any level in the data collection process—including real-world correlations present in the population—are subject to scrutiny, as they may be both creations and creators of structural inequality.

As artificial intelligence absorbs the world's collective knowledge with increasing efficiency and comprehension, our collective knowledge is in turn shaped by the outputs of artificial intelligence. It is thus imperative that we understand how the bias pervading our society is encoded in artificial intelligence. This work constitutes a first step toward understanding and accounting for the social bias present in natural language inference.

Acknowledgments

We are grateful to our many reviewers who offered both candid and thoughtful feedback.

This material is based upon work supported by the JHU Human Language Technology Center of Excellence (HLTCOE), DARPA LORELEI, and the National Science Foundation Graduate Research Fellowship under Grant No. DGE-1232825. The U.S. Government is authorized to reproduce and distribute reprints for Governmental purposes. The views and conclusions contained in this publication are those of the authors and should not be interpreted as representing official policies or endorsements of DARPA, the NSF, or the U.S. Government.

References

Solon Barocas and Andrew D. Selbst. 2016. Big data's disparate impact. *California Law Review*, 104(3):671–732.

Tolga Bolukbasi, Kai-Wei Chang, James Y. Zou, Venkatesh Saligrama, and Adam T. Kalai. 2016.

Man is to computer programmer as woman is to homemaker? debiasing word embeddings. In D. D. Lee, M. Sugiyama, U. V. Luxburg, I. Guyon, and R. Garnett, editors, *Advances in Neural Information Processing Systems 29*, pages 4349–4357.

Samuel R. Bowman, Gabor Angeli, Christopher Potts, and Christopher D. Manning. 2015. A large annotated corpus for learning natural language inference. In *Proceedings of the 2015 Conference on Empirical Methods in Natural Language Processing*, pages 632–642, Lisbon, Portugal, September. Association for Computational Linguistics.

Aylin Caliskan-Islam, Joanna J. Bryson, and Arvind Narayanan. 2016. Semantics derived automatically from language corpora necessarily contain human biases. Preprint, arXiv:1608.07187.

Jordan Carpenter, Daniel Preotiuc-Pietro, Lucie Flekova, Salvatore Giorgi, Courtney Hagan, Margaret L. Kern, Anneke E. K. Buffone, Lyle Ungar, and Martin E. P. Seligman. 2017. Real men dont say "cute": Using automatic language analysis to isolate inaccurate aspects of stereotypes. to appear.

Nathanael Chambers and Dan Jurafsky. 2009. Unsupervised learning of narrative schemas and their participants. In *Proceedings of the Joint Conference of the 47th Annual Meeting of the ACL and the 4th International Joint Conference on Natural Language Processing of the AFNLP*, pages 602–610, Suntec, Singapore, August. Association for Computational Linguistics.

Kenneth Ward Church and Patrick Hanks. 1990. Word association norms mutual information, and lexicography. *Computational Linguistics, Volume 16, Number 1, March 1990*, 16(1).

Kate Crawford, Kate Miltner, and Mary L. Gray. 2014. Critiquing big data: Politics, ethics, epistemology. *International Journal of Communication*, 8:1663–1672.

Kate Crawford. 2013. Think again: Big data. http://atfp.co/2k9jaBT. Accessed 2017-01-26.

Kate Crawford. 2016. Artificial intelligence's white guy problem. http://nyti.ms/2jVLJUh. Accessed 2017-01-22.

Ted Dunning. 1993. Accurate methods for the statistics of surprise and coincidence. *Computational Linguistics, Special Issue on Using Large Corpora: I*, 19(1).

Liye Fu, Cristian Danescu-Niculescu-Mizil, and Lillian Lee. 2016. Tie-breaker: Using language models to quantify gender bias in sports journalism. In *Proceedings of the IJCAI workshop on NLP meets Journalism*.

Sture Holm. 1979. A simple sequentially rejective multiple test procedure. *Scandinavian Journal of Statistics*, 6(2):65–70.

Dirk Hovy and Shannon L. Spruit. 2016. The social impact of natural language processing. In *Proceedings of the 54th Annual Meeting of the Association for Computational Linguistics (Volume 2: Short Papers)*, pages 591–598, Berlin, Germany, August. Association for Computational Linguistics.

Dekang Lin and Patrick Pantel. 2001. Dirt – discovery of inference rules from text. In *Proceedings of the seventh ACM SIGKDD international conference on Knowledge discovery and data mining*, pages 323–328. ACM.

Emiel van Miltenburg. 2016. Stereotyping and bias in the Flickr30K dataset. In Jens Edlund, Dirk Heylen, and Patrizia Paggio, editors, *Proceedings of the Workshop on Multimodal Corpora (MMC-2016)*, pages 1–4, May.

Peter Young, Alice Lai, Micah Hodosh, and Julia Hockenmaier. 2014. From image descriptions to visual denotations. *Transactions of the Association of Computational Linguistics*, 2:67–78.

A Short Review of Ethical Challenges in Clinical Natural Language Processing

Simon Šuster[1,2], Stéphan Tulkens[1] and Walter Daelemans[1]

[1]CLiPS, University of Antwerp
[2]Antwerp University Hospital
{simon.suster,stephan.tulkens,walter.daelemans}@uantwerpen.be

Abstract

Clinical NLP has an immense potential in contributing to how clinical practice will be revolutionized by the advent of large scale processing of clinical records. However, this potential has remained largely untapped due to slow progress primarily caused by strict data access policies for researchers. In this paper, we discuss the concern for privacy and the measures it entails. We also suggest sources of less sensitive data. Finally, we draw attention to biases that can compromise the validity of empirical research and lead to socially harmful applications.

1 Introduction

The use of notes written by healthcare providers in the clinical settings has long been recognized to be a source of valuable information for clinical practice and medical research. Access to large quantities of clinical reports may help in identifying causes of diseases, establishing diagnoses, detecting side effects of beneficial treatments, and monitoring clinical outcomes (Agus, 2016; Goldacre, 2014; Murdoch and Detsky, 2013). The goal of clinical natural language processing (NLP) is to develop and apply computational methods for linguistic analysis and extraction of knowledge from free text reports (Demner-Fushman et al., 2009; Hripcsak et al., 1995; Meystre et al., 2008). But while the benefits of clinical NLP and data mining have been universally acknowledged, *progress in the development of clinical NLP techniques has been slow*. Several contributing factors have been identified, most notably difficult access to data, limited collaboration between researchers from different groups, and little sharing of implementations and trained models (Chapman et al., 2011). For comparison, in biomedical NLP, where the working data consist of biomedical research literature, these conditions have been present to a much lesser degree, and the progress has been more rapid (Cohen and Demner-Fushman, 2014). The main contributing factor to this situation has been the sensitive nature of data, whose processing may in certain situations put patient's privacy at risk.

The ethics discussion is gaining momentum in general NLP (Hovy and Spruit, 2016). We aim in this paper to gather the ethical challenges that are especially relevant for *clinical NLP*, and to stimulate discussion about those in the broader NLP community. Although enhancing privacy through restricted data access has been the norm, we do not only discuss the right to privacy, but also draw attention to the social impact and biases emanating from clinical notes and their processing. The challenges we describe here are in large part not unique to clinical NLP, and are applicable to general data science as well.

2 Sensitivity of data and privacy

Because of legal and institutional concerns arising from the sensitivity of clinical data, it is difficult for the NLP community to gain access to relevant data (Barzilay, 2016; Friedman et al., 2013). This is especially true for the researchers not connected with a healthcare organization. Corpora with transparent access policies that *are* within reach of NLP researchers exist, but are few. An often used corpus is MIMICII(I) (Johnson et al., 2016; Saeed et al., 2011). Despite its large size (covering over 58,000 hospital admissions), it is only representative of patients from a particular clinical domain (the intensive care in this case) and geographic location (a single hospital in the United States). Assuming that such a specific sample is representative of a larger population is an example of sampling bias

80

Proceedings of the First Workshop on Ethics in Natural Language Processing, pages 80–87,
Valencia, Spain, April 4th, 2017. © 2017 Association for Computational Linguistics

(we discuss further sources of bias in section 3). Increasing the size of a sample without recognizing that this sample is atypical for the general population (e.g. not all patients are critical care patients) could also increase sampling bias (Kaplan et al., 2014).[1] We need more large corpora for various medical specialties, narrative types, as well as languages and geographic areas.

Related to difficult access to raw clinical data is the lack of available *annotated* datasets for model training and benchmarking. The reality is that annotation projects do take place, but are typically constrained to a single healthcare organization. Therefore, much of the effort put into annotation is lost afterwards due to impossibility of sharing with the larger research community (Chapman et al., 2011; Fan et al., 2011). Again, exceptions are either few— e.g. THYME (Styler IV et al., 2014), a corpus annotated with temporal information—or consist of small datasets resulting from shared tasks like the i2b2 and ShARe/CLEF. In addition, stringent access policies hamper reproduction efforts, impede scientific oversight and limit collaboration, not only between institutions but also more broadly between the clinical and NLP communities.

There are known cases of datasets that had been used in published research (including reproduction) in its full form, like MiPACQ[2], Blulab, EMC Dutch Clinical Corpus and 2010 i2b2/VA (Albright et al., 2013; Kim et al., 2015; Afzal et al., 2014; Uzuner et al., 2011), but were later trimmed down or made unavailable, likely due to legal issues. Even if these datasets were still available in full, their small size is still a concern, and the comments above regarding sampling bias certainly apply. For example, a named entity recognizer trained on 2010 i2b2/VA data, which consists of 841 annotated patient records from three different specialty areas, will due to its size only contain a small portion of possible named entities. Similarly, in linking clinical concepts to an ontology, where the number of output classes is larger (Pradhan et al., 2013), the small amount of training data is a major obstacle to deployment of systems suitable for general use.

---

[1] Sampling bias could also be called selection bias; it is not inherent to the individual documents, but stems from the way these are arranged into a single corpus.

[2] The access to the MiPACQ corpus will be re-enabled in the future within the Health NLP Center for distributing linguistic annotations of clinical texts (Guergana Savova, personal communication).

2.1 Protecting the individual

Clinical notes contain detailed information about patient-clinician encounters in which patients confide not only their health complaints, but also their lifestyle choices and possibly stigmatizing conditions. This confidential relationship is legally protected in US by the HIPAA privacy rule in the case of individuals' medical data. In EU, the conditions for scientific usage of health data are set out in the General Data Protection Regulation (GDPR). Sanitization of sensitive data categories and individuals' informed consent are in the forefront of those legislative acts and bear immediate consequences for the NLP research.

The GDPR lists general principles relating to processing of personal data, including that processing must be lawful (e.g. by means of consent), fair and transparent; it must be done for explicit and legitimate purposes; and the data should be kept limited to what is necessary and as long as necessary. This is known as data minimization, and it includes sanitization. The scientific usage of health data concerns "special categories of personal data". Their processing is only allowed when the data subject gives explicit consent, or the personal data is made public by the data subject. Scientific usage is defined broadly and includes technological development, fundamental and applied research, as well as privately funded research.

Sanitization Sanitization techniques are often seen as the minimum requirement for protecting individuals' privacy when collecting data (Berman, 2002; Velupillai et al., 2015). The goal is to apply a procedure that produces a new version of the dataset that looks like the original for the purposes of data analysis, but which maintains the privacy of those in the dataset to a certain degree, depending on the technique. Documents can be sanitized by replacing, removing or otherwise manipulating the sensitive mentions such as names and geographic locations. A distinction is normally drawn between anonymization, pseudonymization and de-identification. We refer the reader to Polonetsky et al. (2016) for an excellent overview of these procedures.

Although it is a necessary first step in protecting the privacy of patients, sanitization has been criticized for several reasons. First, it affects the integrity of the data, and as a consequence, their utility (Duquenoy et al., 2008). Second, although sanitization in principle promotes data access and sharing, it may often not be sufficient to eliminate the need for consent. This is largely due to the well-known fact that original sensitive data can be re-identified through deductive disclosure (Amblard et al., 2014; De Mazancourt et al., 2015; Hardt et al., 2016; Malin et al., 2013; Tene, 2011).[3] Finally, sanitization focuses on protecting the individual, whereas ethical harms are still possible on the group level (O'Doherty et al., 2016; Taylor et al., 2017). Instead of working towards increasingly restrictive sanitization and access measures, another course of action could be to work towards heightening the perception of scientific work, emphasizing professionalism and existence of punitive measures for illegal actions (Fairfield and Shtein, 2014; Mittelstadt and Floridi, 2016).

Consent Clinical NLP typically requires a large amount of clinical records describing cases of patients with a particular condition. Although obtaining consent is a necessary first step, obtaining explicit informed consent from each patient can also compromise the research in several ways. First, obtaining consent is time consuming by itself, and it results in financial and bureaucratic burdens. It can also be infeasible due to practical reasons such as a patient's death. Next, it can introduce bias as those willing to grant consent represent a skewed population (Nyrén et al., 2014). Finally, it can be difficult to satisfy the informedness criterion: Information about the experiment sometimes can not be communicated in an unambiguous way, or experiments happen at speed that makes enacting informed consent extremely hard (Bird et al., 2016).

The alternative might be a default opt-in policy with a right to withdraw (opt-out). Here, consent can be presumed either in a broad manner—allowing unspecified future research, subject to ethical restrictions—or a tiered manner—allowing certain areas of research but not others (Mittelstadt and Floridi, 2016; Terry, 2012). Since the information about the intended use is no longer uniquely tied to each research case but is more general, this could facilitate the reuse of datasets by several research teams, without the need to ask for consent each time. The success of implementing this approach in practice is likely to depend on public trust and awareness about possible risks and oppor-

tunities. We also believe that a distinction between academic research and commercial use of clinical data should be implemented, as the public is more willing to allow research than commercial exploitation (Lawrence, 2016; van Staa et al., 2016).

Yet another possibility is open consent, in which individuals make their data publicly available. Initiatives like Personal Genome Project may have an exemplary role, however, they can only provide limited data and they represent a biased population sample (Mittelstadt and Floridi, 2016).

Secure access Since withholding data from researchers would be a dubious way of ensuring confidentiality (Berman, 2002), the research has long been active on secure access and storage of sensitive clinical data, and the balance between the degree of privacy loss and the degree of utility. This is a broad topic that is outside the scope of this article. The interested reader can find the relevant information in Dwork and Pottenger (2013), Malin et al. (2013) and Rindfleisch (1997).

Promotion of knowledge and application of best-of-class approaches to health data is seen as one of the ethical duties of researchers (Duquenoy et al., 2008; Lawrence, 2016). But for this to be put in practice, ways need to be guaranteed (e.g. with government help) to provide researchers with access to the relevant data. Researchers can also go to the data rather than have the data sent to them. It is an open question though whether medical institutions—especially those with less developed research departments—can provide the infrastructure (e.g. enough CPU and GPU power) needed in statistical NLP. Also, granting access to one healthcare organization at a time does not satisfy interoperability (cross-organizational data sharing and research), which can reduce bias by allowing for more complete input data. Interoperability is crucial for epidemiology and rare disease research, where data from one institution can not yield sufficient statistical power (Kaplan et al., 2014).

Are there less sensitive data? One criterion which may have influence on data accessibility is whether the data is about living subjects or not. The HIPAA privacy rule under certain conditions allows disclosure of personal health information of **deceased persons**, without the need to seek IRB agreement and without the need for sanitization (Huser and Cimino, 2014). It is not entirely clear

---

[3]Additionally, it may be due to organizational skepticism about the effectiveness of sanitization techniques, although it has been shown that automated de-identification systems for English perform on par with manual de-identification (Deleger et al., 2013).

though how often this possibility has been used in clinical NLP research or broader.

Next, the work on **surrogate data** has recently seen a surge in activity. Increasingly more health-related texts are produced in social media (Abbasi et al., 2014), and patient-generated data are available online. Admittedly, these may not resemble the clinical discourse, yet they bear to the same individuals whose health is documented in the clinical reports. Indeed, linking individuals' health information from online resources to their health records to improve documentation is an active line of research (Padrez et al., 2015). Although it is generally easier to obtain access to social media data, the use of social media still requires similar ethical considerations as in the clinical domain. See for example the influential study on emotional contagion in Facebook posts by Kramer et al. (2014), which has been criticized for not properly gaining prior consent from the users who were involved in the study (Schroeder, 2014).

Another way of reducing sensitivity of data and improving chances for IRB approval is to work on **derived data**. Data that can not be used to reconstruct the original text (and when sanitized, can not directly re-identify the individual) include text fragments, various statistics and trained models. Working on randomized subsets of clinical notes may also improve the chances of obtaining the data. When we only have access to trained models from disparate sources, we can refine them through ensembling and creation of silver standard corpora, cf. Rebholz-Schuhmann et al. (2011).

Finally, clinical NLP is also possible on **veterinary texts**. Records of companion animals are perhaps less likely to involve legal issues, while still amounting to a large pool of data. As an example, around 40M clinical documents from different veterinary clinics in UK and Australia are stored centrally in the VetCompass repository. First NLP steps in this direction were described in the invited talk at the Clinical NLP 2016 workshop (Baldwin, 2016).

3   Social impact and biases

Unlocking knowledge from free text in the health domain has a tremendous societal value. However, discrimination can occur when individuals or groups receive unfair treatment as a result of automated processing, which might be a result of biases in the data that were used to train models.

The question is therefore what the most important biases are and how to overcome them, not only out of ethical but also legal responsibility. Related to the question of bias is so-called *algorithm transparency* (Goodman, 2016; Kamarinou et al., 2016), as this right to explanation requires that influences of bias in training data are charted. In addition to sampling bias, which we introduced in section 2, we discuss in this section further sources of bias. Unlike sampling bias, which is a corpus-level bias, these biases here are already present in documents, and therefore hard to account for by introducing larger corpora.

Data quality   Texts produced in the clinical settings do not always tell a complete or accurate patient story (e.g. due to time constraints or due to patient treatment in different hospitals), yet important decisions can be based on them.[4] As language is situated, a lot of information may be implicit, such as the circumstances in which treatment decisions are made (Hersh et al., 2013). If we fail to detect a medical concept during automated processing, this can not necessarily be a sign of negative evidence.[5] Work on identifying and imputing missing values holds promise for reducing incompleteness, see Lipton et al. (2016) for an example in sequential modeling applied to diagnosis classification.

Reporting bias   Clinical texts may include bias coming from both patient's and clinician's reporting. Clinicians apply their subjective judgments to what is important during the encounter with patients. In other words, there is separation between, on the one side, what is observed by the clinician and communicated by the patient, and on the other, what is noted down. Cases of more serious illness may be more accurately documented as a result of clinician's bias (increased attention) and patient's recall bias. On the other hand, the cases of stigmatized diseases may include suppressed information. In the case of traffic injuries, documentation may even be distorted to avoid legal consequences (Indrayan, 2013).

---

[4]A way to increase data completeness and reduce selection bias is the use of nationwide patient registries, as known for example in Scandinavian countries (Schmidt et al., 2015).

[5]We can take timing-related "censoring" effects as an example. In event detection, events prior to the start of an observation may be missed or are uncertain, which means that the first appearance of a diagnosis in the clinical record may not coincide with the occurrence of the disease. Similarly, key events after the end of the observation may be missing (e.g. death, when it occurred in another institution).

We need to be aware that clinical notes may reflect health disparities. These can originate from prejudices held by healthcare practitioners which may impact patients' perceptions; they can also originate from communication difficulties in the case of ethnic differences (Zestcott et al., 2016). Finally, societal norms can play a role. Brady et al. (2016) find that obesity is often not documented equally well for both sexes in weight-addressing clinics. Young males are less likely to be recognized as obese, possibly due to societal norms seeing them as "stocky" as opposed to obese. Unless we are aware of such bias, we may draw premature conclusions about the impact of our results.

It is clear that during processing of clinical texts, we should strive to avoid reinforcing the biases. It is difficult to give a solution on how to actually reduce the reporting bias after the fact. One possibility might be to model it. If we see clinical reports as noisy annotations for the patient story in which information is left-out or altered, we could try to decouple the bias from the reports. Inspiration could be drawn, for example, from the work on decoupling reporting bias from annotations in visual concept recognition (Misra et al., 2016).

Observational bias Although variance in health outcome is affected by social, environmental and behavioral factors, these are rarely noted in clinical reports (Kaplan et al., 2014). The bias of missing explanatory factors because they can not be identified within the given experimental setting is also known as *the streetlight effect*. In certain cases, we could obtain important prior knowledge (e.g. demographic characteristics) from data other than clinical notes.

Dual use We have already mentioned linking personal health information from online texts to clinical records as a motivation for exploring surrogate data sources. However, this and many other applications also have potential to be applied in both beneficial and harmful ways. It is easy to imagine how sensitive information from clinical notes can be revealed about an individual who is present in social media with a known identity. More general examples of dual use are when the NLP tools are used to analyze clinical notes with a goal of determining individuals' insurability and employability.

4 Conclusion

In this paper, we reviewed some challenges that we believe are central to the work in clinical NLP.

Difficult access to data due to privacy concerns has been an obstacle to progress in the field. We have discussed how the protection of privacy through sanitization measures and the requirement for informed consent may affect the work in this domain. Perhaps, it is time to rethink the right to privacy in health in the light of recent work in ethics of big data, especially its uneasy relationship to the *right to science*, i.e. being able to benefit from science and participate in it (Tasioulas, 2016; Verbeek, 2014). We also touched upon possible sources of bias that can have an effect on the application of NLP in the health domain, and which can ultimately lead to unfair or harmful treatment.

Acknowledgments

We would like to thank Madhumita and the anonymous reviewers for useful comments. Part of this research was carried out in the framework of the Accumulate IWT SBO project, funded by the government agency for Innovation by Science and Technology (IWT).

References

Ahmed Abbasi, Donald Adjeroh, Mark Dredze, Michael J. Paul, Fatemeh Mariam Zahedi, Huimin Zhao, Nitin Walia, Hemant Jain, Patrick Sanvanson, Reza Shaker, et al. 2014. Social media analytics for smart health. *IEEE Intelligent Systems*, 29(2):60–80.

Zubair Afzal, Ewoud Pons, Ning Kang, Miriam C.J.M. Sturkenboom, Martijn J. Schuemie, and Jan A. Kors. 2014. ContextD: an algorithm to identify contextual properties of medical terms in a Dutch clinical corpus. *BMC Bioinformatics*, 15(1):373.

David B. Agus. 2016. Give Up Your Data to Cure Disease, The New York Times, February 6. `https://goo.gl/0REG0n`.

D. Albright, A. Lanfranchi, A. Fredriksen, W. F. Styler, C. Warner, J. D. Hwang, J. D. Choi, D. Dligach, R. D. Nielsen, J. Martin, W. Ward, M. Palmer, and G. K. Savova. 2013. Towards comprehensive syntactic and semantic annotations of the clinical narrative. *Journal of the American Medical Informatics Association*, 20(5):922–930.

Maxime Amblard, Karën Fort, Michel Musiol, and Manuel Rebuschi. 2014. L'impossibilité de l'anonymat dans le cadre de l'analyse du discours. In *Journée ATALA éthique et TAL*.

Timothy Baldwin. 2016. VetCompass: Clinical Natural Language Processing for Animal Health. Clinical NLP 2016 keynote. `https://goo.gl/ScGFa2`.

Regina Barzilay. 2016. How NLP can help cure cancer? NAACL'16 keynote. `https://goo.gl/hi5nrq`.

Jules J. Berman. 2002. Confidentiality issues for medical data miners. *Artificial Intelligence in Medicine*, 26(1):25–36.

Sarah Bird, Solon Barocas, Kate Crawford, Fernando Diaz, and Hanna Wallach. 2016. Exploring or Exploiting? Social and Ethical Implications of Autonomous Experimentation in AI. In *Workshop on Fairness, Accountability, and Transparency in Machine Learning*.

Cassandra C. Brady, Vidhu V. Thaker, Todd Lingren, Jessica G. Woo, Stephanie S. Kennebeck, Bahram Namjou-Khales, Ashton Roach, Jonathan P. Bickel, Nandan Patibandla, Guergana K. Savova, et al. 2016. Suboptimal Clinical Documentation in Young Children with Severe Obesity at Tertiary Care Centers. *International Journal of Pediatrics*, 2016.

Wendy W. Chapman, Prakash M. Nadkarni, Lynette Hirschman, Leonard W. D'Avolio, Guergana K. Savova, and Özlem Uzuner. 2011. Overcoming barriers to NLP for clinical text: the role of shared tasks and the need for additional creative solutions. *Journal of the American Medical Informatics Association*, 18(5):540–543.

Kevin Bretonnel Cohen and Dina Demner-Fushman. 2014. *Biomedical natural language processing*. John Benjamins Publishing Company.

Hugues De Mazancourt, Alain Couillault, Gilles Adda, and Gaëlle Recourcé. 2015. Faire du TAL sur des données personnelles : un oxymore ? In *TALN 2015*.

Louise Deleger, Katalin Molnar, Guergana Savova, Fei Xia, Todd Lingren, Qi Li, Keith Marsolo, Anil Jegga, Megan Kaiser, Laura Stoutenborough, and Imre Solti. 2013. Large-scale evaluation of automated clinical note de-identification and its impact on information extraction. *Journal of the American Medical Informatics Association*, 20(1):84.

Dina Demner-Fushman, Wendy W. Chapman, and Clement J. McDonald. 2009. What can natural language processing do for clinical decision support? *Journal of Biomedical Informatics*, 42(5):760–772.

Penny Duquenoy, Carlisle George, and Anthony Solomonides. 2008. Considering something ELSE: Ethical, legal and socio-economic factors in medical imaging and medical informatics. *Computer Methods and Programs in Biomedicine*, 92(3):227–237.

Cynthia Dwork and Rebecca Pottenger. 2013. Toward practicing privacy. *Journal of the American Medical Informatics Association*, 20(1):102–108.

Joshua Fairfield and Hannah Shtein. 2014. Big data, big problems: Emerging issues in the ethics of data science and journalism. *Journal of Mass Media Ethics*, 29(1):38–51.

Jung-wei Fan, Rashmi Prasad, Romme M. Yabut, Richard M. Loomis, Daniel S. Zisook, John E. Mattison, and Yang Huang. 2011. Part-of-speech tagging for clinical text: wall or bridge between institutions. In *AMIA Annual Symposium Proceedings*.

Carol Friedman, Thomas C. Rindflesch, and Milton Corn. 2013. Natural language processing: state of the art and prospects for significant progress, a workshop sponsored by the National Library of Medicine. *Journal of Biomedical Informatics*, 46(5):765–773.

Ben Goldacre. 2014. The NHS plan to share our medical data can save lives but must be done right. `https://goo.gl/MH2eC0`.

Bryce W. Goodman. 2016. A Step Towards Accountable Algorithms?: Algorithmic Discrimination and the European Union General Data Protection. In *NIPS Symposium on Machine Learning and the Law*.

Moritz Hardt, Eric Price, and Nati Srebro. 2016. Equality of opportunity in supervised learning. In *NIPS*.

William R. Hersh, Mark G. Weiner, Peter J. Embi, Judith R. Logan, Philip R.O. Payne, Elmer V. Bernstam, Harold P. Lehmann, George Hripcsak, Timothy H. Hartzog, James J. Cimino, and Joel H. Saltz. 2013. Caveats for the use of operational electronic health record data in comparative effectiveness research. *Medical care*, 51(8 0 3).

Dirk Hovy and Shannon L. Spruit. 2016. The social impact of natural language processing. In *Proceedings of the 54th Annual Meeting of the Association for Computational Linguistics (Volume 2: Short Papers)*, pages 591–598, Berlin, Germany, August. Association for Computational Linguistics.

George Hripcsak, Carol Friedman, Philip O. Alderson, William DuMouchel, Stephen B. Johnson, and Paul D. Clayton. 1995. Unlocking clinical data from narrative reports: a study of natural language processing. *Annals of internal medicine*, 122(9):681–688.

Vojtech Huser and James J. Cimino. 2014. Don't take your EHR to heaven, donate it to science: legal and research policies for EHR post mortem. *Journal of the American Medical Informatics Association*, 21(1):8–12.

Abhaya Indrayan. 2013. Varieties of bias to guard against. `https://goo.gl/SqnuZY`.

Alistair EW Johnson, Tom J. Pollard, Lu Shen, Li-wei H. Lehman, Mengling Feng, Mohammad Ghassemi, Benjamin Moody, Peter Szolovits, Leo Anthony Celi, and Roger G. Mark. 2016. MIMIC-III, a freely accessible critical care database. *Scientific data*, 3.

Dimitra Kamarinou, Christopher Millard, and Jatinder Singh. 2016. Machine Learning with Personal Data. *Queen Mary School of Law Legal Studies Research Paper*, (247/2016).

Robert M. Kaplan, David A. Chambers, and Russell E. Glasgow. 2014. Big data and large sample size: a cautionary note on the potential for bias. *Clinical and translational science*, 7(4):342–346.

Youngjun Kim, Ellen Riloff, and John F. Hurdle. 2015. A study of concept extraction across different types of clinical notes. In *AMIA Annual Symposium Proceedings*, volume 2015, page 737. American Medical Informatics Association.

Adam D.I. Kramer, Jamie E. Guillory, and Jeffrey T. Hancock. 2014. Experimental evidence of massive-scale emotional contagion through social networks. *Proceedings of the National Academy of Sciences*, 111(24):8788–8790.

Neil Lawrence. 2016. Data Analysis, NHS and Industrial Partners. https://goo.gl/rRIcu5.

Zachary C. Lipton, David Kale, and Randall Wetzel. 2016. Modeling Missing Data in Clinical Time Series with RNNs. *arXiv preprint arXiv:1606.04130*.

Bradley A. Malin, Khaled El Emam, and Christine M. O'Keefe. 2013. Biomedical data privacy: problems, perspectives, and recent advances. *Journal of the American Medical Informatics Association*, 20(1):2–6.

Stéphane M. Meystre, Guergana K. Savova, Karin C. Kipper-Schuler, John F. Hurdle, et al. 2008. Extracting information from textual documents in the electronic health record: a review of recent research. *Yearbook of Medical Informatics*, 35:128–44.

Ishan Misra, C. Lawrence Zitnick, Margaret Mitchell, and Ross B. Girshick. 2016. Seeing through the Human Reporting Bias: Visual Classifiers from Noisy Human-Centric Labels. In *The IEEE Conference on Computer Vision and Pattern Recognition*.

Brent Daniel Mittelstadt and Luciano Floridi. 2016. The ethics of big data: current and foreseeable issues in biomedical contexts. *Science and engineering ethics*, 22(2):303–341.

Travis B. Murdoch and Allan S. Detsky. 2013. The inevitable application of big data to health care. *JAMA*, 309(13):1351–1352.

Olof Nyrén, Magnus Stenbeck, and Henrik Grönberg. 2014. The European Parliament proposal for the new EU General Data Protection Regulation may severely restrict European epidemiological research. *European Journal of Epidemiology*, 29(4):227–230.

Kieran C. O'Doherty, Emily Christofides, Jeffery Yen, Heidi Beate Bentzen, Wylie Burke, Nina Hallowell, Barbara A. Koenig, and Donald J. Willison. 2016. If you build it, they will come: unintended future uses of organised health data collections. *BMC Medical Ethics*, 17(1).

Kevin A. Padrez, Lyle Ungar, Hansen Andrew Schwartz, Robert J. Smith, Shawndra Hill, Tadas Antanavicius, Dana M. Brown, Patrick Crutchley, David A. Asch, and Raina M. Merchant. 2015. Linking social media and medical record data: a study of adults presenting to an academic, urban emergency department. *BMJ quality & safety*.

Jules Polonetsky, Omer Tene, and Kelsey Finch. 2016. Shades of Gray: Seeing the Full Spectrum of Practical Data De-identification. *Santa Clara Law Review*, 56(3).

Sameer Pradhan, Noemie Elhadad, Brett R. South, David Martinez, Amy Vogel, Hanna Suominen, Wendy W. Chapman, and Guergana Savova. 2013. Task 1: Share/clef ehealth evaluation lab. In *Online Working Notes of CLEF*.

Dietrich Rebholz-Schuhmann, Antonio Jimeno Yepes, Chen Li, et al. 2011. Assessment of NER solutions against the first and second CALBC Silver Standard Corpus. *Journal of Biomedical Semantics*, 2(5):S11.

Thomas C. Rindfleisch. 1997. Privacy, information technology, and health care. *Communications of the ACM*, 40(8):92–100.

Mohammed Saeed, Mauricio Villarroel, Andrew T. Reisner, Gari Clifford, Li-Wei Lehman, George Moody, Thomas Heldt, Tin H. Kyaw, Benjamin Moody, and Roger G. Mark. 2011. Multiparameter Intelligent Monitoring in Intensive Care II (MIMIC-II): a public-access intensive care unit database. *Critical care medicine*, 39(5):952.

Morten Schmidt, S.A. Schmidt, Jakob Lynge Sandegaard, Vera Ehrenstein, Lars Pedersen, and Henrik Toft Sørensen. 2015. The danish national patient registry: a review of content, data quality, and research potential. *Clinical Epidemiology*, 7(449):e490.

Ralph Schroeder. 2014. Big data and the brave new world of social media research. *Big Data & Society*, 1(2):2053951714563194.

William Styler IV, Steven Bethard, Sean Finan, Martha Palmer, Sameer Pradhan, Piet de Groen, Brad Erickson, Timothy Miller, Chen Lin, Guergana Savova, and James Pustejovsky. 2014. Temporal annotation in the clinical domain. *Transactions of the Association for Computational Linguistics*, 2:143–154.

John Tasioulas. 2016. Van Hasselt Lecture 2016: Big Data, Human Rights and the Ethics of Scientific Research. https://goo.gl/QREHUN.

Linnet Taylor, Luciano Floridi, and Bart van der Sloot. 2017. *Group Privacy: New Challenges of Data Technologies*. Springer International Publishing.

Omer Tene. 2011. Privacy: The new generations. *International Data Privacy Law*, 1(1):15–27.

Nicolas P. Terry. 2012. Protecting patient privacy in the age of big data. *University of Missouri-Kansas City Law Review*, 81(2).

Özlem Uzuner, Brett R. South, Shuying Shen, and Scott L. DuVall. 2011. 2010 i2b2/va challenge on concepts, assertions, and relations in clinical text. *Journal of the American Medical Informatics Association*, 18(5):552–556.

Tjeerd-Pieter van Staa, Ben Goldacre, Iain Buchan, and Liam Smeeth. 2016. Big health data: the need to earn public trust. *BMJ*, 354:i3636.

Sumithra Velupillai, D. Mowery, Brett R. South, Maria Kvist, and Hercules Dalianis. 2015. Recent advances in clinical natural language processing in support of semantic analysis. *Yearbook of Medical Informatics*, 10:183–193.

Peter-Paul Verbeek. 2014. *Op de vleugels van Icarus*. Lemniscaat.

Colin A. Zestcott, Irene V. Blair, and Jeff Stone. 2016. Examining the presence, consequences, and reduction of implicit bias in health care: A narrative review. *Group Processes & Intergroup Relations*.

Goal-Oriented Design for Ethical Machine Learning and NLP

Tyler Schnoebelen
Decoded AI
`tyler@aya.yale.edu`

Abstract

The argument made in this paper is that to act ethically in machine learning and NLP requires focusing on goals. NLP projects are often classificatory systems that deal with human subjects, which means that goals from people affected by the systems should be included. The paper takes as its core example a model that detects criminality, showing the problems of training data, categories, and outcomes. The paper is oriented to the kinds of critiques on power and the reproduction of inequality that are found in social theory, but it also includes concrete suggestions on how to put goal-oriented design into practice.

1 Introduction

Ethics asks us to consider how we live and how we discern right and wrong in particular circumstances. Ethicists differ on what they consider fundamental: the actor's moral character and dispositions (virtue ethics), the duties and obligations of the actor given their role (deontology), or the outcomes of the actions (consequentialism). Computational linguists do not need to answer a question of primacy, but the three themes of virtues, duties, and consequences do need to be considered.

This paper uses goals to draw out each of the three themes. Goals are states of affairs that people would like to achieve, maintain, or avoid in the face of changes and obstacles. The use of "goals" here is expansive so that it includes not just designers and users of a system, but also those who are (or would be) affected by the system.

NLP practitioners design and build technologies that connect to law, finance, education and main other domains that substantially affect peo-ple, often those with less access to resources and information. Privileged positions come with responsibilities. Namely, to recognize that systems affect people unevenly. To design with virtues, duties, and consequences in mind is to recognize the limits of one's perspective and then design systems with these limitations in mind.

2 Wicked problems

Simple NLP problems and simple NLP projects require you to identify stakeholders, articulate their goals, and build a plan. Another category of complex problems includes those that are only actually complex until they are decomposed into multiple simple problems.

A third category is wicked problems: those in which you can articulate goals but they are fundamentally in conflict (Rittel and Webber, 1973). For example, a traffic planner wants to build a highway because they want less congestion. But community members don't want their neighborhood cut in half because it destroys their goal of affiliation.

Wicked problems have no definitive solution because there are multiple valid viewpoints: you cannot take for granted that there is a single objective that will let you judge your solution as correct and finished.

We often shield ourselves from ethical problems by ignoring populations who would throw light on a project's wicked complexity. This is a good indication of an ethical problem: turning a blind eye to people who will be affected by the system but who are difficult to reach or who may have inconveniently conflicting goals.

3 An easy unethical project

In order to illustrate the ethical implications of goal-oriented design, let's take an example from machine learning that most readers will find straight-forwardly problematic. Here are two conclusions from an abstract on automated infer-

Proceedings of the First Workshop on Ethics in Natural Language Processing, pages 88–93,
Valencia, Spain, April 4th, 2017. © 2017 Association for Computational Linguistics

ence of criminality using faces (Wu and Zhang, 2016):

> All four classifiers perform consistently well and produce evidence for the validity of automated face-induced inference on criminality… Also, we find some discriminating structural features for predicting criminality, such as lip curvature, eye inner corner distance, and the so-called nose-mouth angle.

Can the goal for this project be simply stated? It seems to be, "Improve safety by having computers automatically detect the criminality of people's faces." This goal inherently categorizes people by degrees of criminality based on physical characteristics. It takes the perspective of the safety-minded, yet anyone categorized as criminal has legitimate goals to consider. Regardless of how many iterations the models go through, meeting the main goal will always create a group of criminal-looking people who will not agree with that definition and its consequences. This is a wicked problem.

In the United States, people of color have radically different experiences with the criminal justice system than white people. Attempting to use U.S. police data for training will not work: the criminal justice system in the U.S. is systemically biased, as can be seen in Hetey et al. (2016), which shows racial biases in Oakland police stops, searches, handcuffings, and arrests.

The Hetey et al. data is not merely counts of police actions on different kinds of civilians; it is also an examination of the differences in the aggressiveness of the language used by the police with African-American men. In other parts of the justice system, language—non-standard dialects—causes crucial testimony to be ignored (Rickford and King, 2016). Linguistic profiling is common in housing and many other areas (Baugh, 2016).

Ignoring the social and ideological uses of language means ignoring some of the way NLP techniques are applied. There are multiple companies working on models that use language data to decide who to give loans to. As with police stops, the features detected are not intentionally racially biased but they have the same effect in excluding specific individual from access to credit because of who they look, sound, or read like.

Such wicked problems are adjudicated by acts of authority. Neither wicked problems nor adjudication are inherently unethical. But dismissing the claims and goals of affected populations usually is. Such populations get hit by a double whammy: they are unlikely to be represented by technologists and other stakeholders and they have much less room to maneuver in whatever system is built.

4 The trouble with training data

The data for Wu and Zhang (2016) comes from China and includes only men, but it is ethically safer to assume that data from the ministry of public security and various police departments is biased than it is to assume that it is balanced and representative.

Interrogating training data is important for building effective machine learning models and it's also important for building ethical ones. Machine learning techniques depend upon training data, which causes two kinds of problems. The first problem is that whatever you build, it's biased towards the contexts that you can sample and the ways you get it annotated. Some populations are overrepresented and some are underrepresented.

The second problem with training data is that whatever your categories are, they are wrong. Categories can still be meaningful and useful, but it is a mistake to consider them to be natural or uncontestable. As Bowker and Star (1999) discuss, categorization always valorizes some point of view and erases others.

For example, gender detection is common in NLP. These projects typically begin with the assumption that a binary division of humans is relevant. But as Bamman et al. (2014) show, even binary models with high accuracy are descriptively inadequate. This is also the central point of intersectionality: people are not just the sum of different demographic characteristics (Crenshaw, 1989).

Goals for binary-gender detection projects are generally couched in terms of understanding people. But to what end and in which ways? Making goals explicit can help uncover latent biases in your mental model of what kind of people there are in the world and how you believe they move through it.

5 What you think of people

The ethics you adopt has a lot to do with what you think of human beings. In the case of Wu and Zhang (2016), tying facial structure to criminality suggests that some humans are "bad".

Plenty of serious thinkers have considered people to be fundamentally good. For example, that's what Confucian thinkers like Mencius and Wang Yang Ming believed (Chan, 2008).

Evidence suggests that individual choices—our goodness and our badness—are strongly dependent upon context. For example, what happens when you give theology students a chance to help a stranger? Darley and Batson (1973) demonstrate how localized the choices are: students in a rush to give a talk do not help—even when the talk they are hurrying to is about The Good Samaritan.

People commonly remember psychologist Walter Mischel's Marshmallow Test as proof that traits like self-control are destiny: certain kinds of children resist taking a marshmallow and they grow up to be successful. But the idea that people have durable traits is precisely not Mischel's conclusion. Rather, it is that people are fundamentally flexible: if you reframe how you think about a situation, you change how you react to it (Mischel, 2014).

People seem stable and consistent because they tend to be put in the same situations; in those situations they have the same role, and the same kinds of relationships to you. How do we keep getting into the same situations? The answer requires us to appreciate individual's agentive choices as well as to recognize the social structures that give rise to and constrain those choices. The systems we build enable, enforce, and constrain choices.

Defining goals, building models, and adjudicating conflict are clear exercises of power. But the powerful have another benefit. "Power means not *having* to act, or more accurately, the capacity to be more negligent and casual about any single performance" (Scott, 1990). Systems are not equally hospitable to all people and require some to perform acrobatics and contortions to get by.

Deontologists are the ethicists who focus on duties and obligations. As people in relative positions of power, we have an outsized impact on systems and therefore greater obligations to the people who are marginalized or victimized by them (Kamm, 2008).

6   Outcomes and reiterations

Utilitarians are consequentialist ethicists famous for focusing on the goodness of outcomes (Foot, 1967; Taurek, 1977; Parfit, 1978; Thomson, 1985). Outcomes are complicated: let's say criminal recognition worked. The odds are that it would make the world marginally safer for many people. But none of us have built a system with zero false positives. So a "working" criminal recognition system would make the lives of some innocent people who were treated as criminals much, much worse. Goal-oriented ethical design requires thinking about outcomes, with a special focus on which systems are created and maintained, and how disparate the outcomes are for the people subject to the system.

To think ethically is to think self-skeptically: "What is the worst possible way this technology could be used and how sound are my mitigation strategies?" Recently, a number of American consulting firms attempted to answer a Request for Proposals from an oil-rich country that wanted to understand social media sentiment on government projects like the building of a new stadium. But stated and elicited goals and use cases are not necessarily how something will be used or even what is actually desired.

The RFP stayed open for over a year, suggesting that consulting firms had difficulty finding NLP practitioners willing to take the stated goal at face value. It has subsequently been shown that, in fact, this project was intended to identify dissidents. The ability to identify sentiment about government projects can give a voice to people about those projects, which seems positive. But the worst-case scenario is that it can find people who are negative about the government for the government to track, regulate, discipline, and punish.

Considering the system-wide consequences of models leads us back to criminality recognition. It is one thing to identify an actual perpetrator of a crime, but to identify someone who has not committed a crime is to invite harassment from the police. Corporations could also use these models to make it hard to get a job, go into stores, or open bank accounts. In short, it could become nearly impossible for certain innocent individuals to operate within the law.

Systems shape the choices people are allowed to make and therefore they shape the people—not just the people suspected of being criminals, but everyone else, too. People who are not identified as criminals by the system may come to believe it works and that others who look bad are bad. In social theory terms, "subjects regulated by such structures are, by virtue of being subjected to them, formed, defined, and reproduced in accordance with the requirements of those structures" (Butler, 1999).

It seems handy to have something else make choices that we probably would have made anyhow. Even without any algorithms, there are more choice points in our lives than we can possibly give thoughtful consideration to. That's one reason why status quos maintain themselves: we tend to do the things we've tended to do (Bourdieu, 1977; Giddens, 1984; Butler, 1999).

The more consistent our systems are and the more rapidly they converge on consistency, the more they are likely to reiterate—and possibly exaggerate—what already exists. The actions a system takes may be small. But the ramifications may not be, as is the case with news recommendation engines operating in an already partisan context.

Routines in industry often serve to reduce anxiety. But *whose* anxiety? Each human or algorithmic choice offers the possibility of disturbing the status quo, but the vast majority of the time, they reproduce what came before. By considering the goals of people affected by the systems we build, we have a better chance of seeing how much people have to conform or contort themselves to receive benefits and avoid problems. In turn, these perspectives give us a better ability to abandon projects or reconceive them to give people ways of thwarting and hindering unethical instruments and effects of power.

7 Practical recommendations

NLP practitioners are used to thinking critically about models and algorithms. Taking an ethical stance means looking at goals just as critically, which in turn requires deeper interrogation of the training data, the categories, and the effects of the system. It also means seriously considering how the outputs of the specific system being built become inputs for other systems. But how does one do this other than "thinking harder?"

Perform a premortem (Klein, 2007). In a premortem, a team at the beginning of a project imagines the project was completed and turned out to be a complete disaster. They narrate, individually and collectively, the stories of the failures. This is a generally useful way of identifying weaknesses in design, planning, and implementation. Premortems can also be used to diagnose ethical problems. Ideally, participants approach the premortem from a place of true concern for people, but premortems can be helpful even if participants are orienting to problems of human resources, public relations, and customer service.

Ask for justifications. There are lots of things you could be doing, but why do managers and executives want to do *this*? Any of the following replies should put you on Ethical High Alert:

1. Everyone else is doing it and we have to keep up
2. No one else is doing it so we can lead the pack
3. It makes money
4. It's legal
5. It's inevitable

Projects that get these responses may be ethical, but these are terrible justifications in any event (for more on problematic justifications see Pope and Vasquez, 2016). You may get an idea because competitors are doing it and you certainly want to check on legality, but we shouldn't confuse wishes, plans, and circumstances with justifications. Even if markets and the law worked to promote ethical behavior (a big if), they will necessarily lag behind new ethical problems that computational linguists, data scientists and A.I. practitioners bring forth (Moor, 1985).

List the people affected. Which groups are specifically represented in the training data and which ones are left out? Who will use the system? Who will the system itself affect, distinguishing people immediately affected from those affected as the system outputs become inputs to other systems. How awful is it to be a false positive or a false negative? Who is most/least vulnerable to the negative effects of the system? The point of making a list is to keep technical models from becoming unmoored from human beings.

Is it a WMD? Cathy O'Neill describes the three characteristics of Weapons of Math Destruction: they are opaque to the people they affect, they affect important aspects of life (education, housing, work, justice, finance/credit), and they can do real damage.

What values are enshrined? We orient ethics around dilemmas of preventing harm, but it is also worth asking whether our systems bring about good. Which values are served and which are eschewed by a planned technology? A noncomprehensive list to consider: freedom, peace, security, dignity, respect, justice, equality.

Principles and values come into conflict—there's even an adage, "it's not a principle unless it costs you something". For example, a project centered on security may have negative implications for equality. Conflict is not to be avoided, it's to be made explicit—and most difficultly, it is to be made explicit to people affected. Sweeping concerns under the rug or otherwise obfuscating them are convenient solutions, not ethical ones.

8 Conclusion

Technology does not just appear and impact society; it is the product of society, carrying with it the baggage of what has come before and usually reproducing it, discriminatory warts and all. Technology does not just appear: we make it.

But as Bruno Latour points out, "If there is one thing toward which 'making' does not lead, it is to the concept of a human actor fully in command" (Latour, 2003). At a construction site you can witness builders who may have mastery but certainly not full control: materials resist, personnel get sick, the weather won't cooperate, the planning department requires another form, the client is late with payment but fresh with a new idea.

Mastery and expertise do not imply control over objects and people; they imply practice and the ability to translate that practice into both plans and improvisations.

An important aspect of virtue ethics is practicing and developing dispositions towards moral choices (Annas, 1998). To develop habits of bravery, justice, self-control, and other virtues means practicing them. By focusing on goals, we focus on the connections between systems and people. We talk to people about their goals and their situations. We reason through surface conflicts that can be solved and discover where compromise is impossible so that we know when to reimagine our systems and when to abandon them. Done consistently, this kind of design develops habits of thinking and feeling that enable and refine our capacity to be ethical and build ethically.

It is necessary to acknowledge and address Crawford (2016)'s critique: most of the people who build technology come from privileged backgrounds, which makes it difficult for our imagination and our empathy to extend out to everyone our systems will affect.

The implication extends us beyond what is comfortable for many people and organizations: to not only to attend to issues of diversity and representation, but to go out and educate communities who will be affected so that they, too, can voice their goals and values. In other words, the practice of ethical design among NLP experts leads to greater ethical capacity—but ethics are too important to be left only to experts.

References

Julia Annas. 1998. Virtue and eudaimonism. *Social Philosophy and Policy*, 15(1):37–55.

David Bamman, Jacob Eisenstein, and Tyler Schnoebelen. 2014. Gender identity and lexical variation in social media. *Journal of Sociolinguistics*, 18(2):135–160.

John Baugh. 2016. Linguistic Profiling and Discrimination. *The Oxford Handbook of Language and Society*:349–368.

Pierre Bourdieu. 1977. *Outline of a Theory of Practice*. Cambridge University Press, Cambridge, England.

Geoffrey C. Bowker and Susan Leigh Star. 1999. *Sorting things out: classification and its consequences*. MIT Press, Cambridge, MA.

Judith Butler. 1999. *Gender Trouble*. Routledge, New York.

Wing-tsit Chan. 2008. *A source book in Chinese philosophy*. Princeton University Press.

Kate Crawford. 2016. Artificial Intelligence's White Guy Problem. *New York Times*.

Kimberle Crenshaw. 1989. Demarginalizing the intersection of race and sex: A black feminist critique of antidiscrimination doctrine, feminist theory and anti racist politics. *University of Chicago Legal Forum*:139–167.

John M. Darley and C. Daniel Batson. 1973. " From Jerusalem to Jericho": A study of situational and dispositional variables in helping behavior. *Journal of personality and social psychology*, 27(1):100–108.

Philippa Foot. 1967. The problem of abortion and the doctrine of double effect. *Oxford Review*, 5:5–15.

Anthony Giddens. 1984. *The Constitution of Society: Outline of the Theory of Structuration*. University of California Press, Berkeley, CA.

Rebecca C Hetey, Benoît Monin, Amrita Maitreyi, and Jennifer L Eberhardt. 2016. Data for Change: A Statistical Analysis of Police Stops, Searches, Handcuffings, and Arrests in Oakland, Calif., 2013-2014.

Frances Myrna Kamm. 2008. *Intricate ethics: Rights, responsibilities, and permissible harm*. Oxford University Press.

Gary Klein. 2007. Performing a project premortem. *Harvard Business Review*, 85(9):18–19.

Bruno Latour. 2003. The Promises of Constructivism. In *Chasing technoscience: Matrix for materiality*. Indiana University Press, Bloomington, IN.

Walter Mischel. 2014. *The marshmallow test: understanding self-control and how to master it*. Random House.

James H. Moor. 1985. What is computer ethics? *Metaphilosophy*, 16(4):266–275.

Derek Parfit. 1978. Innumerate ethics. *Philosophy & Public Affairs*:285–301.

Kenneth S. Pope and Melba JT Vasquez. 2016. *Ethics in psychotherapy and counseling: A practical guide*. John Wiley & Sons.

John R. Rickford and Sharese King. 2016. Language and linguistics on trial: Hearing Rachel Jeantel (and other vernacular speakers) in the courtroom and beyond. *Language*, 92(4):948–988.

Horst WJ Rittel and Melvin M. Webber. 1973. Dilemmas in a general theory of planning. *Policy sciences*, 4(2):155–169.

James Scott. 1990. *Domination and the Arts of Resistance: Hidden Transcripts*. Yale University Press, New Haven, CT.

John M. Taurek. 1977. Should the numbers count? *Philosophy & Public Affairs*:293–316.

Judith Jarvis Thomson. 1985. The trolley problem. *The Yale Law Journal*, 94(6):1395–1415.

Xiaolin Wu and Xi Zhang. 2016. Automated Inference on Criminality using Face Images. *arXiv:1611.04135 [cs]*, November. arXiv: 1611.04135.

Ethical Research Protocols for Social Media Health Research

Adrian Benton
Center for Language and
Speech Processing
Johns Hopkins University
adrian@cs.jhu.edu

Glen Coppersmith
Qntfy
glen@qntfy.com

Mark Dredze
Human Language Technology
Center of Excellence
Johns Hopkins University
mdredze@jhu.edu

Abstract

Social media have transformed data-driven research in political science, the social sciences, health, and medicine. Since health research often touches on sensitive topics that relate to ethics of treatment and patient privacy, similar ethical considerations should be acknowledged when using social media data in health research. While much has been said regarding the ethical considerations of social media research, health research leads to an additional set of concerns. We provide practical suggestions in the form of guidelines for researchers working with social media data in health research. These guidelines can inform an IRB proposal for researchers new to social media health research.

1 Introduction

Widely available social media data – including Twitter, Facebook, discussion forums and other platforms – have emerged as grounds for data-driven research in several disciplines, such as political science (Tumasjan et al., 2011), public health (Paul and Dredze, 2011), economics (Bollen et al., 2011), and the social sciences in general (Schwartz et al., 2013). Researchers have access to massive corpora of online conversations about a range of topics as never before. What once required painstaking data collection or controlled experiments, can now be quickly collected and analyzed with computational tools. The impact of such data is especially significant in health and medicine, where advances in our understanding of disease transmission, medical decision making, human behavior and public perceptions of health topics could directly lead to saving lives and improving quality of life.

Health research often touches on sensitive topics that relate to ethics of treatment and patient privacy. Based on decades of research experience and public debate, the research community has developed an extensive set of guidelines surrounding ethical practices that guide modern research programs. These guidelines focus on human subjects research, which involves research with data from living individuals. The core principles of human subjects research were codified in the Belmont Report (National Commission, 1978), which serves as the essential reference for institutional review boards (IRBs) in the United States. IRB guidelines include a range of exemptions from full review for research protocols that consider certain types of data or populations. For example, research projects that rely on online data sources may be exempt since the data are publicly available. Historically, public data exemptions included previously compiled databases containing human subject data that have entered the public domain. The recent proposal to modernize the U.S. Common Rule for the Protection of Human Subjects acknowledges the widespread use of social media for health research, but does little to clarify the ethical obligations of social media health researchers, generally reducing oversight necessary for research placed under expedited review (National Research Council, 2014).

A more participatory research model is emerging in social, behavioral, and biomedical research, one in which potential research subjects and communities express their views about the value and acceptability of research studies. This participatory model has emerged alongside a broader trend in American

Proceedings of the First Workshop on Ethics in Natural Language Processing, pages 94–102,
Valencia, Spain, April 4th, 2017. © 2017 Association for Computational Linguistics

society, facilitated by the widespread use of social media, in which Americans are increasingly sharing identifiable personal information and expect to be involved in decisions about how to further share the personal information, including health-related information that they have voluntarily chosen to provide.

In general, it provides a more permissive definition of what qualifies as exempt research. It suggests exempting observational studies of publicly available data where appropriate measures are taken to secure sensitive data, and demonstrably benign behavioral intervention studies.

The intersection of these ethics traditions and social media research pose new challenges for the formulation of research protocols. These challenges are further complicated by the discipline of the researchers conducting these studies. Health research is typically conducted by researchers with training in medical topics, who have an understanding of human subjects research protocols and issues regarding IRBs. In contrast, social media research may be conducted by computer scientists and engineers, disciplines that are typically unaccustomed to these guidelines (Conway, 2014).

Although this dichotomy is not absolute, many researchers are still unclear on what measures are required by an IRB before analyzing social media data for health research. Conversations by the authors with colleagues have revealed a wide range of "standard practice" from IRBs at different institutions. In fact, the (excellent) anonymous reviews of this paper stated conflicting perceptions on this point. One claimed that online data did not necessarily qualify for an exemption if account handles were included, whereas another reviewer states that health research solely on public social media data did not constitute human subjects research.

The meeting of non-traditional health researchers, health topics, and non-traditional data sets has led to questions regarding ethical and privacy concerns of such research. This document is meant to serve as a guide for researchers who are unfamiliar with health-related human subjects research and want to craft a research proposal that complies with requirements of most IRBs or ethics committees.

How are we to apply the ethical principles of human subjects research to projects that analyze publicly available social media posts? What protections or restrictions apply to the billions of Twitter posts publicly available and accessible by anyone in the world? Are tweets that contain personal information – including information about the author or individuals known to the author – subject to the same exemptions from full IRB review that have traditionally been granted to public data sources? Are corpora that include public data from millions of individuals subject to the same informed consent requirements of traditional human subjects research? Should researchers produce annotations on top of these datasets and share them publicly with the research community? The answers to these and other questions influence the design of research protocols regarding social media data.

Ethical issues surrounding social media research have been discussed in numerous papers, a survey of which can be found in McKee (2013) and Conway (2014). Additionally, Mikal et al. (2016) used focus groups to understand the perceived ethics of using social media data for mental health research. Our goal in this paper is complementary to these ethics surveys: we want to provide practical guidance for researchers working with social media data in human subjects research. We, ourselves, are not ethicists; we are practitioners who have spent time considering practical suggestions in consultation with experts in ethics and privacy. These guidelines encapsulate our experience implementing privacy and ethical ideals and principles.

These guidelines are not meant as a fixed set of standards, rather they are a starting point for researchers who want to ensure compliance with ethical and privacy guidelines, and they can be included with an IRB application as a reflection of current best practices. We intend these to be a skeleton upon which formal research protocols can be developed, and precautions when working with these data. Readers will also note the wide range of suggestions we provide, which reflects the wide range of research and associated risk. Finally, we include software packages to support implementation of some of these guidelines.

For each guideline, we reference relevant discussions in the literature and give examples of how these guidelines have been applied. We hope that this serves as a first step towards a robust discussion of ethical guidelines for health-related social media research.

2 Discussion

The start of each research study includes asking core questions about the benefits and risks of the proposed research. What is the potential good this particular application allows? What is the potential harm it may cause and how can the harm be mitigated? Is there another feasible route to the good with less potential harm?

Answers to these questions provide a framework within which we can decide which avenues of research should be pursued. Virtually all technology is dual-use: it can be used for good or ill. The existence of an ill use does not mean that the technology should not be developed, nor does the existence of a good mean that it should.

To focus our discussion on the pragmatic, we will use mental health research as a concrete use case. A research community has grown around using social media data to assess and understand mental health (Resnik et al., 2013; Schwartz et al., 2013; Preotiuc-Pietro et al., 2015; Coppersmith et al., 2015a; De Choudhury et al., 2016). Our discussion on the benefits and risks of such research is sharpened by the discrimination and stigma surrounding mental illness. The discrimination paired with potentially lethal outcomes put the risks and benefits of this type of research in stark relief – not sufficiently protecting users'/subjects' privacy, may exacerbate the challenge, discourage individuals from seeking treatment and erode public trust in researchers. Similarly, insufficient research results in a cost measured in human lives – in the United States, more than 40,000 die from suicide each year (Curtin et al., 2016). Mental health may be an extreme case for the gravity of these choices, but similar risk and benefits are present in many other health research domains. Clearly identifying the risks and the potential reward helps to inform the stance and guidelines one should adopt.

We found it helpful to enumerate facts and observations that inform each research protocol decision:

- We want to make a positive impact upon society, and one significant contribution we may provide is to better understand mental illness. Specifically, we want to learn information that will aid mental health diagnosis and help those challenged by mental illness. Thus, the driving force behind this research is to prevent suffering from mental illness.

- Intervention has great potential for good and for harm. Naturally, we would like to help those around us that are suffering, but that does not mean that we are properly equipped to do so. Interventions enacted at a time of emotional crisis amplify the risks and benefits. The approach we have taken in previous studies was to observe and understand mental illness, not to intervene. This is likely true for many computer and data science research endeavors, but that does not absolve the consideration of interventions. Ultimately, if the proposed research is successful it will inform the way that medicine is practiced, and thus will directly or indirectly have an effect on interventions.

- Machine learning algorithms do not learn perfectly predictive models. Errors and misclassifications will be made, and this should be accounted for by the researcher. Even less clearly error-prone systems, such as databases for sensitive patient data, are liable to being compromised.

- Social media platforms, like Twitter, are often public broadcast media. Nevertheless, much has been written about the perception that users do not necessarily treat social media as a purely public space (McKee, 2013). Mikal et al. (2016) found that many Twitter users in focus groups do have a skewed expectation of privacy, even in an explicitly public platform like Twitter, driven by *"users' (1) failure to understand data permanence, (2) failure to understand data reach, and (3) failure to understand the big data computational tools that can be used to analyze posts"*.

Our guidelines emerge from these tenets and our experience with mental health research on social media, where we try to strike a balance between enabling important research with the concerns of risk to the privacy of the target population. We encourage all researchers to frame their own research tenets first to establish guiding principles as to how research should proceed.

3 Guidelines

In contrast to others (Neuhaus and Webmoor, 2012; McKee, 2013; Conway, 2014) who have offered broad ethical frameworks and high-level guidance in social media health research, we offer specific suggestions grounded in our own experience conducting health research with social media. At the same time, the risk of a study varies depending on the type of health annotations collected and whether the research is purely observational or not. Therefore, we do not provide hard rules, but different options given the risk associated with the study.

Researchers familiar with human subjects research may ask how our guidelines differ from those recommended for all such research, regardless of connections with social media data. While the main points are general to human subjects research, we describe how these issues specifically arise in the context of social media research, and provide relevant examples. Additionally, social media raises some specific concerns and suggestions described below, such as (1) concern of inadvertently compromising user privacy by linking data, even when all the linked datasets are public, (2) using alternatives to traditionally obtained informed consent, (3) additional steps to de-identify social media data before analysis and dissemination, and (4) care when attributing presenting information in public forums. Furthermore, our intended audience are readers unfamiliar with human subjects research guidelines, as opposed to seasoned researchers in this area.

3.1 Institutional Review Board

In the United States, all federally-funded *human subject* research must be approved by a committee of at least five persons, with at least one member from outside of the institution (Edgar and Rothman, 1995). This committee is the Institutional Review Board (IRB), and in practice, many American institutions require all performed research to be sanctioned by the IRB. Ethics committees serve a similar role as IRBs in European Union member states (European Parliament and Council of the European Union, 2001). These committees have different regulations, but typically make similar approval judgments as IRBs (Edwards et al., 2007).

Human subjects are any living individual about whom an investigator conducting research obtains "(1) Data through intervention or interaction with the individual, or (2) Identifiable private information" (US Department of HHS, 2009). Collecting posts, examining networks, or in any way observing the activity of people means that social media health research qualifies as human subjects research (O'Connor, 2013) and requires the review of an IRB. The distinction between social media research that involves human subjects and research that does not is nebulous, as the inclusion of individuals in research alone is insufficient. For example, research that requires the annotation of corpora for training models involves human annotators. But since the research does not study the actions of those annotators, the research does not involve human subjects. By contrast, if the goal of the research was to study *how* humans annotate data, such as to learn about how humans interpret language, then the research may constitute human subjects research. When in doubt, researchers should consult their appropriate IRB contact.

IRB review provides a series of exemption categories that exempt research protocols from a full review by the IRB. Exemption category 4 in section 46.101 (b) concerns public datasets (US Department of HHS, 2009):

> *Research involving the collection or study of existing data, documents, records, pathological specimens, or diagnostic specimens, if these sources are publicly available or if the information is recorded by the investigator in such a manner that subjects cannot be identified, directly or through identifiers linked to the subjects.*

Since these projects pose a minimal risk to subjects, they require minimal review. Since most social media projects rely on publicly available data, and do not include interventions or interactions with the population, they may qualify for IRB exempt status (Hudson and Bruckman, 2004). Such research still requires an application to the IRB, but with a substantially expedited and simplified review process. This is an important point: research that involves human subjects, even if it falls under an exemption, must obtain an exemption from the IRB. Research that does not involve human subjects need not obtain any approval from the IRB.

3.2 Informed Consent

Obtain informed consent when possible.

A fundamental tenant of human subjects research is to obtain informed consent from study participants. Research that analyzes public corpora that include millions of individuals cannot feasibly obtain informed consent from each individual (O'Connor, 2013). Therefore, the vast majority of research that analyzes collected social media posts cannot obtain such consent. Still, we advocate for informed consent where possible due to the central role of consent in human subjects research guidelines. In cases where researchers solicit data from users, such as private Facebook or Twitter messages, informed consent may be required (Celli et al., 2013). Be explicit about how subject data will be used, and how it will be stored and protected. OurDataHelps[1], which solicits data donations for mental health research, provides such information.

Even if you have not explicitly dealt with consent while collecting public subject data, attaching a "statement of responsibility" and description of how the data were compiled and are to be used will give you, the researcher, a measure of accountability (Neuhaus and Webmoor, 2012; Vayena et al., 2013). This statement of responsibility would be posted publicly on the research group's website, and contains a description of the type of data that are collected, how they are being protected, and the types of analyses that will be conducted using it. Users could explicitly choose to opt-out their data from the research by providing their account handle. An IRB or ethics committee may not explicitly request such a statement[2], but it serves to ensure trust in subjects who typically have no say in how their online data are used.

3.3 User Interventions

Research that involves user interventions may not qualify for an IRB exemption.

Research that starts by analyzing public data may subsequently lead to interacting with users

---

or modifying user experience. For example, research may start with identifying public Twitter messages on a given topic, and then generating an interaction with the user of the message. The well known study of Kramer et al. (2014) manipulated Facebook users' news feeds to vary the emotional content and monitor how the feed influenced users' emotional states. This study raised particularly strong ethical reservations since informed consent agreements were never obtained, and was followed by an "Editorial Expression of Concern". While we cannot make definitive judgements as to what studies can receive IRB exemptions, interacting with users often comes with testing specific interventions, which typically require a full IRB review. In these cases, it is the responsibility of the researchers to work with the IRB to minimize risks to study subjects, and such risk minimization may qualify for expedited IRB review (McKee, 2013). In short, researchers should be careful not to conflate exemptions for public datasets with blanket permission for all social media research.

3.4 Protections for Sensitive Data

Develop appropriate protections for sensitive data.

Even publicly available data may include sensitive data that requires protection. For example, users may post sensitive information (e.g. diagnoses, personal attributes) that, while public, are still considered sensitive by the user. Furthermore, algorithms may infer latent attributes of users from publicly posted information that can be considered sensitive. This is often the case in mental health research, where algorithms identify users who may be challenged by a mental illness even when this diagnosis isn't explicitly mentioned by the user. Additionally, domain experts may manually label users for different medical conditions based on their public statements. These annotations, either manually identified or automatically extracted, may be considered sensitive user information even when derived from public data.

Proper protections for these data should be developed before the data are created. These may include:

1. Restrict access to sensitive data. This may include placing such data on a protected server, restricting access using OS level permissions, and encrypting the drives. This is common practice for medical record data.

---

[1] https://ourdatahelps.org

[2] Although some IRBs do require such a statement and the ability for users to opt-out of the study. See the University of Rochester guidelines for social media research: https://www.rochester.edu/ohsp/documents/ohsp/pdf/policiesAndGuidance/Guideline_for_Research_Using_Social_Media.pdf

2. Separate annotations from user data. The raw user data can be kept in one location, and the sensitive annotations in another. The two data files are linked by an anonymous ID so as not to rely on publicly identifiable user handles.

The extent to which researchers should rely on these and other data protections depends on the nature of the data. Some minimal protections, such as OS level permissions, are easy to implement and may be appropriate for a wide range of data types. For example, the dataset of users who self-identified as having a mental condition as compiled in Coppersmith et al. (2015a) was protected in this way during the *3rd Annual Frederick Jelinek Summer Workshop*. More extreme measures, such as the use of air-gapped servers – computers that are physically removed from external networks – may be appropriate when data is particularly sensitive and the risk of harm is great. Certainly in cases where public data (e.g. social media) is linked to private data (e.g. electronic medical records) greater restrictions may be appropriate to control data access (Padrez et al., 2015).

3.5 User Attribution

De-identify data and messages in public presentations to minimize risk to users.

While messages posted publicly may be freely accessible to anyone, users may not intend for their posts to have such a broad audience. For example, on Twitter many users engage in public conversations with other users knowing that their messages are public, but do not expect a large audience to read their posts. Public users may be aware that their tweets can be read by anyone, but posted messages may still be intended for their small group of followers (Hudson and Bruckman, 2004; Quercia et al., 2011; Neuhaus and Webmoor, 2012; O'Connor, 2013; Kandias et al., 2013). The result is that while technically and legally public messages may be viewable by anyone, the author's intention and care with which they wrote the message may not reflect this reality. Therefore, we suggest that messages be de-identified or presented without attribution in public talks and papers unless it is necessary and appropriate to do otherwise. This is especially true when the users discuss sensitive topics, or are identified as having a stigmatized condition.

In practice, we suggest:

1. Remove usernames and profile pictures from papers and presentations where the tweet includes potentially sensitive information (McKee, 2013).

2. Paraphrase the original message. In cases where the post is particularly sensitive, the true author may be identifiable through text searches over the relevant platform. In these cases, paraphrase or modify the wording of the original message to preserve its meaning but obscure the author.

3. Use synthetic examples. In many cases it may be appropriate to create new message content in public presentations that reflects the type of content studied without using a real example. Be sure to inform your audience when the examples are artificial.

Not all cases require obfuscation of message authorship; in many situations it may be perfectly acceptable to show screen shots or verbatim quotes of real content with full attribution. When making these determinations, you should consider if your inclusion of content with attribution may bring unwanted attention to the user, demonstrate behavior the user may not want to highlight, or pose a non-negligible risk to the user. For example, showing an example of an un-anonymized tweet from someone with schizophrenia, or another stigmatized condition, can be much more damaging to them than posting a tweet from someone who smokes tobacco. While the content may be publicly available, you do not necessarily need to draw attention to it.

3.6 User De-identification in Analysis

Remove the identity of a user or other sensitive personal information if it is not needed in your analysis.

It is good practice to remove usernames and other identifying fields when the inclusion of such information poses risk to the user. For example, in the 2015 CLPsych shared task, tweets were de-identified by removing references to usernames, URLs, and most metadata fields (Coppersmith et al., 2015b). Carefully removing such information can be a delicate process, so we encourage the use of existing software for this task: `https://github.com/qntfy/deidentify_twitter`. This tool is clearly not a panacea for social media health researchers, and depending on the sensitivity of the data, more time-consuming de-identification measures will need to be taken. For example, before analyzing a collection of breast cancer message board posts, Benton et al. (2011) trained a model to de-identify several fields: named entities such as person names, locations, as well as phone numbers and addresses. When analyzing text data, perfect anonymization may be impossible to achieve, since a Google search can often retrieve the identity of a user given a single message they post.

3.7 Sharing Data

> Ensure that other researchers will respect ethical and privacy concerns.

We strongly encourage researchers to share datasets and annotations they have created so that others can replicate research findings and develop new uses for existing datasets. In many cases, there may be no risk to users in sharing data and such data should be freely shared. However, where there may be risk to users, data should not be shared blindly without concern for how it will be used.

First, if protective protocols of the kind described above were established for the data, new researchers who will use the data should agree to the same protocols. This agreement was implemented in the MIMIC-III hospital admissions database, by Johnson et al. (2016). Researchers are required to present a certificate of human subjects training before receiving access to a de-identified dataset of hospital admissions. Additionally, the new research team may need to obtain their own IRB approval before receiving a copy of the data.

Second, do not share sensitive or identifiable information if it is not required for the research. For example, if sensitive annotations were created for users, you may instead share an anonymized version of the corpus where features such as, for example, individual posts they made, are not shared. Otherwise, the original user handle may be recovered using a search for the message text. For NLP-centric projects where models are trained to predict sensitive annotations from text, this means that either opaque feature vectors should be shared (disallowing others from preprocessing the data differently), or the messages be replaced with de-identified tokens, allowing other researchers to use

token frequency statistics as features, but not, for example, gazetteers or pre-trained word vectors as features in their models.

It is also important to refer to the social media platform terms of service before sharing datasets. For example, section F.2 of Twitter's Developer Policy restricts sharing to no more than 50,000 tweets and user information objects per downloader per day.[3]

3.8 Data Linkage Across Sites

> Be cautious about linking data across sites, even when all data are public.

While users may share data publicly on multiple platforms, they may not intend for combinations of data across platforms to be public (McKee, 2013). For example, a user may create a public persona on Twitter, and a less identifiable account on a mental health discussion forum. The discussions they have on this health forum should not be inadvertently linked to their Twitter account by an overzealous researcher, since it may "out" their condition to the Twitter community.

There have been several cases of identifying users in anonymized data based on linking data across sources. Douriez et al. (2016) describe how the New York City Taxi Dataset can be deanonymized by collecting taxi location information from four popular intersections. Narayanan and Shmatikov (2008) showed that the identify of users in the anonymized Netflix challenge data can be revealed by mining the Internet Movie Database.

Combinations of public data can create new sensitivities and must be carefully evaluated on a case-by-case basis. In some cases, users may explicitly link accounts across platforms, such as including in a Twitter profile a link to a LinkedIn page or blog (Burger et al., 2011). Other times users may not make these links explicit, intentionally try to hide the connections, or the connections are inferred by the researcher, e.g. by similarity in user handles. These factors should be considered when conducting research that links users across multiple platforms. It goes without saying that linking public posts to private, sensitive fields (electronic health records) should be handled with the utmost care (Padrez et al., 2015).

---

[3] https://dev.twitter.com/overview/
terms/agreement-and-policy

4   Conclusion

We have provided a series of ethical recommendations for health research using social media. These recommendations can serve as a guide for developing new research protocols, and researchers can decide on specific practices based on the issues raised in this paper. We hope that researchers new to the field find these guidelines useful to familiarize themselves with ethical issues.

References

Adrian Benton, Lyle Ungar, Shawndra Hill, Sean Hennessy, Jun Mao, Annie Chung, Charles E. Leonard, and John H. Holmes. 2011. Identifying potential adverse effects using the web: A new approach to medical hypothesis generation. *Journal of biomedical informatics*, 44(6):989–996.

Johan Bollen, Huina Mao, and Xiaojun Zeng. 2011. Twitter mood predicts the stock market. *Journal of computational science*, 2(1):1–8.

John D. Burger, John Henderson, George Kim, and Guido Zarrella. 2011. Discriminating gender on twitter. In *Empirical Methods in Natural Language Processing (EMNLP)*, pages 1301–1309.

Fabio Celli, Fabio Pianesi, David Stillwell, and Michal Kosinski. 2013. Workshop on computational personality recognition (shared task). In *Workshop on Computational Personality Recognition*.

Mike Conway. 2014. Ethical issues in using Twitter for public health surveillance and research: developing a taxonomy of ethical concepts from the research literature. *Journal of Medical Internet Research*, 16(12):e290.

Glen Coppersmith, Mark Dredze, Craig Harman, and Kristy Hollingshead. 2015a. From ADHD to SAD: analyzing the language of mental health on Twitter through self-reported diagnoses. In *NAACL Workshop on Computational Linguistics and Clinical Psychology*.

Glen Coppersmith, Mark Dredze, Craig Harman, Kristy Hollingshead, and Margaret Mitchell. 2015b. CLPsych 2015 shared task: Depression and ptsd on Twitter. In *Workshop on Computational Linguistics and Clinical Psychology: From Linguistic Signal to Clinical Reality*, pages 31–39.

Sally C. Curtin, Margaret Warner, and Holly Hedegaard. 2016. Increase in suicide in the United States, 1999-2014. *NCHS data brief*, 241:1–8.

Munmun De Choudhury, Emre Kiciman, Mark Dredze, Glen Coppersmith, and Mrinal Kumar. 2016. Discovering shifts to suicidal ideation from mental health content in social media. In *Conference on Human Factors in Computing Systems (CHI)*, pages 2098–2110.

Marie Douriez, Harish Doraiswamy, Juliana Freire, and Cláudio T. Silva. 2016. Anonymizing nyc taxi data: Does it matter? In *IEEE International Conference on Data Science and Advanced Analytics (DSAA)*, pages 140–148.

Harold Edgar and David J. Rothman. 1995. The institutional review board and beyond: Future challenges to the ethics of human experimentation. *The Milbank Quarterly*, 73(4):489–506.

Sarah J. L. Edwards, Tracey Stone, and Teresa Swift. 2007. Differences between research ethics committees. *International journal of technology assessment in health care*, 23(01):17–23.

European Parliament and Council of the European Union. 2001. Directive 2001/20/EC.

James M. Hudson and Amy Bruckman. 2004. "Go away": participant objections to being studied and the ethics of chatroom research. *The Information Society*, 20(2):127–139.

Alistair E. W. Johnson, Tom J. Pollard, Lu Shen, Liwei H. Lehman, Mengling Feng, Mohammad Ghassemi, Benjamin Moody, Peter Szolovits, Leo Anthony Celi, and Roger G. Mark. 2016. MIMIC-III, a freely accessible critical care database. *Scientific data*, 3.

Miltiadis Kandias, Konstantina Galbogini, Lilian Mitrou, and Dimitris Gritzalis. 2013. Insiders trapped in the mirror reveal themselves in social media. In *International Conference on Network and System Security*, pages 220–235.

Adam D. I. Kramer, Jamie E. Guillory, and Jeffrey T. Hancock. 2014. Experimental evidence of massive-scale emotional contagion through social networks. *Proceedings of the National Academy of Sciences*, 111(24):8788–8790.

Rebecca McKee. 2013. Ethical issues in using social media for health and health care research. *Health Policy*, 110(2):298–301.

Jude Mikal, Samantha Hurst, and Mike Conway. 2016. Ethical issues in using Twitter for population-level depression monitoring: a qualitative study. *BMC medical ethics*, 17(1):1.

Arvind Narayanan and Vitaly Shmatikov. 2008. Robust de-anonymization of large sparse datasets. In *IEEE Symposium on Security and Privacy*, pages 111–125.

National Commission. 1978. *The Belmont Report: Ethical Principles and Guidelines for the Protection of Human Subjects of Research-the National Commission for the Protection of Human Subjects of Biomedical and Behavioral Research*. US Government Printing Office.

National Research Council. 2014. *Proposed revisions to the common rule for the protection of human subjects in the behavioral and social sciences*. National Academies Press.

Fabian Neuhaus and Timothy Webmoor. 2012. Agile ethics for massified research and visualization. *Information, Communication & Society*, 15(1):43–65.

Dan O'Connor. 2013. The apomediated world: regulating research when social media has changed research. *Journal of Law, Medicine, and Ethics*, 41(2):470–483.

Kevin A. Padrez, Lyle Ungar, H. Andrew Schwartz, Robert J. Smith, Shawndra Hill, Tadas Antanavicius, Dana M. Brown, Patrick Crutchley, David A. Asch, and Raina M. Merchant. 2015. Linking social media and medical record data: a study of adults presenting to an academic, urban emergency department. *Quality and Safety in Health Care*.

Michael J. Paul and Mark Dredze. 2011. You are what you tweet: Analyzing twitter for public health. In *International Conference on Weblogs and Social Media (ICWSM)*, pages 265–272.

Daniel Preotiuc-Pietro, Johannes Eichstaedt, Gregory Park, Maarten Sap, Laura Smith, Victoria Tobolsky, H. Andrew Schwartz, and Lyle Ungar. 2015. The role of personality, age and gender in tweeting about mental illnesses. In *Workshop on Computational Linguistics and Clinical Psychology: From Linguistic Signal to Clinical Reality*.

Daniele Quercia, Michal Kosinski, David Stillwell, and Jon Crowcroft. 2011. Our Twitter profiles, our selves: Predicting personality with Twitter. In *IEEE Third International Conference on Privacy, Security, Risk and Trust (PASSAT)*, pages 180–185.

Philip Resnik, Anderson Garron, and Rebecca Resnik. 2013. Using topic modeling to improve prediction of neuroticism and depression. In *Empirical Methods in Natural Language Processing (EMNLP)*, pages 1348–1353.

H. Andrew Schwartz, Johannes C. Eichstaedt, Margaret L. Kern, Lukasz Dziurzynski, Richard E. Lucas, Megha Agrawal, Gregory J. Park, Shrinidhi K. Lakshmikanth, Sneha Jha, Martin E. P. Seligman, and Lyle H. Ungar. 2013. Characterizing geographic variation in well-being using tweets. In *International Conference on Weblogs and Social Media (ICWSM)*.

Andranik Tumasjan, Timm O. Sprenger, Philipp G. Sandner, and Isabell M. Welpe. 2011. Election forecasts with twitter: How 140 characters reflect the political landscape. *Social science computer review*, 29(4):402–418.

US Department of HHS. 2009. Code of federal regulations. title 45. *Public Welfare CFR*, 46.

Effy Vayena, Anna Mastroianni, and Jeffrey Kahn. 2013. Caught in the web: informed consent for online health research. *Sci Transl Med*, 5(173):1–3.

Say the Right Thing Right: Ethics Issues in Natural Language Generation Systems

Charese Smiley & Frank Schilder
Thomson Reuters R&D
610 Opperman Drive
Eagan, MN 55123
USA
`FirstName.LastName@tr.com`

Vassilis Plachouras & Jochen L. Leidner
Thomson Reuters R&D
30 South Colonnade
London E14 5EP
United Kingdom
`FirstName.LastName@tr.com`

Abstract

We discuss the ethical implications of Natural Language Generation systems. We use one particular system as a case study to identify and classify issues, and we provide an ethics checklist, in the hope that future system designers may benefit from conducting their own ethics reviews based on our checklist.

1 Introduction

With the advent of big data, there is increasingly a need to distill information computed from these datasets into automated summaries and reports that users can quickly digest without the need for time-consuming data munging and analysis. However, with automated summaries comes not only the added benefit of easy access to the findings of large datasets but the need for ethical considerations in ensuring that these reports accurately reflect the true nature of the underlying data and do not make any misleading statements.

This is especially vital from a Natural Language Generation (NLG) perspective because with large datasets, it may be impossible to read every generation and reasonable-sounding, but misleading, generations may slip through without proper validation. As users read the automatically generated summaries, any misleading information can affect their subsequent actions, having a real-world impact. Such summaries may also be consumed by other automated processes, which extract information or calculate sentiment for example, potentially amplifying any misrepresented information. Ideally, the research community and industry should be building NLG systems which avoid altogether behaviors that promote ethical violations. However, given the difficulty of such a task, before

we reach this goal, it is necessary to have a list of best practices for building NLG systems.

This paper presents a checklist of ethics issues arising when developing NLG systems in general and more specifically from the development of an NLG system to generate descriptive text for macro-economic indicators as well as insights gleaned from our experiences with other NLG projects. While not meant to be comprehensive, it provides high and low-level views of the types of considerations that should be taken when generating directly from data to text.

The remainder of the paper is organized as follows: Section 2 covers related work in ethics for NLG systems. Section 3 introduces an ethics checklist for guiding the design of NLG systems. Section 4 describes a variety of issues we have encountered. Section 5 outlines ways to address these issues emphasizing various methods we propose should be applied while developing an NLG system. We present our conclusions in Section 6.

2 Related work

Many of the ethical issues of NLG systems have been discussed in the context of algorithmic journalism (Dörr and Hollnbuchner, 2016). They outline a general framework of moral theories following Weischenberg *et al.* (2006) that should be applied to algorithmic journalism in general and especially when NLG systems are used.

We are building on their framework by providing concrete issues we encounter while creating actual NLG systems.

Kent (2015) proposes a concrete checklist for robot journalism[1] that lists various guidelines for utilizing NLG systems in journalism. He also points out that a link back to the source data is

---

[1] `http://mediashift.org/2015/03/an-ethical-checklist-for-robot-journalism/`

Proceedings of the First Workshop on Ethics in Natural Language Processing, pages 103–108,
Valencia, Spain, April 4th, 2017. © 2017 Association for Computational Linguistics

QUESTION	EXAMPLE RESPONSE	SECTION
Human consequences		
Are there ethical objections to building the application?	No objections anticipated	4.3
How could a user be disadvantaged by the system?	No anticipated disadvantages to user	4.4-4.7
Does the system use any Personally Identifiable Information?	No PII collected or used	4.5
Data issues		
How accurate is the underlying data?*	Data is drawn from trusted source	4
Are there any misleading rankings given?	Yes, detected via data validation	4.1
Are there (automatic) checks for missing data?	Yes, detected via data validation	4.2
Does the data contain any outliers?	Yes, detected via data validation	4.2
Generation issues		
Can you defend how the story is written?*	Yes via presupposition checks and disclosure	5
Does the style of the automated report match your style?*	Yes, generations reviewed by domain experts	5
Who is watching the machines?*	Conducted internal evaluation and quality control	5
Provenance		
Will you disclose your methods?*	Disclosure text	4.4
Will you disclose the underlying data sources?	Provide link to open data & source for proprietary data	4.4

Table 1: An ethics checklist for NLG systems. There is an overlap with questions from the checklist Thomas Kent proposed and they are indicated by ∗.

essential and that such systems should at least in the beginning go through rigorous quality checks.

A comprehensive overview of ethical issues on designing computer systems can be found in (IEEE, 2016). More specifically, Amodei et al. (2016) propose an array of machine learning-based strategies for ensuring safety in general AI systems, mostly focussing on autonomous system interacting with a real world environment. Their research questions encompass avoiding negative side effects, robustness to distributional shift (i.e. the machine's situational awareness) and scalable oversight (i.e. autonomy of the machine in decision-making). The last question is clearly relevant to defining safeguards for NLG systems as well. Ethical questions addressing the impact of specifically NLP systems are addressed by Hovy and Spruit (2016).

To ensure oversight of an AI system, they draw inspiration from semi-supervised reinforcement learning and suggest to learn a reward function either based on supervised or semi-supervised active learning. We follow this suggestion and propose creating such a reward-based model for NLG systems in order to learn whether the generated texts may lay outside of the normal parameters.

Actual NLG systems are faced with word choice problem and possible data problems. Such systems, however, normally do not address the ethical consequences of the choices taken, but see Joshi et al. (1984) for an exception. Choosing the appropriate word in an NLG system was already addressed by (Ward, 1988; Barzilay and Lee, 2002), among others. More recently, Smiley et al. (2016), for example, derive the word choice

of verbs describing the trend between two data points from an extensive corpus analysis. Grounding the verb choice in data helps to correctly describe the intensity of a change.

The problem of missing data can taint every data analysis and lead to misleading conclusions if not handled appropriately. Equally important as the way one imputes missing data points in the analysis is the transparent description of how data is handled. NLG system designers, in particular, have to be very careful about which kind of data their generated text is based on. To our knowledge, this problem has not been systematically addressed in the literature on creating NLG systems.

At the application level, Mahamood and Reiter (2011) present an NLG system for the neonatal care domain, which arguably is particularly sensitive as far as medical sub-domains are concerned. They generate summaries about the health status of young babies, including affective elements to calm down potentially worried parents to an appropriate degree. If a critically ill baby has seen dramatic deterioration or has died, the system appropriately does not generate any output, but refers to a human medic.[2]

3 Ethics Checklist

While there is a large body of work on metrics and methodologies for improving data quality (Batini et al., 2008), reaching a state where an NLG system could automatically determine edge cases (problems that occur at the extremes or outside of normal data ranges) or issues in the data, is a dif-

---

[2]Ehud Reiter, personal communication

	2009	2010	2011	2012	2013	2014
Curaçao	76.15609756	..	77.47317073	..	..	77.82439024

Table 2: Life expectancy at birth, total (years) for Curaçao.

	2006	2007	2008	2009	2010	2011
South Sudan	..	..	15,550,136,279	12,231,362,023	15,727,363,443	17,826,697,892

Table 3: GDP (current US$) for South Sudan.

ficult task. Until such systems are built, we believe it could be helpful to have some guidance in the form of an ethics checklist, which could be integrated in any existing project management process.

In Table 1, we propose such a checklist, with the aim to aid the developers of NLG systems on how to address the ethical issues arising from the use of an NLG system, and to provide a starting point for outlining mechanisms and processes to address these issues. We divided the checklist up into 4 areas starting with questions on developing NLP systems in general. The table also contains the response for a system we designed and developed and pointers to sections of the paper which discuss methods that could be deployed to make sure the issues raised by the questions are adequately addressed. The checklist was derived from our own experience with NLG systems as well as informed by the literature. We do not assert its completion, but rather offer it as a starting point that may be extended by others; also, other kinds of NLP systems may lead to specific checklists following the same methodology.

4   Current issues

This section consists of issues encountered when developing an NLG system for generating summaries for macro-economic data (Plachouras et al., 2016). To illustrate these issues we use World Bank Open Data,[3] an open access repository of global development indicator data. While this repository contains a wealth of data that can be used for generating automatic summaries, it also contains a variety of edge cases that are typical of large datasets. Managing edge cases is essential not only due to issues of grammaticality (e.g. noun-number agreement, subject-verb agreement), but because they can lead to misstatements and misrepresentations of the data that a user might act on. These issues are discussed in turn

in this section.

4.1   Ranking

It is common to provide a ranking among entities with values that can be ordered. However, when there are a small number of entities, ranking may not be informative especially if the size of the set is not also given. For example, if there is only one country reporting in a region for a particular indicator an NLG engine could claim that the country is either the highest or lowest in the region. A region like North America, for which World Bank lists Bermuda, Canada, and the United States will sometimes only have data for 2 countries as Bermuda is dramatically smaller, so clarity in which countries are being compared for a given indicator and timespan is essential.

4.2   Time series

Missing Data: Enterprise applications will usually contain Terms of Use of products stating that data may be incomplete and calculations may include missing points. However, users may still assume that content shown by an application is authoritative leading to a wrong impression about the accuracy of the data. Table 3 shows the life expectancy for Curaçao from 2009-2015. Here we see that 2010, 2012, and 2013 are missing. NLG systems should check for missing values and should be informed if calculations are performed on data with missing values or if values presented to the user have been imputed.

Leading/trailing empty cells: Similar to issues with missing data, leading/trailing zeros and missing values in the data may be accurate or may signal that data was not recorded during that time period or that the phenomena started/ended when the first or last values were reported. For example, Table 3 shows empty leading values for South Sudan, a country that only recently became independent.

Small Changes: The reported life expectancy of St. Lucia was very stable in the late 1990s. In 1996, World Bank gives a life expectancy of

---

[3] http://data.worldbank.org

71.1574878 and in 1997, 71.15529268. Depending on our algorithm, one generation would say that there was *no change* in St. Lucia's life expectancy between 1996 and 1997 if the number was rounded to 2 decimal places. If the difference is calculated without rounding then the generation would say that there was *virtually no change*. Using the second wording allows for a more precise accounting of the slight difference seen from one year to the next.

Temporal scope: It is common to report activity occurring from a starting from the current time and extending to some fixed point in the past (e.g. *over the past 10 years*). While this is also a frequent occurrence in human written texts and dialogues, it is quite ambiguous and could refer to the start of the first year, the start of the fiscal calendar on the first year, a precise number of days extending from today to 10 years ago, or a myriad of other interpretations. Likewise, what it meant by the current time period is also ambiguous as data may or may not be reported for the current time period. If, for example, the Gross Domestic Product (GDP) for the current year is not available the generation should inform the user that the data is current as of the earliest year available.

4.3 Ethical Objections

Before beginning any NLG project, it is important to consider whether there are any reasons why the system should not be built. A system that would cause harm to the user by producing generations that are offensive should not be built without appropriate safeguards. For example, in 2016, Microsoft released Tay, a chatbot which unwittingly began to generate hate speech due to lack of filtering for racist content in its training data and output.[4]

4.4 Provenance

In the computer medium, authority is ascribed based on number of factors (Conrad et al., 2008): the user may have a prior trust distribution into humans and machines (on the "species" and individual level), they may ascribe credibility based on the generated message itself. Only being transparent about where data originated permits humans to apply their prior beliefs, whereas hiding whether generated text originated from a machine or a human leaves the user in the dark about how to use

their prior beliefs to ascribe trust (or not). Once users are informed about the provenance of the information, they are enabled to decide for themselves whether or how much they trust a piece of information output by a system, such as a natural language summary.

As pointed out by Kent (2015) disclaimers on the completeness and correctness of the data should be added to the generation, or website where it's shown. Ideally, a link to the actual data source should also be provided and in general a description of how the generation is carried out in order to provide full transparency to the user. For example, such description should state whether the generated texts are personalized to match the profile of each user.

4.5 Personalization

One of the advantages of NLG systems is the capability to produce text customized to the profile of individual users. Instead of writing one text for all users, the NLG system can incorporate the background and context of a user to increase the communication effectiveness of the text. However, users are not always aware of personalization. Hence, insights they may obtain from the text can be aligned with their profile and history, but may also be missing alternative insights that are weighed down by the personalization algorithm. One way to address this limitation is to make users aware of the use of personalization, similar to how provenance can be addressed.

4.6 Fraud Prevention

In sensitive financial systems, in theory a rogue developer could introduce fraudulent code that generates overly positive or negative-sounding sentiment for a company, for their financial gain. A code audit can bring attempts to manipulate any code base to light, and pair programming may make any attempts less likely.

4.7 Accessibility

In addition to providing misleading texts, the accessibility of the texts generated automatically is an additional way in which users may be put in a disadvantaged position by the use of an NLG system. First, the readability of the generated text may not match the expectations of the target users, limiting their understanding due to the use of specialized terminology, or complex structure. Second, the quality of the user experience may be af-

---

fected if the generated text has been constructed without considering the requirements of how users access the text. For example, delivering a text through a text-to-speech synthesizer may require to expand numerical expressions or to construct shorter texts because of the time required for the articulation of speech.

5   Discussion

The research community and the industry should aim to design NLG systems that do not promote unethical behavior, by detecting issues in the data and automatically identifying cases where the automated summaries do not reflect the true nature of the data.

There are a couple of methods we want to highlight because they address the problems of solving ethical issues from two different angles. The first method we called *presupposition check* draws principled way of describing pragmatic issues in language by adding semantic and pragmatic constraints informed by Grice's Cooperative Principles and presupposition (Grice, 1975; Beaver, 1997): Adding formal constraints to the generation process will make NLG more transparent, and less potentially misleading (Joshi, 1982).

If an NLG system, for example, is asked to generate a phrase expressing the minimum, average or maximum of a group of numbers ("The smallest/average/largest (Property) of (Group) is (Value)"), an automatic check should be installed that determines whether the cardinality of the set comprising that group is greater than one. If this check only finds one entity, the generation should be licensed and the system avoids that user is misled into believing the very notion of calculating a minimum, average or maximum actually makes sense. Instead, in such a situation a better response may be "There is only one (Property) in (Group), and it is (Value)." (cf. work on the NLG of gradable properties by van Deemter (2006)).

A second method to ensure that the output of the generated system is valid involves evaluating and monitoring the quality of the text. A model can be trained to identify problematic generations based on an active learning approach. For example, interquartile ranges can be computed for numerical data used for the generation determining outliers in the data. In addition, the fraction of missing data points and the number of input elements in aggregate functions can be estimated from the respective data. Then, domain experts can rate whether the generated text is acceptable or not as a description of the respective data. The judgements can be used to train a classifier that can be applied to future data sets and generations.

6   Conclusions

We analyzed how the development of an NLG system can have ethical implications considering in particular data problems and how the meaning of the generated text can be potentially misleading. We also introduced best practice guidelines for creating an NLP system in general and transparency in interaction with a user.

Based on the checklist for the NLG systems we proposed various methods for ensuring that the right utterance is generated. We discussed in particular two methods that future research should focus on: (a) the validation of utterances via a presupposition checker and (b) a better evaluation framework that may be able to learn from feedback and improve upon that feedback.

Checklists can be collected as project management artifacts for each completed NLP project in order to create a learning organization, and they are a useful resource that inform Ethics Review Boards, as introduced by Leidner and Plachouras (2017).

Acknowledgments

We would like to thank Khalid Al-Kofahi for supporting this work.

References

Dario Amodei, Chris Olah, Jacob Steinhardt, Paul Christiano, John Schulman, and Dan Mané. 2016. Concrete problems in AI safety. *arXiv preprint arXiv:1606.06565*.

Regina Barzilay and Lillian Lee. 2002. Bootstrapping lexical choice via multiple-sequence alignment. In *Proceedings of the 2002 Conference on Empirical Methods in Natural Language Processing*, pages 164–171. Association for Computational Linguistics, July.

Carlo Batini, Federico Cabitza, Cinzia Cappiello, and Chiara Francalanci. 2008. A comprehensive data quality methodology for Web and structured data. *Int. J. Innov. Comput. Appl.*, 1(3):205–218, July.

David Beaver. 1997. Presupposition. In Johan van Benthem and Alice ter Meulen, editors, *The Hand-*

book of *Logic and Language*, pages 939–1008. Elsevier, Amsterdam.

Anja Belz and Ehud Reiter. 2006. Comparing automatic and human evaluation of nlg systems. In *In Proc. EACL'06*, pages 313–320.

Jack G. Conrad, Jochen L. Leidner, and Frank Schilder. 2008. Professional credibility: Authority on the Web. In *Proceedings of the 2nd ACM Workshop on Information Credibility on the Web*, WICOW 2008, pages 85–88, New York, NY, USA. ACM.

Konstantin Nicholas Dörr and Katharina Hollnbuchner. 2016. Ethical challenges of algorithmic journalism. *Digital Journalism*, pages 1–16.

Paul Grice. 1975. Logic and conversation. In P. Cole and J. Morgan, editors, *Syntax and Semantics III: Speech Acts*, pages 41–58. Academic Press, New York, NY, USA.

Dirk Hovy and Shannon L. Spruit. 2016. The social impact of natural language processing. In *Proceedings of the 54th Annual Meeting of the Association for Computational Linguistics*, volume 2, pages 591–598.

IEEE, editor. 2016. *Ethically Aligned Design: A Vision For Prioritizing Wellbeing With Artificial Intelligence And Autonomous Systems*. IEEE - advanced Technology for Humanity.

Aravind Joshi, Bonnie Webber, and Ralph M. Weischede. 1984. Preventing false inferences. In *Proceedings of the 10th International Conference on Computational Linguistics and 22nd Annual Meeting of the Association for Computational Linguistics*, pages 134–138, Stanford, California, USA, July. Association for Computational Linguistics.

Aravind Joshi. 1982. Mutual beliefs in question-answering systems. In Neil S. Smith, editor, *Mutual Knowledge*, pages 181–197. Academic Press, London.

Thomas Kent. 2015. "an ethical checklist for robot journalism. Online, cited 2017-01-25, http://mediashift.org/2015/03/an-ethical-checklist-for-robot-journalism/.

Jochen L. Leidner and Vassilis Plachouras. 2017. Ethical by design: Ethics best practices for natural language processing. In *Proceedings of the Workshop on Ethics & NLP held at the EACL Conference, April 3-7, 2017*, Valencia, Spain. ACL.

Saad Mahamood and Ehud Reiter. 2011. Generating affective natural language for parents of neonatal infants. In *Proceedings of the 13th European Workshop on Natural Language Generation*, ENLG 2011, pages 12–21, Nancy, France. Association for Computational Linguistics.

Leo L. Pipino, Yang W. Lee, and Richard Y. Wang. 2002. Data quality assessment. *Commun. ACM*, 45(4):211–218, April.

Vassilis Plachouras, Charese Smiley, Hiroko Bretz, Ola Taylor, Jochen L. Leidner, Dezhao Song, and Frank Schilder. 2016. Interacting with financial data using natural language. In Raffaele Perego, Fabrizio Sebastiani, Javed A. Aslam, Ian Ruthven, and Justin Zobel, editors, *Proceedings of the 39th International ACM SIGIR Conference on Research and Development in Information Retrieval, Pisa, Italy, July 17-21, 2016*, SIGIR 2016, pages 1121–1124. ACM.

Ehud Reiter. 2007. An architecture for data-to-text systems. In *Proceedings of the Eleventh European Workshop on Natural Language Generation*, ENLG '07, pages 97–104, Stroudsburg, PA, USA. Association for Computational Linguistics.

Frank Schilder, Blake Howald, and Ravi Kondadadi. 2013. Gennext: A consolidated domain adaptable nlg system. In *Proceedings of the 14th European Workshop on Natural Language Generation*, pages 178–182, Sofia, Bulgaria, August. Association for Computational Linguistics.

Charese Smiley, Vassilis Plachouras, Frank Schilder, Hiroko Bretz, Jochen L. Leidner, and Dezhao Song. 2016. When to plummet and when to soar: Corpus based verb selection for natural language generation. In *The 9th International Natural Language Generation Conference*, page 36.

Kees van Deemter. 2006. Generating referring expressions that involve gradable properties. *Computational Linguistics*, 32(2):195–222.

Nigel Ward. 1988. Issues in word choice. In *Proceedings of the 12th Conference on Computational Linguistics-Volume 2*, pages 726–731. Association for Computational Linguistics.

Siegfried Weischenberg, Maja Malik, and Armin Scholl. 2006. Die Souffleure der Mediengesellschaft. *Report über die Journalisten in Deutschland. Konstanz: UVK*, page 204.

Author Index

Association for Computational Linguistics
209 N. Eighth Street
Stroudsburg, Pennsylvania 18360

ISBN 978-1-5108-3864-2